NEW YORK CITY

|CONDENSED|

 dani valent

LONELY PLANET PUBLICATIONS
Melbourne • Oakland • London • Paris

contents

Lonely Planet Condensed – New York City
1st edition – April 2000

Published by
Lonely Planet Publications Pty Ltd
A.C.N. 005 607 983
192 Burwood Rd, Hawthorn,
Victoria 3122, Australia

Lonely Planet Offices
Australia PO Box 617, Hawthorn, VIC 3122
USA 150 Linden St, Oakland, CA 94607
UK 10a Spring Place, London NW5 3BH
France 1 rue du Dahomey, 75011 Paris

Photographs
All of the images in this guide are available
for licensing from Lonely Planet Images.
email: lpi@lonelyplanet.com.au

Front cover photographs
Top: Manhattan skyline
    (Greg Elms)
Bottom: Utility hole cover
    (Richard I'Anson)

ISBN 1 86450 046 8

Text & maps © Lonely Planet 2000
Photos © photographers as indicated 2000

Printed by The Bookmaker International Ltd
Printed in China

how to use this book

KEY TO SYMBOLS

⊠ address
☎ telephone number
✆ email/web site address
Ⓜ nearest subway station
Ⓡ nearest train station
Ⓑ nearest bus route (M3 to M6 means you can take buses M3, M4, M5 & M6)
⚓ nearest ferry wharf
🚗 car access

✈ nearby airport
ⓘ tourist information
🕐 opening hours
Ⓢ cost, entry charge
♿ wheelchair access
🚸 child-friendly
✕ on-site or nearby eatery
V vegetarian, or with a good vegetarian selection

COLOUR-CODING

Each chapter has a different colour code which is reflected on the maps for quick reference.

MAPS & GRID REFERENCES

The fold-out maps on the front and back covers are numbered from 1 to 5. All sights and venues in the text have map references which indicate where to find them, eg (2, G5) means Map 2, grid reference G5. When a map reference appears immediately after a name, the sight is labelled on the map; when it appears after an address (eg with most restaurants, hotels etc), only the street is marked on the map.

PRICES

Multiple prices (eg $14/10/35) usually indicate adult/concession/family entry charges. Where the last 'price' listed is free (eg $14/10/free), children are not charged admittance. Concession prices can include child, pensioner and/or student discounts. Most family tickets cover 2 adults and 2 children.

WARNING & REQUEST

Things change – prices go up, schedules change, good places go bad and bad places improve or go bankrupt. So, if you find things better or worse, recently opened or long since closed, please tell us and help make the next edition even more accurate. Everyone who writes to us will find their name and possibly excerpts from their correspondence in one of our publications (let us know if you *don't* want your letter published or your name acknowledged). They will also receive the latest issue of *Planet Talk*, our quarterly printed newsletter, or *Comet*, our monthly email newsletter. Subscriptions to both newsletters are free. The very best contributions will be rewarded with a free guidebook.

Send all correspondence to the Lonely Planet office closest to you (p. 123).

Lonely Planet books provide independent advice. Lonely Planet does not accept advertising in guidebooks, nor payment in exchange for listing or endorsing any place or business. Lonely Planet writers do not accept discounts or payments in exchange for positive coverage of any sort.

facts about new york city

New York is exhilarating, mad, bursting with spectacle and possibility and hope. At any given moment – now, now and now! – the city is expressing itself. The skyscrapers punch the sky in gleamy victory and there's a guy flossing his teeth on the subway. There's a novel being written in the public library and a dame is shopping Madison Ave with a parrot on her shoulder. There's a constant chatter: people are talking to one another, to you ('where'd you get that sandwich?'), muttering or singing for anyone who's listening. Inanimate objects are just as conversational. There's the hum of machines and

buildings, the hymn of taxis and trains and street signs that read 'don't even *think* about parking here' because 'no standing' is way too wishy-washy. It's the buzz, it's abuzz, it's New York, and there is nowhere to match it in the world.

New York excels in the quantity of its qualities. Other cities have great buildings, museums, restaurants and performances. But no city puts it all together with as much energy and prideful aplomb as this one. Dense, immense, intense – there is no other place with as much

upfront allure. The bagels have the most cream cheese, the panhandlers have the best stories, you can take your dog to church, you can pray to Mecca (or Wiccan) in the street, sell lobster bisque from a hot dog stand and no-one will bat an eyelid. There's a general refusal to be baffled; the answer to any kind of difference, strangeness or outright lunacy is a shrugged 'this is New York'.

Kim Grant

Jazz Age gem – the Chrysler Building

New York is a feast of humans being everything they can be: good, bad, funny, friendly and indifferent. They're engaging in a spontaneous rap, getting the toddler off to analysis, or appearing from nowhere with umbrellas to sell in a rainstorm. A large proportion of them are immigrants, whether from Teaneck or Timbuktu and, like them, you can pursue any dream you want to here. It's not easy – it's expensive, it's relentless and a lot of its residents are struggling just to survive. At its best though, New York is the most intoxicating, energising metropolis we've got. Be warned – many visitors find it extremely hard to leave!

HISTORY

The area now known as New York City was occupied by Native Americans for more than 11,000 years – the name 'Manhattan' was derived from local Munsee Indian words. The first recorded European visitor was Giovanni da Verrazano, in 1524, but Henry Hudson was the first to claim the land for his sponsors, the Dutch East India Company, in 1609.

Colonial Era

The Dutch established their first trading post, Nieuw Amsterdam, in 1624, consolidating their claim 2 years later by reputedly buying Manhattan Island from the Indians for about 60 guilders' worth of gifts. In 1647 Peter Stuyvesant was sent to impose order on the unruly colony, but his intolerant religious and moral views led to unrest. Few resisted the 1664 bloodless takeover by the British, who renamed the colony New York.

Minor opposition to British colonial rule developed but many New Yorkers, with familial ties to the UK, resisted a war for independence. In fact, New York was a British stronghold, and George III's troops controlled the city for most of the War of American Independence.

Boom Years

George Washington was sworn in as the republic's first president in New York in 1789, but the founding fathers disliked the city, then a bustling and dirty seaport of 33,000 people: Thomas Jefferson described it as 'a cloacina of all the depravities of human nature'. By 1830 it had exploded to a metropolis of 250,000.

Manhattan's distinctive street grid was imposed by the Planning Commission in 1811, and the Croton Aqueduct, completed in 1842, brought 283.7 million litres of fresh water into the city daily, greatly improving public health. Commerce and infrastructure boomed.

Growing Pains

New York's explosive growth continued in the late 19th century; its population of half a million more than doubled between 1850 and 1880. Corrupt politicians milked millions from public-works projects, while industrial barons amassed tax-free fortunes. The poorest New Yorkers worked in dangerous factories and lived in squalid apartment blocks, where a tenement culture developed. Meanwhile multimillionaire philanthropists poured money into public institutions like the New York Public Library and Carnegie Hall.

The severely limited space in the downtown business district left no room for growth – the only way to go was up, and by the late 19th century Manhattan had a cluster of new multistorey office buildings called 'skyscrapers'. An expanding network of subways and elevated trains ('els') made the city's outer reaches accessible and areas beyond the official borders grew. In 1898 the independent districts of Queens, Staten Island, the Bronx and Brooklyn became 'boroughs' of a consolidated New York City.

With another wave of European immigrants, the population of the new metropolis leapt from 3 million in 1900 to 7 million in 1930. The Depression caused enormous distress, but Mayor Fiorello La Guardia fought municipal corruption and expanded the social service network, and civic planner Robert Moses remade the city's landscape with public-works projects – many of which were contro-

> **Incoming...**
> 'I support a very specific type of immigration control. I think we should only let people born in other countries get into New York.' – Humorist Fran Lebowitz

versial because they destroyed working-class neighbourhoods. One of Moses' worst mistakes was to design highways at the expense of public transport, resulting in the congested roads of today's city.

Decline & Renewal

After WWII, New York became the world's premier city, but it soon suffered the middle-class flight to the suburbs. Television production, manufacturing and even the fabled Brooklyn Dodgers baseball team moved to the West Coast. By the 1970s, the unreliable, graffiti-ridden subway system had become a symbol of New York's psychic and economic tailspin. Only a massive federal loan program saved the city from bankruptcy. Led by a colourful 3-term mayor named Ed Koch, New York regained much of its swagger in the 1980s. The city, though periodically torn by racial conflict, elected its first African American mayor, David Dinkins, in 1989. After his largely ineffectual single term, he was ousted by the city's overwhelmingly Democratic voters and replaced with Rudy Giuliani, a socially liberal Republican. By the mid-90s, billions were being made on Wall St.

New York City Today

The hard-nosed Giuliani has overseen a 50% drop in crime, the city's 100th birthday (1998), the gentrification of Times Square and the East Village, and the sprucing up of Harlem. Strangely enough, New Yorkers have entered the new millennium with the somewhat grudging feeling that, perhaps, the 'Capital of the World' has found a way to thrive as well as survive. Giuliani's second term is up at the beginning of 2002; he's not allowed to run for a third consecutive term.

Bright lights; big city – Times Square

ORIENTATION

New York City sits at the mouth of the Hudson River where it meets the west end of Long Island Sound and opens to the sea. The city (actually some 50 islands with 309 sq miles/800 sq km land mass) comprises 5 boroughs: Manhattan, Staten Island, Brooklyn, Queens and The Bronx.

Popular tourist sites are concentrated in the southern end of Manhattan. Most of the island is easy to navigate, thanks to a grid system of named or numbered avenues running north-south, cut across by numbered streets that run east-west. Navigation can be trickier in the oldest part of the city, from 14th St to the southern tip of Manhattan, as streets snake along haphazardly. Broadway, the only avenue to cut diagonally across the island, runs from the southern tip of the island all the way to the state capital Albany. Above Washington Square, Fifth Ave serves as the dividing line between the 'East Side' and the 'West Side'. Manhattan has no official suburbs and its many neighbourhoods don't always have fixed boundaries (p. 29).

The Bronx is the most northerly borough and the only one on the mainland. It includes the run-down South Bronx, north suburban Fieldston and the quiet fishing community of City Island. Brooklyn, on the western tip of Long Island, is the most populous of the outer boroughs, with 2.5 million people. Queens, adjoining Brooklyn on Long Island, is the largest and most ethnically diverse borough in the city, with some 2 million people speaking 120 different languages. The 'forgotten borough' of Staten Island often threatens secession from the city. It's the smallest borough (population 380,000) and can be reached by the famous and free Staten Island Ferry.

ENVIRONMENT

New York has come a long way in improving air and waterway quality but the city's streets are anything but pristine, and its infrastructure is in desperate need of improvement. Summer heat and air pollution produce brownouts, and heavy rain can shut down the subways: sometimes it seems as though the operational veneer of the city is a very thin skin indeed.

Green awareness is growing, but recycling efforts remain patchy and unnecessary consumption rife (NYC produces a massive 23,000 tons of waste daily). The Hudson River used to be a dumping ground for 758 million litres of sewage daily but that changed with the opening of a sewage treatment plant on W 125th St in 1986. You can catch striped bass, blueback herring, yellow perch and blue crab in the Hudson, and health officials say they're safe to eat.

Whatever the conditions of the air and water, visitors will probably suffer most from the 24hr noise pollution in New York – the car horns, sirens and trucks bedevil those used to quieter environs.

Winter steam rises from under New York City's dirty boulevards.

Angus Oborn

GOVERNMENT & POLITICS

New York has a long record of voting for the Democratic Party, though there are conservative pockets in the blue collar sections of Queens and Brooklyn, and suburban-flavoured Staten Island is almost exclusively Republican. Despite the Democratic tradition, socially liberal Republican reformers can be elected mayor, as has been proved by Rudolph Giuliani.

City politics is often a hot topic for New Yorkers. Given that their town has the population of a small nation and that its residents are chatty, opinionated folk, the intensity of debate can be quite high. The image many outsiders have of New York as an unwieldy metropolis is at odds with the important role played by local activism in the community – childcare, soup kitchens and community gardens are just a few of the resident-run projects that keep the city feeling neighbourly.

The city's political structure includes 5 borough presidents (for community-level works and patronage), a city-wide comptroller and a public advocate. New York also has a city council of 51 elected officials who represent individual neighbourhoods. They are supposed to provide a check on mayoral power, but have been criticised for lack of political input.

ECONOMY

New York could stand alone as its own city state. It is either the nation's leader or a major player in the worlds of finance, tourism, shipping and transportation, and is still a prestige address for major US corporations and nearly all prominent foreign concerns.

Though the city fell seriously behind in manufacturing in the post WWII era, it is still the country's leading producer of fashion

did you know?
- there are 7.5 million New Yorkers
- over 35 million people visit the city each year (28 million domestic and 7 million international)
- tourists spend $14 billion supporting 131,000 jobs & 25,000 businesses
- NYC has 65,000 hotel rooms
- a tiny studio apartment in Manhattan can cost $1200 a month
- Over 200 feature films are shot in New York City each year

and the world's communications centre. And even in this time of electronic 24hr global communications, New York is still the leading financial centre.

SOCIETY & CULTURE

New York City is a singular example of racial diversity – about 30% of residents are foreign-born, buttressing its reputation as the nation's 'melting pot'. Downtown, Chinatown and Little Italy are easily recognisable, the East Village and southern Harlem is Hispanic, and African Americans are still the dominant group in Harlem proper. Washington Heights is home to many former citizens of the Dominican Republic and El Salvador.

Many other ethnic groups have dispersed to the boroughs. Most of the Jewish population, once in the Lower East Side, have moved to The Bronx, Brooklyn and Queens, though the Upper West Side remains strongly Jewish. Koreans have made their niche in Flushing and Ecuadorians and Colombians have settled in Queens (also home to a large Greek colony in Astoria).

Despite intermittent flarings of racial tension, New York is one of the US's best-integrated cities. This isn't to say it's one big happy family (it isn't), but millions of New Yorkers of all ethnicities live in close proximity, usually without incident. This is as much by necessity as due to any glowing humanist tendencies – it would be very exhausting to maintain your prejudices here.

Etiquette
There isn't any particular look you can adopt to fit in – practically anything goes, unless you're intending to dine in a fine restaurant (where jacket and tie are required) or a leather bar (BYO whip). The best pose is confidence – you really can do *anything* in this town.

Even the most go-ahead tourist can be marked as an outsider in many tiny ways – by actually looking up at the buildings, crossing the street at a corner instead of jaywalking, or attempting to read the *New York Times* on a packed subway train without first folding it lengthwise and then in half.

Smoking Smoking cigarettes is as fashionable as farting on the subway. Cancer sticks are banned in government buildings, offices, public transport, taxis, concert venues and theatres. Cigarettes are not allowed in most restaurants (p. 76), though you can puff proud in most clubs and bars.

Arts
Literature New York's literary scene has been dominated by the likes of F Scott Fitzgerald, Henry James, Edith Wharton, Jay McInerney and Tom Wolfe. For an overview of the city in literature, pick up Shaun O'Connell's *Remarkable, Unspeakable, New York*, a survey of how American writers have regarded the metropolis over 2 centuries. For New York reads, see p. 62.

Film Martin Scorsese is celebrated for bringing the dark side of NYC to life, and comic artist Woody Allen turns out a film most every year. Sidney Lumet represents an older, more idealistic liberal sensibility, and Spike Lee foregrounds an African American perspective. Harmony Korine is the most exciting young film-maker working in New York today.

Music New York is home to some of the foremost classical music and operatic organisations in the world, and leading composers and conductors, including Gustav Mahler, Arturo Toscanini, Leonard Bernstein and John Cage, have achieved fame and fortune here.

Ragtime owes its popularity to Scott Joplin and Irving Berlin. Jazz hit the mainstream in New York thanks to George Gershwin and Duke Ellington, who once declared: 'the whole world revolves around New York. Very little happens anywhere else unless someone in New York presses the button'. Trumpeter Dizzy Gillespie and saxophonist Charlie Parker ushered in bebop, which gave way to the freer expressions of Miles Davis and

Sonny Rollins. Wynton Marsalis and Joshua Redman now lead the way.

Popular-music icons like Bob Dylan, The Doors and Jimi Hendrix found validation and increased popularity in New York. Powercouple Lou Reed and Laurie Anderson are among the most influential New York-based contemporary musicians. Iggy Pop is kicking on in Alphabet City and the not-so-nasty Beastie Boys still rap it up.

Dance New York has incubated most of the USA's prominent dance companies and choreographers, including Martha Graham. Russian-born choreographer George Balanchine founded the NYC Ballet (now directed by Peter Martins). The Alvin Ailey, Martha Graham and Paul Taylor companies and the Dance Theater of Harlem perform annually.

Theatre Broadway has hosted the work of most prestigious American playwrights, including Eugene O'Neill, Sam Shepard, August Wilson, David Mamet, Neil Simon and Arthur Miller. Tin Pan Alley composers George Gershwin and Cole Porter produced many of the most enduring musicals. Such is the allure of New York's stages that George M Cohan (theatre producer, actor and playwright who wrote *Give My Regards to Broadway*) said: 'When you are away from old Broadway, you are only camping out'.

Painting Edward Hopper is one of the best-known painters associated with New York. Others include Thomas Cole and Frederic Edwin Church (Hudson River School), impressionists Childe Hassam and Mary Cassatt, Marcel Duchamp and Man Ray (school of Dada), abstract expressionists Jackson Pollock and Willem de Kooning, and Andy Warhol (pop art).

Photography Influential figures associated with New York include Alfred Stieglitz and Man Ray, both of whom helped develop photography as an art form. Other notables include prominent photojournalists Margaret Bourke-White and Alfred Eisenstaedt, and fashion photographers Weegee (Arthur H Fellig), William Klein and Richard Avedon. American-born photographers Stephen Meisel, Herb Ritts and Annie Liebowitz are as famous for their commercial works as their artistic endeavours.

Cats – one of the long-running Andrew Lloyd Webber mega-musicals on Broadway.

highlights

I t's not very 'New York' to race around sightseeing – most residents have never been to the Statue of Liberty and only distantly remember a childhood trip to the Met. Quintessential New York experiences are often chance encounters with locals, mooching in cafes, hearing subway buskers or watching a basketball game on a local court.

That said, the highlight attractions here are all world-beaters: postcard sights are breathtaking, museums and galleries are boggling in their brilliance and some neighbourhoods are crackling with history and atmosphere.

You may notice that you're not the only visitor in town, especially if you get stuck in a 3hr queue for the Empire State Building. Avoid delays by getting up early in order to be among the first for every site. A **CityPass** (www.citypass.net) lets you bypass ticket lines for 6 major attractions (and saves 50% on admission). Ask for it at participating venues (see individual information boxes), or pre-purchase via the Website.

However you spend your time, you can't really go wrong, as New York's vibrancy and character is sure to infiltrate even the most insulated tourist itinerary.

NYC Lowlights

It's overwhelming – it's fast, expensive and crowded, and there's too much to see and do. It's too hot in summer and too cold in winter, and the shoulder seasons are too damn short. The hotel rooms are small, you've got to queue for the sights, elbow your way onto the subway, and sometimes you've even got to pay $10 for a sandwich.

This is a subjective list of what we don't like; lots of people can handle this stuff but it isn't us:

- shopping at the Manhattan Mall or the South Street Seaport
- eating in Mulberry St, Little Italy
- door snobs at entertainment venues
- the lack of efficient airport transport
- low level environmental awareness (how many napkins do people need?)
- salad bars
- queuing up for brunch when you're really hungry

Stopping Over?

One Day Whiz up the Empire State Building to get your bearings then head over to MoMA for an art attack. Stroll up Madison Ave for some boutique-browsing or buying. Duck into Central Park before taking the subway or a taxi to Greenwich Village for dinner.

Two Days Catch the early ferry to the Statue of Liberty and Ellis Island and return to the Financial District to pop into the Stock Exchange. Take a ride up the World Trade Center (North Tower) where you can have a drink or dinner.

Three Days After a sleep in and lazy brunch over the *New York Times*, visit the American Museum of Natural History or the Met, then shop and gallery hop in SoHo til it's time to dine.

Big yellow taxis clog New York's arterials.

Kim Grant

AMERICAN MUSEUM OF NATURAL HISTORY (2, E4)

The museum was founded in 1869 on the basis of a mastodon's tooth and a few thousand beetles. It now has over 32 million artefacts in its collection. It is most famous for its 3 large **dinosaur halls**, which have been significantly renovated and now provide information about the latest discoveries of how these behemoths behaved and theories as to why they disappeared. Knowledgeable guides roam the dinosaur halls ready to answer questions, and there are 'please touch' displays that allow you to handle, among other items, the skullcap of a **pachycephulosaurus**, a planteating dinosaur that roamed the earth 65 million years ago.

The treasures of the 4 floors of the permanent collection include the scary-looking plaster blue whale that hangs from the ceiling above the **Hall of Ocean Life**. There's a strong ecological slant to newer exhibitions – the **Hall of Biodiversity**, tells the story of earth's diversity and the threats to it from environmental degradation.

While some of the mammal halls still have a gloomy, Victorian-era look, the museum is aggressively updating the facility with 'electronic newspaper' video terminals and excellent look-and-learn displays.

There's an **IMAX screen** in a beautiful old theatre and a spectacular **Center for Earth and Space**, including a redesigned **planetarium** and **Big Bang Theater**, which re-creates the birth of the universe.

Mostly, the museum does an exceptional job of letting visitors of all ages be as educated or entertained as they wish. Staff are helpful, and there are also plenty of places to sit down and rest and lots of toilets.

INFORMATION

- ✉ Central Park West & 79th St, Upper West Side
- ☎ 769-5100
- Ⓜ 81st St
- 🚌 M7, M10, M11, M79
- 🕐 10am-5.45pm (to 8.45pm Fri-Sat)
- 💲 $9.50/6; $14/8.50 with IMAX; temporary exhibits extra; CityPass
- ⓘ audio tours; free guided tours hourly (10.15am-3.15pm); kids' Discovery Room ☎ 769-5304
- ℮ www.amnh.org
- ♿ good
- 🍴 Diner Saurus, Ocean Life Food Court

Neil Setchfield

Kim Grant

Dry bones make for lively exhibits.

DON'T MISS
- Star of India • blue whale • barosaurus

BROOKLYN BRIDGE   (3, J8)

Regarded by many as the most beautiful bridge in the world and a magnificent example of fine urban design, the Brooklyn Bridge is the first steel suspension bridge ever built, and its 478m span between the 2 support towers was the world's longest when it opened in 1883.

It remains a compelling symbol of US achievement and a superbly graceful structure, though its construction was plagued by budget overruns and the deaths of 20 workers, including designer John Roebling, the inventor of wire cable, who died in 1869 of tetanus poisoning after being knocked off a pier. His son took charge of the project but succumbed to the bends while working on the excavation and supervised operations from a telescope in his sick room. Twelve pedestrians were trampled in a panic that the bridge was collapsing during the opening ceremony.

There's no fear of collapse today, as the bridge enters its 2nd century following an extensive renovation in the early 1980s. The pedestrian walkway that begins just east of City Hall affords a wonderful view of Lower Manhattan, and you can stop at observation points under both stone support towers and view brass panorama histories of the waterfront at various points in New York's history.

Once you reach the Brooklyn side (about a 20min walk) you can bear right to walk down to Cadman Plaza West to a park that will bring you to Middagh St, which runs east to west in the heart of Brooklyn Heights. Continuing left brings you to Brooklyn's downtown area, which includes the ornate Borough Hall and Fulton St pedestrian mall.

From Saturday Night Fever *to* 9-to-5 – *Brooklyn workers cross the bridge to Manhattan.*

Kim Grant

DON'T MISS
• walking or cycling across the bridge at sunset • an evening riverside promenade in Brooklyn Heights • boat trip under the bridge (p. 52-3)

CENTRAL PARK   (2)

This large rectangular park, right in the middle of Manhattan, is for many what makes New York liveable. On weekends it's packed with joggers, skaters, musicians and tourists, but north of 72nd St the crowds thin out, and it's easier to appreciate the landscaping. Though the park is quite safe during the day, it's best to stick to peopled areas after dark.

Central Park's 337 hectares were set aside in 1856, on the marshy northern fringe of the city. The project received wide support: the rich wanted a setting for pony and carriage rides while the social-minded wanted workers to have an alternative retreat to saloons. The naturalist landscaping was innovative, with forested groves, winding paths and informal ponds.

In the 1960s and 70s the park hosted legendary rock concerts (such as Simon & Garfunkel) and hippy 'be-ins'. The Public Theater, the Metropolitan Opera and the New York Philharmonic also began their **free summer performances** at this time. Recent events have included a performance by Baaba Maal and an audience with the Dalai Lama.

The roadway encircling the park and the path around Jacqueline Kennedy Onassis reservoir are extra popular with runners, in-line skaters and bikers (p. 44).

Bikes and boats are available for rent in good weather at the Loeb Boathouse (☎ 517-2233) on the East Drive near 74th St. **Ice-skating** is possible from October to May at the Wollman Rink (☎ 396-1010), which is mid-park at 62nd St, and at the less crowded Lasker Rink (☎ 534-7639), which is uptown near E 106th St.

INFORMATION

- ⊠ bounded by 59th & 110th Sts, Fifth Ave & Central Park West
- ☎ Dairy Visitor & Information Center 794-6564, 360-3444
- 🚇 5th Ave (N, R), Columbus Circle, 72nd St (B, C), 81st St, 86th St (B, C), 103rd St (B, C), Cathedral Pkwy (B, C), Central Park Nth
- 🚌 M1 to M5, M7, M10, M18, M72, M79, M86
- ⊙ 6am-1am
- $ free
- ⓘ free music, theatre (see Joseph Papp, p. 86) and family events
- 🖥 www.central parknyc.org
- ♿ good
- ✗ Park View Restaurant, Tavern on the Green, kiosks

Angus Oborn

Kim Grant

Bethesda Terrace at the people's park

DON'T MISS • The Ramble • Strawberry Fields • The Carousel • Wildlife Center • fishing • a horse-drawn carriage ride ($34/30min)

CHINATOWN (3, G7)

Though the first Chinese sailors and traders arrived in the 1780s, New York's Chinatown didn't grow quickly. In 1859 there were only about 150 Chinese in Lower Manhattan, clustered between Pell and Doyers Sts and in the southern part of Mott St. The community expanded in the 1870s, largely as a consequence of an influx of overlanders from California, but its growth was stunted by the Chinese Exclusion Act, which prevented men from having their families join them from China.

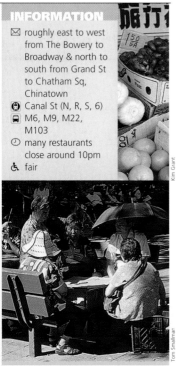

INFORMATION

- ✉ roughly east to west from The Bowery to Broadway & north to south from Grand St to Chatham Sq, Chinatown
- Ⓖ Canal St (N, R, S, 6)
- 🚌 M6, M9, M22, M103
- 🕑 many restaurants close around 10pm
- ♿ fair

Card players in Columbus Park, Chinatown

Chinatown began to grow after the Exclusion Act was repealed in 1943, but immigration quotas kept a lid on the community's expansion. In 1965, the 20,000 Chinese New Yorkers were still mostly male. When the quotas were relaxed in 1968, a further 20,000 Chinese were allowed to enter and New York suddenly became the biggest Chinese city in the western hemisphere, growing beyond Chinatown and into the boroughs, particularly Flushing, Queens and Sunset Park, Brooklyn.

Today Chinatown is a thriving community of more than 120,000 residents, many living and working in their mini-society without using a word of English. The 1990s saw an influx of Vietnamese immigrants. Chinatown has also expanded east and north – you can now find Chinese businesses in the area above Canal St, particularly Grand St, which has busy fruit stands and fish stores open into the evening.

The Chinese shopping district begins past Baxter St, with stands selling fresh, exotic produce. At the southern end of Mott St is a busy restaurant strip, the **Eastern States Buddhist Temple** (No 64), and the **Church of the Transfiguration** (No 29), historically Irish and Italian but today holds services in Chinese. For a self-guided walk through Chinatown, see p. 47.

DON'T MISS
- Museum of Chinese in the Americas (p. 31) • shopping along Baxter, Canal & Grand Sts • a Chinese or Vietnamese meal

ELLIS ISLAND & IMMIGRATION MUSEUM   (3, P2)

Ellis Island was New York's main immigration station from 1892 to 1954 – more than 12 million people passed through here. Its early years were busiest: in 1907 an all-time high of 1 million new Americans arrived. Later, Ellis Island also operated as a hospital for soldiers and a detention station for deportees and illegal aliens. When the island was abandoned in 1954, only one inmate needed to be rehoused: a sailor detained for the dastardly crime of overstaying his shore leave.

A $160 million restoration has turned the impressive red-brick main building into an **Immigration Museum** with a series of galleries on the history of the island. The exhibitions begin at the **Baggage Room**, and continue up to 2nd-storey rooms where medical inspections took place. The doctors had an initial look-see down to 6 seconds; if further investigation was necessary, the immigrant's clothes were marked with chalk.

Pick up the 'telephones' to hear the voices of Ellis Island immigrants, or take the 50min audio tour to hear actors reading from immigrants' letters. A film describes the immigrant experience, and exhibits show how the influx changed the USA. There's also an interesting wall display of Tin Pan Alley sheet music that was aimed at the new foreign-born audience.

The exhibits emphasise that, contrary to popular myth, most of the ship-borne immigrants were processed within 8hrs and that conditions were generally clean and safe. The 101m-long **Registry Room** includes a beautiful vaulted tile ceiling made by immigrants from Spain. But walking though the registry today surely can't compare to the days when the same room housed a queue of 5000 confused and tired people waiting to be interviewed by overworked immigration officers.

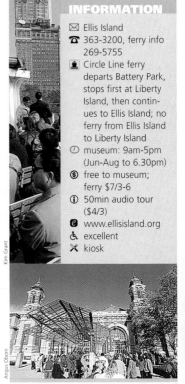

INFORMATION

✉ Ellis Island
☎ 363-3200, ferry info 269-5755
🚢 Circle Line ferry departs Battery Park, stops first at Liberty Island, then continues to Ellis Island; no ferry from Ellis Island to Liberty Island
🕐 museum: 9am-5pm (Jun-Aug to 6.30pm)
$ free to museum; ferry $7/3-6
ⓘ 50min audio tour ($4/3)
🌐 www.ellisisland.org
♿ excellent
✗ kiosk

Gateway to the States – Ellis Island

DON'T MISS
• exhibits: Through America's Gate, Ellis Island Chronicles and Treasures from Home • Ellis Island Stories play • Statue of Liberty and city views

EMPIRE STATE BUILDING (2, N6)

New York's original skyline symbol is a limestone classic built in just 410 days during the depths of the Depression at a cost of $41 million. Located on the site of the original Waldorf-Astoria Hotel, the 102-storey Empire State Building opened in 1931 and was immediately the most exclusive business address in the city.

The famous antenna was originally intended to be a zeppelin mooring mast, but the Hindenberg disaster put a stop to that plan. One airship accidentally met up with the building: a B25 crashed into the 79th floor on a foggy day in July 1945, killing 14 people.

About 16,000 people work in the building and a staggering 35,000 people visit the observatory every day. The building's top 30 floors are floodlit in seasonal and holiday colours (eg green for St Patrick's Day, red and green for Christmas and pink for Gay Pride weekend in June).

Reaching the observatories on the 86th and 102nd floors means standing in line for tickets and elevators on the concourse level and sometimes being confronted with another line at the top. If you can't get there early, it's worth waiting until late evening to avoid the worst of the crush. An alternative crowd-beating solution is to buy a combination ticket which includes the silly-but-fun **New York Skyride**, on the 2nd floor; queues are never long here.

Once you're up there you can stay as long as you want. There are **coin-operated telescopes** and diagrams to help you identify what you're gawking at. Due to the fact that Manhattan is so compact, you can usually point out where you're staying, where you've been and make a mental map of your plans for the rest of the day.

Elevators? Pah!

Every year there is a foot race up the 1860 stairs from street level to the 102nd floor. The record, set by Australian Paul Crake, is 10mins 15secs.

A king kong of a view over the Chrysler Building from the Empire State

GREENWICH VILLAGE   (3, C4)

Greenwich Village is one of the city's most popular neighbourhoods, and a symbol throughout the world for all things outlandish and bohemian. It began as a trading port for Indians, who liked the easy access to the shores of what is now Hoboken, New Jersey, just across the Hudson River. Dutch settlers established tobacco plantations, and the peaceful wooded area was named Greenwich Village by their English successors. As the city began to develop a large servant class, Greenwich Village became New York's most prominent black neighbourhood until many of those residents moved to Harlem just before the 1920s in search of better housing. The brownstone buildings they abandoned are now some of the most fashionable and valuable properties in the city.

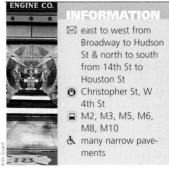

INFORMATION

- ✉ east to west from Broadway to Hudson St & north to south from 14th St to Houston St
- Ⓧ Christopher St, W 4th St
- 🚍 M2, M3, M5, M6, M8, M10
- ♿ many narrow pavements

Its reputation as a creative enclave can be traced back at least 100 years when artists and writers such as Walt Whitman, Edgar Allen Poe and Edna St Vincent Millay moved in. By the 1940s the area was known as a gathering place for gays. The West Village today is a mixed neighbourhood – some of bars and bookshops cater to gays and lesbians but there are plenty of straight-friendly venues.

The centre of 'the Village' is dominated by **New York University** (3, D5), owner of most property around **Washington Square Park** (3, D5). South-west of the park, there is a lively, crowded collection of cafes, shops and restaurants. Beyond 7th Ave is the West Village, a pleasant neighbourhood of crooked streets and town houses that is loaded with buildings of architectural or historical importance – look for bronze landmark plaques explaining their significance. A self-guided walk of Greenwich Village is on p. 48.

Quoth artist Marcel Duchamp:

'New York is a work of art – a complete work of art ... A real bohemia. Delightful. Why, Greenwich Village was full of people doing absolutely *nothing*.'

Above: Stone couples, Stonewall Place
Top: Even the Fire Station is artsy

DON'T MISS
- cafes • New York's narrowest house (p. 48) • Forbes Galleries
- jazz clubs • Minetta Lane intersection of W 4th & W 11th St

METROPOLITAN MUSEUM OF ART (2, D6)

Commonly called 'The Met', this vast museum is New York's most popular single-site tourist attraction. When you enter the **Great Hall**, pick up a floor plan and work out what you'd most like to see before fatigue sets in – the riches of the Met are quite overwhelming. The first choice is between 2 ancient worlds, the Egyptian, to your right as you enter, and the Greek & Roman, to your left.

If you begin with the **Egyptian Art** section in the northern wing, start with the tomb of Pernebi, then keep left to pass several mummies and some incredibly well-preserved wall paintings. Farther on you come to the entire Temple of Dendur, saved from submersion in the waters behind the Aswan Dam.

Exit behind the temple and head to the **American Wing**, starting with a valuable collection of baseball cards. Continue left through exhibits of furniture and clocks. Along an enclosed garden are displays of Tiffany stained-glass and the entire façade of the Branch Bank of the US.

You then pass through the dark **Medieval Galleries**, with artefacts, jewellery and religious art. Turn right to the **Lehman Collection** of Italian, Impressionist and modern art. If you continue to the northeastern corner, you come upon the 20th century art collection (and the elevator to the roof garden).

Heading back toward Fifth Ave you pass through the Rockefeller collection of **Africa, Oceania & the Americas** and into the new **Greek & Roman Galleries**, before winding up back at the southern side of the Great Hall. On the 2nd floor is the Met's unrivalled collection of **European Paintings** and the **Asian Art** wing.

INFORMATION

- ⊠ Fifth Ave & 82nd St, Upper East Side
- ☎ 879-5500
- ⊖ 86th St (4, 5, 6)
- 🚌 M1-M5
- ⏰ Tues-Thurs & Sun 9.30am-5.15pm, Fri-Sat 9.30am-8.45pm
- 💲 $10/5/free (under 12); CityPass valid
- ⓘ $5 audio tours; free guided tours; free calendars; combo ticket for The Cloisters; film screenings; children's programs
- ♿ good, wheelchairs available; tours for visually handicapped ☎ 535-7710, deaf ☎ 879-0421
- 🄴 www.metmuseum.org
- ✕ bar, cafes & restaurant

Massed culture at The Met

Dale Setchfield

Neil Setchfield

DON'T MISS
- Sarcophagus of Har-khebi • Renoir's *Two Young Girls at the Piano*
- de Kooning's *Woman* • Picasso's *The Dreamer* • van Gogh's *Cypresses* • works from Rodin's *The Gates of Hell* • The Paradise of Bhaishajyaguru • music on the roof garden (Fri & Sat evening)

MUSEUM OF MODERN ART   (2, J6)

The Museum of Modern Art (MoMA) was founded in 1929 and moved to its present location in 1939. It has a world-class collection not to be missed. In its sculpture and painting galleries are a number of works by Picasso, van Gogh's *Starry Night* and Matisse's *Dance 1*. A quiet stand-alone gallery is dedicated solely to Monet's 3-panelled *Water Lilies*.

The **Abby Aldrich Rockefeller Sculpture Garden** is the setting for concerts throughout the year.

The museum places a special emphasis on photography and film, 2 areas of visual expression that tend to get short shrift at the larger Metropolitan Museum of Art. There are daily film screenings in MoMA's 2 basement theatres (entry is free with admission), and an Oscar, awarded to the museum's film department in 1978, is on permanent display along with an impressive collection of film posters.

At least once a year, MoMA puts on an important exhibit of a single major artist's work: recent retrospectives have focused on Jackson

INFORMATION

✉ 11 W 53rd St, b/w Fifth & Sixth Aves, Midtown

☎ 708-9480

⊕ 5th Ave (E, F)

🚌 M1 to M4

🕐 Sat-Tues & Thurs 10.30am-6pm, Fri 10.30am-8:30pm

💲 $9.50/6.50/free (under 16); 'pay what you wish' Fri after 4.30pm; CityPass

♿ good

🌐 www.moma.org

ⓘ audio tour ($4), live jazz in the garden Fri evenings (not July and Aug)

🍴 Sette MoMa Bar & Ristorante

☎ 708-9710

Upside Down & Red Faced

In 1961, Henri Matisse's *Le Bateau*, a gouache of a sailing boat and its reflection, hung upside down in MoMA for nearly 2 months before anyone noticed. The 116,000 visitors to the museum in this period included Matisse's son, Pierre.

Pollock and Alfred Hitchcock. Themed exhibitions often have a speculative aspect: 1999's *Fame After Photography* investigated the cult of celebrity. The gallery also maintains a commitment to emerging artists.

MoMA is all the better for being modest in size; it's much more manageable than the Met. The down side is that your Picasso is often blocked by a couple of kids having their photo taken in front of it. If you're pressed for time or simply undecided about where to go, it's a good idea to rent the $4 audio tour of the museum narrated by chief curator Kirk Varnedoe.

MoMA's fabulous sculpture garden

NEW YORK STOCK EXCHANGE　　(3, K5)

Though 'Wall St' is the widely recognised metaphor for US capitalism, the world's best-known stock exchange is actually around the corner on Broad St, behind a portentous façade reminiscent of a Roman temple.

INFORMATION

- ✉ 8 Broad St & Wall St, Lower Manhattan
- ☎ 656-5165
- Ⓣ Wall St, Broad St
- 🚌 M6
- ⏱ Mon-Fri 9.15am-4.30pm
- 💲 free (tickets from 20 Broad St)
- ⓘ self-guided tours
- ♿ yes
- 🌐 www.nyse.com
- 🍴 Mangia (p. 78)

Tom Smallman

Free tickets allow entrance to the visitors' centre in 45min time periods throughout the day and are usually snapped up by noon. While waiting in line, you'll see dozens of brokers wearing colour-coordinated trading jackets popping out of the NYSE for a quick cigarette or hot dog.

Once you get inside, don't waste too much time in the self-guided 'Interactive Education Center', which is not much more than PR fluff about what a good corporate citizen the NYSE is. The modern business of the exchange isn't explained very well, and there is no information about the famous 1929 stock market crash or even the 1987 debacle that led to restrictions on the computer-programmed stock dumping that triggered it off.

Keep going to the visitors' gallery overlooking the frenetic trading floor where attendants are on hand to explain what everyone is doing. Each of the NYSE's 1600 'seats' is worth about $2.6 million; brokers here handle trade in shares for 10,000 different companies.

If you're lucky, you will receive a ticket for the time period that includes the 4pm end of trading, when a retiring broker or other financial worthy is given the honour of ringing a bell that brings the business day to a close. Cheers arise if the market closes on a high note; groans and oaths abound on a down day.

I'm in the Market for You

George Olsen's song reflects the Jazz Age optimism before the 1929 crash: *'I'll have to see my broker ... cos I'm in the market for you ... You're going up, up, up in my estimation, I want a thousand shares of your caresses too ... We'll count the hugs and kisses, when dividends are due, cos I'm in the market for you.'*

Angus Oborn

NYSE – where bear battles bull daily

ROCKEFELLER CENTER   (2, K6)

Known for its ice rink, Christmas tree, statuary and decorated façades, the Art Deco Rockefeller Center was started in 1931 and took 9 years to complete. Some 200 dwellings were removed to make way for the project, but at the time that was less controversial than the lobby mural by Mexican artist Diego Rivera, which depicted Lenin; it was covered during the opening ceremonies and later destroyed. Its replacement, painted by José Maria Sert, features the more acceptable Abraham Lincoln.

The Center is at its best in winter, when the plaza is converted into an ice-skating rink and the famous Christmas tree sparkles in the chill air. The ritual lighting of the tree occurs at the start of December, complete with skating shows, choirs and kids salivating over Santa.

The **Radio City Musical Hall**, a 6000-seat Art Deco movie palace, had its interior declared a protected landmark. A 1999 refit has restored it to former glory – even the smoking rooms and toilets are elegant. Concerts sell out quickly and tickets to the annual Christmas pageant featuring the corny-but-enjoyable Rockettes dancers are $30-80.

The **NBC TV Network Studio** headquarters are located in the GE Building (not to be confused with the Art Deco General Electric Building at 50th St & Lexington Ave). The **NBC Discovery Center** in the base of the GE Building offers a number of free activities (you can be a weather reporter or a guest on the Jay Leno show). The expensive studio tour is fun but probably only worth it if you're a fan of the American shows taped here. The *Today* show is broadcast from 7 to 9am daily from the plaza south of the fountain area and always draws a crowd.

INFORMATION

- ✉ from 48th St to 51st St, b/w Fifth & Sixth Aves, Midtown
- ☎ 632-3975
- ⊕ Rockefeller Center
- 🚌 M1 to M7, M27, M50
- 💲 outdoor area and GE Bldg lobby free; skating $7.50-11/4-6 (skate hire $4-5)
- ① Radio City Music Hall tours (☎ 632-4041) 10am-5pm (from 11am Sun) ($15/9); NBC studio tours (☎ 664-3700) Mon-Sat 8.30am-7pm, Sun 9.30am-4.30pm ($17.50/15); NBC TV taping info p. 94
- ♿ yes
- ✆ www.radiocity.com www.nbc.com
- ✗ The Sea Grill, American Festival Cafe, Chez Louis

John D Rockefeller Jr's very, very big baby

Kim Grant

Angus Oborn

DON'T MISS
- Prometheus statue • Atlas statue • frescoes on the GE Building
- Radio City Music Hall tours • skating in winter • NBC studio tour

SOLOMON R GUGGENHEIM MUSEUM (2, C6)

The inspired work of Frank Lloyd Wright, the sweeping spiral of the Guggenheim, is a superb sculpture in which the excellent collection of 20th-century paintings is almost an afterthought. The building was commissioned by Solomon Guggenheim in 1943 but construction didn't commence until 1957. Wright died 6 months before the building was finished in 1959. A controversial 1993 extension added a 10 storey tower designed by Gwathmey Siegel.

INFORMATION

✉ 1071 Fifth Ave & 88th St, Upper East Side

☎ 423-3500

🚇 86th St (4, 5, 6)

🚌 M1 to M4

🕐 Sun-Wed 9am-6pm, Fri-Sat 9am-8pm

💲 $12/free (under 12s); 'pay what you wish' Fri evening

ℹ Fri & Sat jazz evening; films on Tues; daily tours; children's & family programs; wine tastings

🄴 www.guggenheim.org

♿ very good; ☎ 423-3539 for information

✕ Museum Café

Angus Oborn

Rick Gerharter

The Guggenheim's immortal coil

The museum has a permanent collection including work by Picasso, Pollock, Chagall, Cézanne and (especially) Kandinsky. In 1976, Justin Thannhauser bequeathed his impressive collection of contemporary art, which now comprises the bulk of the museum's late 19th century and early 20th century art, including Monet, Pissarro, van Gogh and Degas.

The museum's **collection of American Minimalist art** from the 1960s and 70s was enriched by the acquisition of the collection of Panzo di Biumo in 1990. In 1993, the Robert Mapplethorpe Foundation donated 200 photographs to the gallery, spurring the museum to devote the 4th floor of the tower to photography exhibitions.

Temporary exhibitions, often drawn from private collections, take up the bulk of the spiral area and the museum's permanent collection is generally displayed in the offshoot tower galleries. Though the exhibitions tend to work bottom to top, you could consider taking the lift to the 6th floor and letting gravity help you make your way back down. It's great to be able to wander around the spiral without having to worry about missing anything or finding your way out at the end.

DON'T MISS
- Matisse's *The Italian Woman* • Kandinsky's *In the Black Square*
- Mondrian's *New York City I* • van Gogh's *Peasants Lifting Potatoes*
- Picasso's *Moulin de la Galette* • Cézanne's *Man with Crossed Arms*

SOUTH STREET SEAPORT   (3, K7)

The seaport was the central New York port during the 'Golden Age of Sail'. The famous *Flying Cloud* docked here before embarking on her record breaking voyages to San Francisco via Cape Horn. This was also the main East River ferry dock but fell into disuse upon the building of the Brooklyn Bridge and the establishment of deep-water piers on the Hudson River.

Now restored, the 11-block enclave includes historic ships and buildings, an excellent series of small museums with a maritime bent and a lot of sterile shops and restaurants. It's the best and worst in urban design.

The **South Street Seaport Museum** oversees several interesting sights in the area, including 3 galleries, an antique printing shop, a children's activity centre, a maritime crafts centre and the ships. Standing just south of Pier 17 are several **tall-masted sailing vessels**, including the *Peking*, the *Wavertree*, the *Pioneer* and the lightship *Ambrose*. From Pier 16 you can take an hour-long riverboat tour that highlights Manhattan maritime history.

Pier 17 is also the site of the **Fulton Fish Market**, where most of the city's restaurants get their fresh seafood. The nightly working of the market can be seen from midnight to 8am. There are great views of the East River bridges from the building behind the market; this is also the site of the most yawn-inducing shops and restaurants in Manhattan. **Schermerhorn Row**, a block of old warehouses bordered by Fulton, Front and South Sts, contains a visitors' centre, shops, restaurants and a pub.

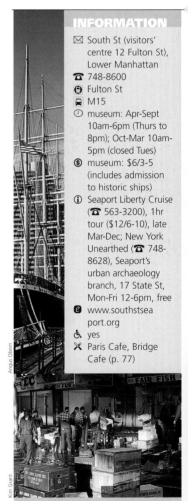

INFORMATION

- ✉ South St (visitors' centre 12 Fulton St), Lower Manhattan
- ☎ 748-8600
- Ⓕ Fulton St
- 🚌 M15
- 🕐 museum: Apr-Sept 10am-6pm (Thurs to 8pm); Oct-Mar 10am-5pm (closed Tues)
- 💲 museum: $6/3-5 (includes admission to historic ships)
- ⓘ Seaport Liberty Cruise (☎ 563-3200), 1hr tour ($12/6-10), late Mar-Dec; New York Unearthed (☎ 748-8628), Seaport's urban archaeology branch, 17 State St, Mon-Fri 12-6pm, free
- ℮ www.southstsea port.org
- ♿ yes
- ✕ Paris Cafe, Bridge Cafe (p. 77)

Fishy Fulton Market

Angus Oborn

Kim Grant

DON'T MISS   • lights on the Brooklyn & Manhattan Bridges • the museum's knot-tying workshop • midnight shopping at the fish market

STATUE OF LIBERTY (4, D2)

This great statue, *Liberty Enlightening the World*, is an all-American icon. French sculptor Frédéric-Auguste Bartholdi spent 10 years in Paris making the 50m figure, thought to be based on the face of his mother and the body of his mistress. The statue was shipped to New York in 1886 and erected on a small island that used to house a gallows. Structurally, it consists of a copper skin attached to an iron skeleton, designed by Gustave Eiffel.

INFORMATION

- ✉ Liberty Island
- ☎ 363-3200
- Ⓗ Bowling Green, South Ferry
- 🚍 M15
- ⚓ depart Battery Park every 20-30mins, 8.30am-late afternoon
- ◷ 9am-5pm (Jun-Aug 6.30pm)
- ⑤ free to statue; ferry $7/3-6
- ⓘ ferry info: ☎ 269-5755, free ranger tours of museum
- ⓔ www.nps.gov/stli
- ♿ to base only
- ✗ refreshment kiosk

Kim Grant

The official opening, held on 28 October 1886, was for dignitaries only, though a million people gathered for a celebratory parade down Broadway. Only 2 women were invited to the ceremonial lunch (held in the Lady's leg) provoking 2 miffed suffragettes to circle the island in a boat, yelling megaphone protests throughout proceedings.

Corrosion of the copper became a serious problem, and for her centennial over $100 million was spent on restoration, including a reworking of the flame, which is now gilded in 24 carat gold leaf. The original leadlight flame is in the museum at the base of the statue.

There are 354 steps from the pedestal to the crown and though the views from ground level are almost as good as those from the top, it's worth making the climb simply to be inside this colossal structure. In summer, only passengers on the first ferry are given tickets to climb to the crown; in autumn, the first 2 boatloads are allowed up. Later arrivals are allowed as far as the base of the statue.

The ticket office for the Circle Line ferry is at Castle Clinton: the boat stops first at Liberty Island, then Ellis Island and then makes its way back to Manhattan, with spectacular views all the way.

She's a Big Girl

The Statue of Liberty has quite a honker – her nose is 1.35m long. Her ears (1m long) are so big that workers sat inside them during construction. The statue can sway about 10cm – if there's a breeze while you're up there, you'll feel it shifting.

Liberté ... égalité ... ferryternité

Kim Grant

TIMES SQUARE   (2, L4)

Before TV, Times Square was the nation's largest space for glittery advertising directed at a mass audience. Dubbed the 'Great White Way' after its bright lights, it has long been celebrated as New York's crossroads. But Times Square fell into a deep decline in the 1960s, as once-proud movie palaces that previously showed first-run films turned into 'triple X' porn theatres, and the square became known as a hang-out for every colourful, crazy or dangerous character in Midtown.

For years the city tried to change Times Square's gamy reputation, and it finally seems to be working, as companies have reinstalled colourful billboards above the street and built theme showcases, such as the Virgin Megastore and the neighbouring Official All Star Cafe, smack in the middle of the square.

INFORMATION

⊠ junction 42nd St, Seventh Ave & Broadway
☎ 768-1500
🚇 42nd St/Times Sq
🚌 M6, M7, M10, M27, M42, M104
ⓘ Embassy Theatre visitors' centre, 1560 Broadway (b/w 46th & 47th Sts) 8am-8pm (information, theatre tickets, free Internet access, banking and exchange facilities); free 2hr walking tour (Fri noon)
ℯ www.timessquare bid.org
♿ good

Strolling around Times Square gives you a good look at the city's many architectural styles, from the Art Deco **McGraw Hill Building** (2, L4), 330 W 42nd St, to the Greek Revival **Town Hall** (2, L5), 113 W 43rd St, and the more recent and garish office blocks on Broadway itself, like the **Morgan Stanley Building** (2, K5), at No 1589.

The neighbourhood's oldest venue, the 1899 **New Victory Theater** (2, L5), has been restored by architect Hugh Hardy for children's productions. The Disney Corporation has reinvigorated the **New Amsterdam** (2, L5), built in 1904, as a permanent home for its theatrical versions of children's classics. Development of **Madame Tussaud's** waxworks, **BB King's Blues Room**, a 550-seat nightclub and restaurant, and also a family-oriented **Galactic Circus** promise to flood the square with even more good clean fun.

Times Square's neon ballroom by day and by night

WORLD TRADE CENTER (3, J5)

The massive twin towers of the World Trade Center rise 107 floors, 405m above the ground. Built between 1966 and 73, the towers house businesses that employ more than 50,000 people among them, and have attracted 2 well-publicised daredevils: George Willig, who used mountain-climbing equipment to scale the side of one building, and circus performer Philippe Petit, who claimed he was able to use a crossbow to run a tightrope across both buildings and put on a show at 400m above the ground without anyone in authority knowing about it.

INFORMATION

✉ West St, Lower Manhattan

☎ 323-2340

🚇 Cortlandt St

🚌 M6, M10, M15, M101, M103

🕐 observatory: 9.30am-9.30pm (Jun-Aug to 11.30pm)

💲 observatory: $7/3.50; City Pass valid

🌐 www.wtc-top.com

♿ good

✗ Windows on the World, Greatest Bar on Earth and Wild Blue (p. 78)

Angus Oborn

Kim Grant

The array of federal and state government offices here made it a tempting target for the terrorists who set off a truck bomb in the underground parking garage on February 26, 1993, killing 6 people. An understated memorial to the victims is just beneath the twin towers on the plaza.

If you just want to see the view, head for the **Top of the World observatory** in the South Tower. On a clear day you can see over 55 miles. If you'd like to hang around for a drink or meal, climb to the North Tower's bar and restaurants (p. 78).

Just across West St is the **World Financial Center** (3, J4; ☎ 945-0505), with 4 office towers surrounding a glass atrium called the **Winter Garden** (p. 40), which hosts free talks, music and dancing through the year. There are also free summer lunchtime and after-work concerts in the World Trade Center Plaza.

Charging Up the Batteries

Battery Park City, a residential development, was built on 1730 tons of rock and dirt excavated for the trade center's foundation. A mile-long promenade, from the World Financial Center south to Battery Park, makes for a pleasant walk, run or bike ride.

The wonderful Winter Garden at the World Financial Center.

sights & activities

MANHATTAN NEIGHBOURHOODS

New York City is sometimes called the city of neighbourhoods. Here's a run-down on some of Manhattan's colourful 'hoods'. Other boroughs are featured on p. 8, Greenwich Village on p. 19 & 48 and Chinatown on p. 16 & 47.

Chelsea, west of Broadway between 14th and 23rd Sts, was once a dry-goods and retail area; it now brims with cafes, art galleries and gay and straight nightlife. The hip **East Village** is bordered by 14th St, Lafayette St, E Houston St and the East River. **Alphabet City** (Aves A, B, C and D) was dangerous and druggy until recently but is now scrubbed fairly clean. The overlapping neighbourhoods of the **Flatiron District** & **Gramercy Park** (with 4 historic parks – **Union Square**, **Gramercy**, **Madison Square** and **Stuyvesant**) are happening places to hang out, shop and eat.

Centred on Mulberry St, north of Canal St, **Little Italy** is a bit of a tourist trap. North of Broome St, the area segues into **NoLita** ('North of Little Italy'), a cool fashion and food district. The **Lower East Side**, birthplace of Jewish New York, is developing as 2 distinct areas either side of Delancey: to the south it's Chinese; the north is a yuppified adjunct of East Village. **Lower Manhattan**, the south tip of the island, has historical sites from the Dutch period and earlier and includes the fabled **Financial District**.

SoHo's cast-iron industrial buildings originally housed textile factories but began to be colonised by artists in the 1950s. Today SoHo ('South of Houston St' down to Canal St) is full of galleries and boutiques. **Tribeca** (the 'Triangle Below Canal' St), roughly bordered by Broadway and Chambers St, has old warehouses and funky restaurants but is not as touristy as SoHo. Fashion photographers come here for the desolation chic.

Teeming **Midtown** (34th St to 59th St) holds many of the city's most popular attractions. The area includes the Rockefeller Center, **Times Square**, the theatre district and Grand Central Station. New York's most thoroughly planned neighbourhood, **Roosevelt Island**, is no wider than a football field in the East River. A 3min aerial tramway scoots over from Manhattan.

New York's most identifiable African American neighbourhood, **Harlem**, is home to gospel churches, jazz clubs and the Apollo Theater. Though it does have racial tensions, a conspicuous police presence keeps most danger at bay. **Spanish Harlem** (El Barrio) is home to a big Latino community. La Marqueta (Park Ave above 110th St; 1, C3) – the colourful collection of produce stalls – is the signature attraction.

Home to New York's greatest concentration of cultural centres, the **Upper East Side** (Fifth Ave above 57th St is the *Museum Mile*) is filled with exclusive hotels and residences. The side streets have some stunning brownstone buildings. On the other side of Central Park, the **Upper West Side** provides comfortable living for monied families. Many celebrities live in the plush apartment buildings that line Central Park West up to 96th St. **Washington Heights** is an unremarkable neighbourhood of large apartment buildings at the northern tip of Manhattan, above Harlem. The area around the Cloisters, which includes Fort Tryon Park, is beautiful in warm weather.

MUSEUMS

Many small countries would burst with cultural pride if they had half of New York City's museums. From major art galleries to small community-based venues and oft-neglected outer borough institutions, the museums in New York make this is one of the richest art and culture zones in the world.

Alternative Museum
(3, E6) This small museum specialises in artworks with a humanitarian outlook or sociopolitical bent, particularly with a high electronic or technological component. Artists exhibited include Andres Serano, Adrian Piper and Heidi Kumao.
✉ **4th fl, 594 Broadway, SoHo** ☎ **966-4444** @ **www.alternative museum.org** 🚇 B'way/ **Lafayette St** 🚌 **M5, M6, M21** ⏰ **Tues-Sat 11am-6pm, closed Aug & Sept** 💲 **suggested $3** ♿ **yes**

American Museum of the Moving Image
Set in the middle of the 75-year-old Kaufman Astoria Studio film production complex, this museum and cinema shows the mastery behind film-making. Sit-com buffs can get all misty eyed on the *Seinfeld* coffee shop set.
✉ **35th Ave & 36th St, Astoria, Queens (4, B3)** ☎ **718-784-0077** @ **www.ammi.org** 🚇 **Steinway St** ⏰ **Tues-Fri 12-5pm, Sat-Sun 11am-6pm** 💲 **$8.50/ 4.50-5.50, children under 4 free** ♿ **yes**

Brooklyn Museum of Art
Excellent collections of African, Islamic and Asian art, Egyptian mummy casings and classical antiquities. Temporary exhibitions of contemporary art get better and better: Mayor

Giuliani tried to ban 1999's *Sensation*, controversial British artworks from the Saatchi collection, including a Virgin Mary splotched with elephant dung.
✉ **200 Eastern Pkwy, Brooklyn (4, D3)** ☎ **718-638-5000** @ **www.brooklynart .org** 🚇 Eastern Pkwy/ **Brooklyn Museum** 🚌 **B41, B48, B71** ⏰ **Wed-Sun 10am-5pm** 💲 **$4/2.50/free** ♿ **yes**

The Cloisters (4, A2)
A lovely complex incorporating fragments of old French and Spanish monasteries. Since 1938, it's housed the Met's collection of medieval frescoes, tapestries and paintings, most of them donated by John D Rockefeller Jnr.
✉ **Fort Tryon Park, Wash Heights** ☎ **923-3700** @ **www.metmuse um.org** 🚇 **190th St** 🚌 **M4** ⏰ **Tues-Sun 9.30am-4.45pm** 💲 **$7/3.50/kids free & free with Met ticket** ♿ **OK**

El Museo del Barrio
(3, E6) Puerto Rican and Latin American art and culture featured with Pre-Columbian artefacts and hand-carved wooden saints. Has temporary local exhibits.
✉ **1230 Fifth Ave & 104th St, Upper E Side** ☎ **831-7272** @ **www .elmuseo.org** 🚇 **103rd St (6)** 🚌 **M1, M2, M3, M4** ⏰ **Wed-Sun 11am-5pm** 💲 **$4/2** ♿ **yes**

Fraunces Tavern Museum (3, L6)
A 1907 restoration of the Queen's Head Tavern, including the Long Room where Washington gave his 1783 farewell address to Continental Army officers. Off-beat New York history displays change periodically. Restaurant on site (p. 77).
✉ **2nd fl, 54 Pearl St, Lwr Manhattan** ☎ **425-1778** 🚇 Bowling Green, **South Ferry** 🚌 **M1, M6, M15** ⏰ **Mon-Fri 10am-4.45pm, Sat-Sun 12-4pm** 💲 **$2.50/1/free**

Frick Collection (2, F6)
An outstanding private collection of European paintings, with works by Bellini, Rembrandt, Titian, Vermeer, Gainsborough, Reynolds, and Constable. The 1914 mansion was part of the Fifth Ave 'millionaires row' of robber baron homes. Under 10s not admitted.
✉ **1 E 70th St & Fifth Ave, Upper E Side** ☎ **288-0700** 🚇 **68th (4, 5, 6)** ⏰ **Tues-Sat 10am-6pm, Sun 1-6pm** 💲 **$7/5** ♿ **yes**

International Center of Photography
(2, B6) The city's most important photography showplace. Artist retrospectives and themed exhibitions are usually excellent. Assiduous curatorial staff oversee a worthy permanent collection.
✉ **1130 Fifth Ave & 94th St, Upper E Side** ☎ **860-1777** @ **www.icp.org**

🚇 96th St (6) 🚌 M1 to M4 🕐 10am-5pm (to 8pm Fri, 6pm Sat-Sun), closed Mon 💲 $6/1-4/free, pay by donation Fri 5-8pm ♿ limited

Intrepid Sea, Air & Space Museum (2, L2)

This somewhat scrappy exhibit should be right up the alley of war machinery fans. The world's fastest plane (the A2 Blackbird), is spookily impressive, and there are some interesting space artefacts. You can see the Berlin Wall fragment without paying entry.
✉ Pier 86, W 46th St & 12th Ave, Midtown
☎ 245-0072 🌐 www.intrepid-museum.com
🚇 42nd St/Port Authority, 50th St (C, E) 🚌 M50 🕐 10am-5pm (to 6pm Sun) 💲 $10/5; CityPass valid ♿ partial

Jewish Museum

(2, B6) Permanent collection showing Jewish life now and in the past through artefacts, dioramas and video. Changing exhibits focus on prominent Jews (eg Sigmund Freud) or Jewish communities (eg Central Asian) and art. A large theatre shows films and TV shows.
✉ 1109 Fifth Ave & 92nd St, Upper E Side
☎ 423-3200 🌐 www.thejewishmuseum.org
🚇 96th St (6) 🚌 M1 to M4 🕐 Sun-Thurs 11am-5.45pm (to 8pm Tues) 💲 $8/$5.50, free Tues 5.45-8pm ♿ yes

Lower East Side Tenement Museum

(3, F7) This excellent museum preserves an important part of the city's heritage. Restored apartments show how people lived in different eras. Watch a video in the

Kim Grant

Jewish Museum

visitors' centre and then take the guided tour into the tenement house across the street. Tours to the Confino Family Apartment are for families.
✉ 90 & 97 Orchard St & Broome St, Lwr E Side
☎ 431-0233 🌐 www.wnet.org/tenement
🚇 Delancey/Essex Sts, Grand St 🚌 M15
🕐 hourly tours Tues-Fri 1-4pm, Thurs 1-7pm; every 30mins Sat-Sun 11am-4.30pm; booking advised 💲 $8/6 ♿ no

Museum for African Art

This vibrant and varied collection includes sculpture, costumes, masks and architectural designs, focusing on sub-Saharan Africa. There are re-creations of African life through storytelling, dance and workshops.
✉ 593 Broadway, near Houston, SoHo (3, E5)
☎ 966-1313

🌐 www.africanart.org
🚇 B'way/Lafayette St, Prince St 🚌 M6, M21
🕐 Tues-Fri 10.30am-5.30pm, Sat-Sun 12-6pm 💲 $5/2.50 ♿ yes

Museum of Chinese in the Americas

(3, G6) The focus here is on Chinese communities in New York and in the Americas generally. Part permanent collection, part changing art or oral history displays, there are also craft workshops, readings and discussions around Chinese holidays.
✉ 70 Mulberry St & Bayard St, Chinatown ☎ 619-4785 🌐 www.moca-nyc.org 🚇 Canal St (N, R, S) 🚌 M6, M103 🕐 Tues-Sat 12-5pm 💲 $3/1/free

Museum of the City of New York (1, E6)

Quieter than it should be, this well-curated museum traces the city's history from beaver trading to futures trading, and features excellent antique dolls' house, teddy bear and toy collections.
✉ 1220 Fifth Ave & 103rd St, Upper E Side
☎ 534-1672 🌐 www.mcny.org 🚇 103rd St (6) 🚌 M1 to M4 🕐 Wed-Sat 10am-5pm, Sun 12-5pm 💲 $5/4/10 family ♿ yes

Museum of Television & Radio

(2, K6) A couch potato's

paradise with over 100,000 US TV and radio shows viewable. Entry fee entitles you to 2hrs viewing or listening in a private booth – go early to secure a spot.
✉ 25 W 52nd St, b/w Fifth & Sixth Aves, Midtown ☎ 621-6800 🌐 www.mtr.org 🚇 5th Ave (E, F) 🚌 M1 to M7 🕐 12-6pm (to 8pm Thurs, 9pm Fri), closed Mon ⑤ $6/4 ♿ yes

Kim Grant

Museum of the City of New York

National Museum of the American Indian

(3, L5) An affiliate of the Smithsonian Institution, the museum occupies part of the grand beaux-arts Customs House. Engrossing displays spur insights into past and present Native American culture through art, crafts, ephemera and thoughtful temporary exhibits.
✉ 1 Bowling Green, Lwr Manhattan ☎ 668-6624

🌐 www.si.edu/nmai 🚇 Bowling Green 🚌 M6, M15 🕐 10am-5pm (to 8pm Thurs) ⑤ free ♿ yes

New Museum of Contemporary Art

(3, E5) This place stays at the vanguard of the contemporary scene by presenting installations, video, book readings, painting and sculpture with a global outlook. Great downstairs drop-in space where you can read, chat and wonder about art.
✉ 583 Broadway, b/w Houston & Prince Sts, SoHo ☎ 219-1222 🌐 www.newmuseum .org 🚇 B'way/Lafayette St, Prince St 🚌 M6, M21 🕐 Wed & Sun 12-6pm, Thurs-Sat 12-8pm ⑤ $5/3/free, all free Thurs 5-8pm ♿ yes

New-York Historical Society Museum

(2, E4) NYC's city's oldest museum has a quirky permanent collection including that of Luman Reed, an early patron of American art. Apposite changing exhibits target locals, making this a great place to get an insight into the New York psyche. The *Kid City* exhibit helps kids learn about the city through play and discovery.
✉ 2 W 77th St & Central Park West, Upper W Side ☎ 873-2400 🌐 www.nyhistory.org 🚇 81st St 🚌 M10, M79

🕐 Tues-Sat 11am-5pm ⑤ $5/3/free ♿ yes

Studio Museum in Harlem

(1, A5) A leading showcase of African American art with a respected artist-in-residence program and a strong permanent collection. It includes the work of photographer James Van Der Zee, who chronicled the Harlem Renaissance of the 1920s and 30s, and objects from the Caribbean and Africa.
✉ 144 W125th St, Harlem ☎ 864-4500 🌐 www.studiomuseum .org 🚇 125th St (A, B, C, D, 2, 3) 🚌 M2, M7, M10, M100, M102 🕐 Wed-Fri 10am-5pm, Sat-Sun 1-6pm ⑤ $5/1-3/free, 1st Sat/month free ♿ yes

Whitney Museum of American Art

(2, F6) The Whitney specialises in contemporary art, with works by Hopper, Pollock, Rothko, de Kooning, O'Keefe and Johns. It's also known for biennial exposés on particular artists or themes. In 1999, it held the massive *American Century* exhibition, part provocation, part elegy.
✉ 945 Madison Ave & E 75th St, Upper E Side ☎ 570-3676 🌐 www .echonyc.com/~whitney 🚇 77th St 🚌 M1 to M4 🕐 Wed & Sat-Sun 11am-6pm, Thurs & Fri 1-8pm ⑤ $8/free, pay by donation 1st Thurs/month 6-8pm ♿ good

ART GALLERIES

New York City has more than 500 galleries, most in SoHo, Chelsea or along 57th St either side of Fifth Ave. The monthly *Gallery Guide* (with a Web site at www.gallery-guide.com) is available free in most galleries; the 'Goings on about Town' section in the *New Yorker* and the entertainment section of the Sunday *New York Times* are also good resources.

Most galleries open Tuesday to Saturday from 11am to 6pm except in summer, when many open Monday to Friday from noon to 5pm or by appointment only, or close entirely. It's best to call ahead from June to September to make sure the gallery is open.

Brooke Alexander Gallery

Large upstairs space that focuses on printmaking, either by artists or by theme. Brooke Alexander, who has a background in publishing and printmaking, is a local gallery identity who has been on the scene for about 30 years. He moved to SoHo in 1985.
✉ 2nd fl, 59 Wooster St, SoHo (3, F5) ☎ 925-4338 ✉ brooke alex@earthlink.onet ⊕ Spring St (C, E, 6) ☒ M6 ⊘ Tues-Sat 10am-6pm ⑤ free

Deitch Projects

Sponsors innovative art on-site or on the streets. Previously exhibited artists include Jeff Koons, Mariko Mori and Ghada Amer. It's worth asking if the *Tourguide?* program (p. 53) is running while you're in town.
✉ 76 Grand St, b/w Wooster & Greene Sts, SoHo (3, F5) ☎ 343-7300 ✉ email@deitch .com ⊕ Canal St (A, C, E) ☒ M6 ⊘ Tues-Sat 10am-6pm ⑤ free ⚐ yes

Dia Center for the Arts (2, P3)

A nonprofit organisation with a 2-decade record of supporting unorthodox art both on-site and around town. The Chelsea headquarters has 4 floors of capital A art. Off-site installations include the **Earth Room**, 141 Wooster St, and the **Broken Kilometer**, 393 W Broadway.
✉ 548 W 22nd St, b/w

Tenth & Eleventh Aves, Chelsea ☎ 989-5566 ✉ www.diacenter.org ⊕ 23rd St (C, E) ☒ M11, M23 ⊘ Wed-Sun 12-6pm ⑤ $6/3, school age children free ⚐ yes

Franklin Bowles Gallery

A longstanding gallery with a mainstay of 20th century master prints and etchings, including Chagall, Miro, Picasso, Horowitz, plus newer artists from the US, South America and Europe.
✉ 444 W Broadway & Prince St, SoHo (3, E5) ☎ 228-4200 ⊕ Prince St ☒ M5, M6, M21 ⊘ 11am-7pm ⑤ free

Franklin Bowles Gallery

Gagosian Gallery

Big name gallery on 2 sites that represents Anselm Kiefer, Chris Burden and Philip Taafe. Gagosian's enthusiasm for Damien Hirst is responsible for introducing the Yorkshireman to a sceptical US audience.
✉ 136 Wooster St,

SoHo (3, E5) & 980 Madison Ave & 76th St, Upper E Side (2, E6) ☎ 228-2828 & 744-2313 ✉ gagosian@aol.com ⊕ Broadway/Lafayette St, Prince St & 77th St ☒ M5, M21 & M1 to M4 ⊘ Tues-Sat 10am-6pm ⑤ free ⚐ yes

Joseph Helman Gallery

Arresting contemporary American and European painting, sculpture and installations in a lovely large space.
✉ 24 E 57th St, b/w Fifth & Sixth Aves, Midtown (2, J6) ☎ 245-2888 ✉ jhgallery@aol.com ⊕ 57th St (B, Q) ☒ M1 to M7, M57 ⊘ Tues-Sat 10am-6pm ⑤ free ⚐ yes

Leo Castelli

This Italian art dealer broke many major artists including Jasper Johns, Robert Rauschenberg and Roy Liechtenstein. Castelli moved his original 77th St premises to SoHo in 1971, one of the first in the downtown art boom, but he has now joined the SoHo exodus and headed back north.
✉ 59 E 79th St, b/w Park & Madison Aves, SoHo (2, E6) ☎ 249-4470 ✉ castelli@aol.com ⊕ 77th St ☒ M1 to M4 ⊘ Tues-Sat 10am-6pm ⑤ free

Matthew Marks

A top notch gallery with a stellar cast spread over 2 Chelsea locations. Artists exhibited here include Willem de Kooning, Nan

Goldin, Tracey Moffat, Jean-Marc Bustamante and Lucian Freud.
✉ **523 W 24th St & 522 W 22nd St, Chelsea (3, A3) ☎ 243-0200 & 243-1650 ⓔ gallery@mmarks.com; www.artnet.com/mmarks.html. Ⓜ 23rd St (C, E) 🚌 M11, M23 🕐 Tues-Sat 11am-6pm $ free ♿ yes**

Paula Cooper

A Chelsea heavyweight showing contemporary art in all media, including video and music installations. Consistently interesting shows have included work by Jonathan Borofsky, Dan Flavin, Zoe Leonard, Sherrie Levine and Robert Wilson.
✉ **534 W 21st St, b/w Tent & Eleventh Aves, Chelsea (3, B2) ☎ 255-1105 Ⓜ 23rd St (C, E) 🚌 M11, M23 🕐 Tues-Sat 10am-6pm $ free**

Pop International Galleries

Pop and neo-pop paintings, sculpture and photography. There's a good selection of classics (Haring, Liechtenstein and Warhol) plus a passing parade of new believers. Sunglasses recommended.
✉ **473 W Broadway, sth of Houston St, SoHo (3, E5) ☎ 533-4262 Ⓜ Prince St 🚌 M5, M6, M21 🕐 10am-7pm $ free**

Mary Boone

In 1996, art dealer Mary Boone shocked the cultural elite by moving her gallery from SoHo to 745 Fifth Ave. Boone, a pioneer in mixing art and commerce in the 1980s, claimed that the 'energy and focus of art has shifted uptown'. But sceptics believed her move was prompted by a distaste for the cafes and shops that sprang up in SoHo, attracting crowds interested in looking at – but not buying – expensive art. Boone was back in the news in 1999 when she was jailed for allowing an artist to hand out live ammunition to gallery-goers.

Tony Shafrazi Gallery

An always interesting and extremely versatile gallery with a populist outlook. Exhibiting artists have included David LaChapelle, Keith Haring, Kenny Scharf and Michael Ray Charles. Tony Shafrazi has recently taken on the estate of Francis Bacon.
✉ **119 Wooster St, b/w Prince & Spring Sts, SoHo (3, F5) ☎ 274-9300 ⓔ tsgallery@aol.com Ⓜ Spring St (C, E), Prince St 🚌 M5, M6, M21 🕐 Tues-Sat 10am-6pm $ free ♿ good**

Zabriskie Gallery

Contemporary photography and painting with Dada, surrealist and early American modernist leanings. The stable includes Pat Adams, Man Ray, Shirley Goldfard and Elie Nadelman.
✉ **4 fl, 41 E 57th St, near Madison Ave, Midtown (2, J7) ☎ 752-1223 ⓔ zabriskieg@worldnet.att.net Ⓜ 59th St (4, 5, 6) 🚌 M1 to M4, M31, M57 🕐 Tues-Sat 10am-5.30pm (Jun-Aug: Mon-Fri 10am-5.30pm) $ free ♿ yes**

NOTABLE BUILDINGS

New York is renowned worldwide for the great height and variety of its buildings. Many significant structures are concentrated from Lower Manhattan to Midtown and the Wall St area is an unrivalled museum of architecture with Federal homes, Greek Revival temples, Gothic churches, Renaissance palazzos and the world's finest collection of early 20th century skyscrapers.

Chrysler Building

(2, L7) William van Alen's 1930 Art Deco masterpiece is adorned with motorcar motifs. Sadly visitors are restricted to admiring the interior and the African marble onyx lights in the lobby. Its needle-sharp stainless-steel spire is lit by night.
✉ **405 Lexington Ave & 42nd St, Midtown Ⓜ 42nd St/Grand Central 🚌 M42, M101 to M104 🕐 Mon-Fri 7am-6pm ♿ good**

Customs House (3, L5)

Simply one of the most sumptuous beaux-arts buildings ever built – with an interior festooned with marine murals. An uncredited cameo sketch of Greta Garbo, at a dockside press

conference, is in the rotunda (towards the back at right).
☒ 1 Bowling Green, Lwr Manhattan ☎ 668-6624 Ⓜ Bowling Green 🚌 M6, M15 ⏱ 10am-5pm, Thurs to 8pm ⑤ free ♿ yes

City Hall

City Hall (3, J5)
Among the first ostentatious buildings built in the city, now a working landmark, this French Renaissance marble monster has been home to the city's government since 1812.
☒ Park Row, Lwr Manhattan ☎ 788-6865 Ⓜ City Hall 🚌 M9, M15, M22 ⏱ call for guided tour info ⑤ free

Equitable Building
The sheer unapologetic bulk of this 41-storey building, opened just before WWI, changed the shape of Manhattan – and world architecture – forever. Its size created such an uproar that 4 years after it was built, New York enacted the nation's first zoning laws requiring building setbacks.
☒ 120 Broadway, b/w Pine & Cedar Sts, Lwr Manhattan (3, K5) Ⓜ Wall St 🚌 M6 ⏱ Mon-Fri 7am-7pm ⑤ free ♿ yes

Federal Hall
The finest surviving example of Classic architecture in Lower Manhattan (1842), it stands on the site of the old City Hall where Washington took his oath of office in 1789, and where the city's courts, libraries, fire trucks and jail cells were. There are historical exhibitions inside.
☒ 26 Wall St & Broad St, Lwr Manhattan (3, K5) ☎ 825-6990 🌐 www.nps.gov/feha Ⓜ Wall St, Rector St 🚌 M6 ⏱ Mon-Fri 9am-5pm; guided tours 12.30-3.30pm ⑤ free ♿ yes

Flatiron Building
(2, P6) People were terrified that all 22 storeys of the world's first skyscraper would topple. Built in 1902, it's famously featured in a haunting 1905 Edward Steichen photo, and remains a popular photographic subject today.
☒ Broadway, Fifth Ave & 23rd St, Chelsea Ⓜ 23rd St (N, R) 🚌 M2, M3, M5 to M7, M23

General Grant National Memorial
(2, A2) Landmark monument where Civil War hero and president, Ulysses S Grant, and his wife, Julia, are buried. It's the largest mausoleum in the country.
☒ Riverside Drive & W 122nd St, Upper W Side ☎ 666-1640 Ⓜ 116th St/Columbia University (1, 9) 🚌 M4, M104 ⏱ 9am-5pm ⑤ free

Grand Central Station (2, L7)
Downgraded as a long-distance terminal, its south façade is marred by a car ramp, but its interior remains breathtaking. A star map decorates the cleaned-up concourse ceiling and Vanderbilt Hall hosts art installations. Grand Central Partnership's neighbourhood tour (☎ 818-1777) starts in front of Philip Morris Building, 120 Park Ave (Fri at 12.30pm).
☒ Park Ave & 42nd St, Midtown Ⓜ 42nd St/Grand Central 🚌 M1 to M4, M42, M101 to M104 ⏱ 5.30am-1.30am ⑤ free ♿ good

New York Public Library (2, L6)
Our favourite place in NYC has a great reading room with original Tiffany lamps and excellent literary-themed exhibits. It's a brilliant open access resource; anyone can walk in and call up a book. There's free Internet access too. Don't miss out – register early.
☒ Fifth Ave & E 42nd St, Midtown ☎ 930-0800 🌐 www.nypl.org Ⓜ 42nd St/Grand

Classic Architecture
As Americans sought to define their new nation, they looked to the ancient societies of Greece and Rome for examples to emulate. Classic architecture, it was felt, gave expression to the aspirations of the young republic. Build on your architectural knowledge by taking a Municipal Arts Society (☎ 935-3960) tour from Grand Central Station Main Concourse (Wed 12.30pm).

Central ⊜ M1 to M5, M42, M104 ⊙ Mon-Sat 11am-6pm (hrs changeable) $ free ♿ yes

Old Police Headquarters (3, F6)
A grand European-style monument built in 1909, it overwhelms its neighbours. In 1988 it was converted into apartments.
✉ **240 Centre St, Little Italy** Ⓢ **Spring St (6), Bowery** ⊜ **M1 (part time service), M6**

Puck Building (3, E6)
This stunning red-brick building was home to the turn-of-the-century humour magazine. It has 2 gold-leaf statues of the portly Puck and is a popular spot for wedding receptions and film shoots.
✉ **295 Lafayette St (behind Mulberry, near Houston St), Little Italy** Ⓢ **Broadway/Lafayette St** ⊜ **M1, M2, M3**

Shrine of St Elizabeth Ann Seton
Delicate Georgian home and adjoining church, dedicated to the first American Catholic saint. The house is the lone survivor of a series of graceful row houses that once hugged the shoreline.
✉ **7 State St, near Pearl St, Lwr Manhattan (3, L5)** ☎ **269-6865** Ⓢ **South Ferry, Bowling Green, Whitehall St**

Kim Grant
Puck atop his building

⊜ **M6, M15** ⊙ **church: Mon-Fri 6.30am-5pm** $ **free** ♿ **no**

United Nations Building (2, L8)
Designed by an international committee of architects, the UNHQ is very much international territory. A nearby park features Henry Moore's *Reclining Figure* and other sculptures.
✉ **First Ave & 46th St, Midtown** ☎ **963-7713** @ **inquiries@un.org** Ⓢ **42nd St/Grand Central** ⊜ **M15, M27, M42, M104** ⊙ **9.15am-4.45pm (closed Sat-Sun Jan-Feb)** $ **$7.50/3.50-5.50; no under 5s; tours every 30mins** ♿ **yes**

Woolworth Building
(3, J5) This was the world's tallest building when it was completed in 1913. Frank Woolworth reputedly paid the $15 million for this 'Cathedral of Commerce' with nickels and dimes. Crane your neck to view the extraordinary ceiling mosaic.
✉ **233 Broadway, Lwr Manhattan** Ⓢ **City Hall** ⊜ **M6** ⊙ **Lobby open 24hrs** $ **free** ♿ **yes**

> **Street Tipping**
> 'You feel that the Americans have practically added a new dimension to space. They move almost as much on the perpendicular as on the horizontal plane. When they find themselves a little crowded, they simply tip a street on end and call it a skyscraper.' – William Archer, *America Today: Observations and Reflections*, 1900

World Financial Center (3, J4)
Cesar Pelli's 1988 building has elegant towers, restaurants, stores and great views of the Hudson. Its centrepiece is the Winter Garden (p. 40).
✉ **West St to North End Ave, Lwr Manhattan** ☎ **945-0505** @ **www.worldfinancialcenter.com** Ⓢ **World Trade Center, Cortlandt St** ⊜ **M9, M10, M22** $ **free** ♿ **yes**

PLACES OF WORSHIP

Cathedral of St John the Divine (2, C3)
This Episcopal cathedral is the USA's largest place of worship and the world's biggest Gothic cathedral. Construction began in 1892 and is continuing – look up to see sculptors carving in the stone! It hosts concerts, lectures and memorial services for famous New Yorkers. High Mass (11am Sun) often features sermons by well-known intellectuals.
✉ **1047 Amsterdam Ave & 112th St, Upper W Side** ☎ **316-7540** Ⓢ **Cathedral Parkway, 116th St/Columbia University (1, 9)** ⊜ **M4, M7, M11** ⊙ **7am-6pm (8pm Sun); tours Tues-Sat 11am, Sun 1pm ($3)**

(⑤) $2 donation ⑤ yes, enter from 113th St

Eldridge St Synagogue

Landmark Moorish synagogue opposite the oldest surviving blocks of tenements in New York.
✉ **12 Eldridge St, Lower E Side (3, G7)** ☎ **219-0888** ㊐ **East Broadway** 🚌 **M9, M15, M22** ⊘ tours Sun 11am-4pm; Tues & Thurs 11.30am & 2.30pm
⑤ $4/2.50 ⑤ yes

First Roumanian-American Congregation

One of the few remaining Orthodox synagogues on the Lower East Side (where 400 once thrived). Has a wonderful ornate wooden sanctuary.
✉ **89 Rivington St, near Orchard St, Lower E Side (3, E7)** ☎ **673-2835** ㊐ **Delancey/Essex Sts** 🚌 **M9, M14** ⊘ 8am-6pm ⑤ yes

Mahayana Buddhist Temple

Unmissable red and yellow building, near the Manhattan Bridge on-ramp. The inside is a functional haven with a huge gold Buddha and stories of his life on the walls.
✉ **133 Canal St, Chinatown (3, G7)** ☎ **925-8787** ㊐ **Grand St** 🚌 **M9, M15, M22, M103** ⊘ varying ⑤ yes

Riverside Church

(1, B2) This 1930 Gothic marvel built by the Rockefellers has an observation deck, the world's largest set of carillon bells and a theatre and events program.
✉ **490 Riverside Dr & 120th St, Upper W Side** ☎ **870-6700** ㊒ www .theriversidechurchny.org

㊐ **125th (1, 9)** 🚌 **M5** ⊘ 9am-4pm ⑤ yes

St Patrick's Cathedral

(2, K6) Built in French Gothic style and one of the city's greatest cathedrals, it serves the 2.2 million Catholics in the NY diocese (but can only seat 2400 of them). Its predecessor is at 263 Mulberry St, Little Italy.
✉ **50th St & Fifth Ave** ☎ **753-2261** ㊐ **5th Ave (E, F), Rockefeller Center,** 🚌 **M1 to M5, M27, M50** ⊘ 6am-9pm, guided tours ⑤ yes

St Paul's steeple

Kim Grant

St Paul's Chapel

This Georgian chapel is the area's last colonial building. President Washington attended services (his personal pew is still on display) in the airy interior with fluted Corinthian columns and Waterford chandeliers.
✉ **Broadway & Fulton St,**

Lwr Manhattan (3, J5)** ☎ **602-0800** ㊒ www .trinitywallstreet.org ㊐ **Fulton St, Broadway/ Nassau St** 🚌 **M6** ⊘ 8am-4pm ⑤ yes

Temple Emanu-El

(2, G6) This is the world's largest reformed Jewish synagogue, and is significant for its Byzantine and Near-Eastern architecture.
✉ **1 E 65th St & Fifth Ave, Upper E Side** ☎ **744-1400** ㊒ www.emanuelnyc .org ㊐ **Lexington Ave (B, Q), 66th St/Hunter College** 🚌 **M1 to M4** ⊘ 10am-5pm (tours Sun-Fri) ⑤ yes

Trinity Church (3, K5)

Richard Upjohn helped launch the American neo-Gothic movement when he designed this 1690 Anglican church. Today's building is a mid-19th century reconstruction (the original burnt down) and features a museum and classical concerts.
✉ **Broadway & Wall St, Lwr Manhattan** ☎ **602-0800** ㊒ www.trinity wallstreet.org ㊐ **Broadway/Nassau St, Rector St** 🚌 **M6** ⊘ 9am-3.45pm (from 10am Sat, 1pm Sun); services: Mon-Sat 8am & noon, Sun 9 & 11.15am ⑤ yes

Harlem Church Services

Harlem's famous **Abyssinian Baptist Church** (☎ 862-7474), 132 W 138th St, has a charismatic pastor and a superb choir. Sunday services start at 9 & 11am and last up to 2hrs. **Canaan Baptist Church** (☎ 866-0301), 132 W 116th St, may be Harlem's friendliest church. The Sunday service is at 10.45am (10am in summer).

Other Harlem churches welcome respectful visitors. Remember to dress neatly, be on time (and stay till the end), and leave your camera in your bag.

PUBLIC ART

The city's museums are full of fine sculpture but there's a lot of street art too. Critic Robert Hughes dismissed a sculpture in front of the **Time Life Building** (2, K5), as 'turd on a pedestal art', but it's not all that bad.

Greenwich Village

A statue of George Washington stands in **Union Square** (3, B5), and there's an arch dedicated to the first president in **Washington Square Park** (3, D5). Bernard Rosenthal's *Alamo* in **Astor Place** (3, D6) is a cube poised on its corner. Give it a spin if you can get past all the skaters.

Lower Manhattan

There's a statue of Colonial patriot Nathan Hale (1890) at **City Hall Park** (2, J5). **Louise Nevelson Plaza**, Maiden Lane, William and Liberty Sts (3, K6), appropriately enough has examples of the American sculptor's work. Also fitting for this part of town is the brash brass bull on Broadway north of Bowling Green. Give his nose a rub for luck.

Midtown

The **Rockefeller Center** (2, K6) is strewn with art, including Paul Manship's *Prometheus* by the skating rink and *News* by Isamu Noguchi, above the entrance of the Associated Press Building. **Vanderbilt Hall** in Grand Central Station (2, L7) hosts vibrant art installations to brighten up commuters' days. Poke your head into the **Pfizer Building**, 42nd St and Second Avenue (2, L8), to look at the fabulous glass ceiling. **Madison Square Park** (2, P6) has statues of Civil War heroes.

Uptown

Bronzes of famous artists stand in **The Mall** (2, G5) in Central Park and Romeo and Juliet (right) embrace at the Delacorte Theater (2, E5). The **Lincoln Center** (2, H3) features Alexander Calder's *Le Guichet* at the Library for the Performing Arts, Henry Moore's *Reclining Figure* in front of the Vivian Beaumont Theatre and Philip Johnson's *Movado Time Sculpture* east of Avery Fisher Hall. In **Harlem** at Fifth Ave and 110th St (1, D6), there's a fine statue of Duke Ellington.

Why for art that haircut Romeo?

PARKS & GARDENS

For a city with a concrete jungle reputation, New York has loads of open space. Some of it's even green. And sometimes you're even allowed on the lawns. Because many residents live in tiny apartments, public parks are highly valued.

Battery Park (3, M5)
Named for the cannons that once protected the harbour, this park offers wonderful water views. It has dozens of statues and monuments, and often hosts musical events. **Peter Minuit Plaza**, at the eastern exit of the park, is reputedly the site of the Manhattan purchase.
✉ **Broadway & Battery Pl, Lwr Manhattan**
🚇 South Ferry, Bowling Green 🚌 M6, M15
💲 free 🚻 yes

Brooklyn Botanic Garden (4, D3)
This 52 acre haven includes extensive conservatories, a wonderful fragrance garden, a meditation area and a fanciful celebrity path. Children's Garden information below.
✉ **1000 Washington Ave, b/w Eastern Pkwy & Empire Blvd, Brooklyn**
☎ 718-622-4433
🌐 www.bbg.org
🚇 Eastern Pkwy/Brooklyn Museum 🚌 B41, B43, B48 & B71
🕐 8am-6pm (from 10am Sat-Sun); closes 1½hrs earlier Oct-Mar); closed Mon 💲 $3/1.50/free, free Tues & Sat till noon 🚻 very good

Bryant Park (2, L6)
Claim a marble bench or folding chair and join the sunbathers or watch a free movie on a summer evening. This was the site of Crystal Palace, which was built in 1853 but burnt down in 15mins in 1858, supposedly by spontaneous combustion.

Battery Park blossoms take the edge off the urban grey.
Kim Grant

✉ **42nd St, Midtown**
☎ 922-9393 🚇 42nd St/Grand Central 🚌 M1 to M5, M42, M104 🕐 6am-dusk 💲 free 🚻 yes

New York Botanical Garden (4, A2)
In the 250 acre gardens there's a Victorian conservatory, a fine rose garden, and a rock garden and museum. Tram, golf cart or guided walking tours focus on different plants and birds. Children's Adventure Garden details below.
✉ **200th St & Kazimiroff Blvd, The Bronx** ☎ 718-817-8700 🌐 www.nybg .org 🚇 Bedford Pk Blvd then bus No BX26 🚉 Metro Nth from Grand Central 🕐 Tues-Sun

10am-6pm; closes 2hrs earlier Nov-Mar
💲 $3/1-2 🚻 yes

Prospect Park (4, D3)
Smaller and calmer than Central Park (built by the same designers), this park offers ice-skating, boating, concerts, a small zoo, the Children's Museum and the Art Deco Brooklyn Public Library.
✉ **Flatbush Ave & Grand Army Plaza, Brooklyn** ☎ 718-965-8951 🌐 www.prospect park.org 🚇 Grand Army Plaza, Prospect Pk 🚌 B41, B69, B71, B75 🕐 6am-1am 💲 free 🚻 yes

Washington Square Park (3, D5) Once a

Little Green Thumbs
The amazing **Children's Adventure Garden** at the New York Botanical Garden includes a Sun, Dirt and Water Gallery, a wetland trail, and a Boulder Maze.
    Founded in 1914 by school teacher Ellen Eddy Shaw, the **Children's Garden** at the Brooklyn Botanic Garden has given over 20,000 children the opportunity to plant, tend and reap flowers, plants and vegetables. Work continues on the garden all year round.

poor cemetery and the site of public executions ('Hangman's Elm' still stands in the north-western corner), this crowded park has comedians, buskers and low-life drug dealers. The arch, originally designed in wood in 1889 by Stanford White for the centennial of George Washington's inauguration, was replaced in stone 6 years later, and adorned with statues of the general in war and peace.
✉ Washington Pl, Greenwich Village ◉ W 4th St 🚌 M2, M3, M5, M6, M8 ⊙ 6am-1am ⑤ free ♿ yes

Winter Garden
Glass and steel atrium centrepiece of the World Financial Center. It hosts free concerts in summer and exclusive black-tie events year round.
✉ World Financial Center, Lwr Manhattan (3, J4) ☎ 945-0505 ❸ www.worldfinancial center.com ◉ World Trade Center, Cortlandt St 🚌 M9, M10, M22 ⑤ free ♿ yes

Washington Square Park

NEW YORK CITY FOR CHILDREN

With its abundance of world-famous sites, tours and attractions, New York is an ideal place to bring children. There are several museums dedicated to children and many annual events that will appeal to kids. The **Big Apple Circus** visits the Lincoln Center each winter and the **Ringling Bros** and **Barnum & Bailey Circus** take over Madison Square Garden every May and June.

Bronx Zoo (4, A3)
One of the biggest and best zoos anywhere, with over 6000 animals, 265 acres of naturalistic enclosures and a kid's zoo (Apr-Oct). Don't miss the Congo Gorilla Forest, a simulated rainforest walk-through, or the Bengali Express, a monorail trip through 'Asia' (May-Oct).
✉ Fordham Rd & Bronx River Pkwy, The Bronx ☎ 718-367-1010 ❸ www.wcs.org

🚃 MetroNorth Getaway packages (☎ 532-4900) ◉ Pelham Pkwy 🚌 Liberty Lines BxM11 Express (☎ 718-652-8400) from Madison Ave ⊙ 10am-5pm (till 5.30pm Sat-Sun & holidays) ⑤ $7.75/4, free Wed (rides extra) ♿ yes

Caroline's Kids Club
Magic, music and clown shows for kids and their parents every weekend in the heart of the theatre district. In the evening, the club is a comedy venue for grown-ups.
✉ 1626 Broadway & 49th St, Times Sq (2, K5) ☎ 757-4100 ❸ www.carolines.com ◉ 50th St (1, 9) 🚌 M6, M7, M10, M27, M50, M104 ⊙ shows Sat-Sun 2pm ♿ yes

Children's Museum of the Arts
If you've been towing your kids around the SoHo galleries and they're looking a bit inspired, bring them straight here where they can draw, paint, make music and join in daily workshops (suitable for 10 months to 10 years). WEE (Wondrous, Experimenting and Exploring) Artist Program, an art and music-making session runs Wed-Fri 10-11.30am for an

Babysitting & Childcare
Nannies and babysitters are happy to come to hotels or private homes to look after your children. The normal fee is around $12/hr plus an agency fee of about 20% and there's usually a 4hr minimum. Though agencies appreciate 48hrs notice, they will usually be able to find someone at the last minute. Best Domestic Services Agency (☎ 685-0351) and Professional Nannies (☎ 692-9510) are reputable agencies.

extra charge (call ahead).
✉ **182 Lafayette St,
near Broome St, SoHo
(3, F6)** ☎ 274-0986
🚇 Spring St (6) 🚌
M103 ⏱ Wed 12-7pm,
Thurs-Sun 12-5pm ⑤ $5

Children's Museum
of Manhattan (2, D3)
Features discovery centers
for toddlers and a postmod-
ern Media Center for kids.
Technologically savvy kids
can work in a TV studio and
the museum also runs crafts
workshops on weekends.
✉ **212 W 83rd St,
Upper W Side** ☎ 721-
1234 🌐 www.cmom.org
🚇 79th St (1, 9)
🚌 M7, M10, M11, M104
⏱ Wed-Sun 10am-5pm
(extended summer hrs)
⑤ $6/3 ♿ yes

New York Aquarium
The perfect place for young
children. There's a touch pool
bursting with small forms of
sea life, an amphitheatre
with marine mammal shows,
and observation windows to
watch the whales and seals.
✉ **Coney Island board-
walk, Coney Is (4, E4)**
☎ 718-265-3400
🚇 NY Aquarium 🚌
B36, B68 ⏱ 10am-5pm
⑤ $8.75/4.50 ♿ yes

New York Hall of
Science
This venue is dedicated to
technology and specialises
in hands-on exhibits where
kids learn through such
things as blowing bubbles
and watching tarantulas eat
crickets. The outdoor Science
Playground has a few early
space-age rockets.
✉ **111th St & 47th Ave,
Corona, Queens (4, B4)**
☎ 718-699-0005
🌐 www.nyhallsci.org
🚌 Grand Central Pkwy

More Kids' Stuff
The following attractions have special exhibitions or
activities for children. See the listings for details.

Coney Island (p. 50)
Fraunces Tavern Museum (p. 30)
Lower East Side Tenement Museum (p. 31)
Metropolitan Museum of Art (p. 20)
American Museum of Natural History (p. 13)
Museum of Television & Radio (p. 31-2)
New-York Historical Society Museum (p. 32)
parks & gardens (p. 15, 39-40)
Wave Hill (p. 42)

---

to Shea Stadium exit to
Flushing Meadows
🚇 Willets Point-Shea
Stadium ⏱ 9.30am-
5pm (Sept-Jun: to 2pm
Thurs-Sun; July-Aug: to
2pm Mon) ⑤ $7.50/5;
free Thurs & Fri 2-5pm
(not summer) ♿ yes

PlaySpace
The perfect place for long,
rainy afternoons for 6
month to 6 year olds. This
indoor playground has a
sandbox, slides, climbing
frames, dress-ups, arts and
crafts and room just to run
around shrieking.
✉ **2473 Broadway &
92nd St, Upper W Side
(2, C3)** ☎ 769-2300
🚇 96th St (1, 2, 3, 9)
🚌 M104 ⏱ 9.30am-
6pm (from 10am Sun);
longer summer hrs
⑤ $6.50 ♿ yes

Sony Wonder
Sure, it's going to make
your kids Sony fans, but
this free Technology Lab is
worth a look – the talking
robot is amazing. Go in the
afternoons to avoid school
groups.
✉ **550 Madison Ave &
56th St, Midtown (2, J6)**
☎ 833-8100 🌐 wonder
techlab.sony.com

🚇 51st St (6), 5th Ave
(E, F), 59th St (4, 5,6)
🚌 M1 to M5, M57
⏱ Tues-Sat 10am-6pm
(Thurs to 8pm), Sun 12-
6pm ⑤ free ♿ yes

Staten Island
Children's Museum
A museum of discovery and
fun. Kids get puzzled, get
active and sometimes get
messy doing anything from
watching insects being
born, to exploring a pirate
ship or inventing a play.
✉ **Snug Harbor Cultural
Center, 1000 Richmond
Terrace, Staten Island
(4, E2)** ☎ 718-273-2060
🚌 from Staten Island
Ferry Terminal: S40
⏱ Tues-Sun 12-5pm
⑤ $4 ♿ yes

Central Park carousel

OFF THE BEATEN TRACK

New York's tracks are beaten down pretty flat, but it's still possible to find places that, though not exactly undiscovered, aren't crawling with people. Often all you need to do to leave the hordes behind is get out of Manhattan.

Conservatory Garden
Yes, it's in Central Park, but this pretty, gated garden is still a hideaway. There are flowers in bloom most of the year, peaceful lily ponds, trellised roses and plenty of secluded benches where you can sit down with a book, a sketch pad or a lover.
✉ **Fifth Ave near 105th St, Central Park, Harlem (1, E6) ⊖ 103rd St (6) 🚌 M1 to M4 ⏲ 8am-dusk ⑤ free ♿ yes**

Isamu Noguchi Garden Museum
The Japanese-American sculptor's work is beautifully presented in 12 galleries and a garden.
✉ **32 Vernon Blvd & 33rd Rd, Long Is City, Queens (4, B3) ☎ 718-721-1932 ⓒ www .noguchi.org ⊖ Broadway 🚌 Sat-Sun shuttle bus departs north-east cnr Park Ave & 70th St hrly 11.30am-3.30pm ⏲ Apr-Oct: Wed-Fri 10am-5pm, Sat-Sun 11am-6pm ⑤ $4/2,**

free guided tour 2pm
♿ partial access

Jackson Heights
This part of Queens is one of the most ethnically diverse parts of New York. The neighbourhoods themselves are somewhat bland but the culture and character found around each of the No 7 train stops is quite exciting. Woodside/61st St is a pub-rich Irish neighbourhood; the 74th St area is a vibrant mix of Korean, Filipino, Indian and lesbian folk; from 82nd St it's more Latino, with large Colombian and Cuban populations, and by 103rd St it's a mix of old Italians and newer immigrants from Pakistan, India and Mexico.
✉ **Roosevelt Ave, Queens (4, B3) ⊖ No 7 train b/w 61st St & 103rd St 🚌 Q32**

Jacques Marchais Center of Tibetan Art
The Buddha statues, clothing and religious objects in the Tibetan-temple-style building make up one of the

largest private collections of Tibetan art outside China.
✉ **338 Lighthouse Ave, Staten Is (1 mile sth of 4, E2) ☎ 718-987-3500 🚌 S74 along Richmond Rd to Lighthouse Ave then 15min walk uphill) 🚇 Staten Is ⏲ Wed-Sun 1-5pm; call ahead for special Sunday events ⑤ $3/1-2.50**

Schomburg Center for Research in Black Culture (4, A5)
Branch of the NY Public Library that holds the nation's largest collection of documents, rare books and photographs; lectures and concerts are regularly held here.
✉ **515 Lenox Ave & 135th St, Harlem ☎ 491-2200 ⓒ www .nypl.org/research/sc ⊖ 135th St 🚌 M1, M7, M102 ⏲ Mon-Wed 12-8pm, Thurs-Sat 10am-6pm, Sun 1-5pm (gallery only) ⑤ free ♿ yes**

Wave Hill
Choose a fine day to visit this Victorian house (1843) and its 27 acres of lovely grounds overlooking the Hudson River. Mark Twain and Theodore Roosevelt are among those who lived here. There are weekend family art sessions with all materials supplied. Eat at the on-site cafe or pack a picnic.
✉ **W 249th St & Independence Ave, Riverdale, The Bronx (4, A2) ☎ 718-549-3200 🚇 MetroNorth to Riverdale ⊖ 207th St**

(A) then Bus No 7; 231st St (1, 9) then Bus No 10 🚌 Liberty Lines (☎ 718-652-8400) express bus to 252nd St ⏰ Tues-Sun 9am-5.30pm 💲 $4/2, free Tues & Sat till noon ♿ yes

Williamsburg
When artists got squeezed out of the East Village by rent hikes and yuppies in the mid-1990s, many of them hopped the East River to Williamsburg, Brooklyn, a traditional Eastern European Jewish neighbourhood. It didn't take long for the real estate sharks to follow them over and these days even Williamsburg is getting pretty tight but it's still a good place to soak up a Polish-meets-postmodernist atmosphere and watch the sun fall behind Manhattan whilst dining at Plan-Eat Thailand (p. 70).
✉ Bedford St, Williamsburg, Brooklyn (4, C3) 🚇 Bedford Ave

QUIRKY NEW YORK

New York will never let you down for the weird and wonderful. If it's not the lady shopping Madison Ave with a macaw on her shoulder, it's either a hot-dog vendor outside MoMA selling lobster bisque or a nightclub with a strict 'look like a tree' dress code. Loopy, kooky or just plain bizarre, New York keeps you interested, amazed, flummoxed and laughing.

Evolution
Fancy a worm lollypop? A tarantula? Freeze dried mice? Insects, bones, fossils, eggs, teeth and lots of icky things in jars – this natural history shop certainly has an eye on the weird prize.
✉ 120 Spring St, near Mercer, SoHo (3, F5) ☎ 343-1114 🚇 Spring St (6) 🚌 M6 ⏰ 11am-7pm

La Nouvelle Justine
Foot worship with your martini? Doggy obedience training with that beer? S&M is on the menu and the cocktails have names like Urophiliac and Gynemimeto-philiac. The atmosphere is easy – you don't have to be hard core to go here.
✉ 101 E 2nd St, E Village (3, E7) ☎ 673-8908 🖥 www.lanouvelle justine.com 🚇 2nd Ave 🚌 M15 ⏰ 7pm-late

Lucky Cheng's
Gorgeous drag waitresses and camp karaoke over 2 floors. The food is good and the cabaret is cute but lounging around in the bar

Hot diggity dogger

is better and less touristy – the drinks are strong and the conversation is always interesting.
✉ 24 First Ave, E Village (3, E7) ☎ 473-0516 🚇 2nd Ave 🚌 M15 ⏰ 6pm-late

Sahara East
The Middle Eastern menu is fine and fiesty but the top attraction in this part of the East Village desert is the water pipes. For $5 a person, you can pack a pipe and suck it in the oasis-ish garden. It's easy to pretend you've got a team of camels waiting outside to take you back to the souk.
✉ 184 First Ave, E Village (3, C7) ☎ 353-9000 🚇 1st Ave 🚌 M15 ⏰ 9am-4am Ⓥ

Fun Times Five
Have a wacky day in New York by fitting in the following:

- the *Passer-By* bar (☎ 206-6847), 436 W 15th St (2, B2) an annex to Gavin Brown's gallery, complete with flashing disco light floor
- techno tenpin bowling at Bowlmor (p. 96)
- eating at *Veselka* (see Jewish Delis p. 73) – you're sure to see something funny
- a trip to the Alternative Museum (p. 30)
- Africa, blood and pretty women – visit Peter Beard's visceral, epic, objectionable installation *The Time is Always Now* (☎ 343-2211), 476 Broome St (2, F5)

KEEPING FIT

Gyms

Even mid-range hotels have small fitness centres these days, and some of the fancier hotels have excellent training facilities. Otherwise, gyms all over the city sell day passes, usually for about $20.

Running

Manhattan has 3 traffic-free spots: Central Park's 6.2 mile roadway loops around the park (closed to cars weekdays from 10am to 3pm and 7 to 10pm weekends); encircling the Jacqueline Kennedy Onassis Reservoir is a soft 1 mile path; and there's great views of the Jersey Shore and the Statue of Liberty from the Hudson River path (23rd St to Battery Park). The **New York Road Runners Club** (☎ 860-4455) has regular runs around the city.

Skating

Central Park, on the mall that runs east of the Sheep Meadow (2, G5), is the place to show off your inline skating skills (or lack thereof). If you're just starting out, rent a pair from the nearby Blades West (☎ 787-3911) at 120 W 72nd St (2, F4) and ask a volunteer at the W 72nd St park entrance to show you how to stop. If you're keen to buy, do so at Paragon (p. 67)

Chelsea Piers has roller rinks and ramps, and there's a path between 14th St and Battery Park along the Hudson. Every Wednesday at 8pm, Blade Night meets on the southern side of Union Square Park (3, B5) for a 2hr skate around the city. Ice skaters also have loads of options, see p. 15 & 23.

Autumnal pedal along Fifth Avenue

Swimming

Much of the swimming done in New York is in expensive private clubs. There are also a number of free summer-opening city pools. Some pools have lap swimming times set aside; the rest of the time they tend to be taken over by dive-bombing kids. See the White Pages Government Listings, New York City Offices and Parks & Recreation, for a list of pools.

Yoga

Yoga is extremely popular in New York. Not only are there a lot of people wanting to align those pesky chakras, but it's also taken off among the body-conscious as a low-impact way of toning up.

Asser Levy Bath

A pleasant 25m pool that has lap swimming on summer weekdays from 7 to 8.30am and 7 to 8.30pm. A less appealing indoor pool operates through the winter. There's a small gym here too.

✉ E23rd St & Asser Levy Pl, E Village (3, A7) ☎ 447-2020 🚇 1st Ave 🚌 M16, M21, M23 ⏰ Jun-Aug: Mon-Fri 7am-8.30pm, Sat-Sun 9am-6pm (call for winter hrs) ⓢ free

Chelsea Piers (2, P2)

This massive gym has a thousand ways to make you sweat. Choose – if you can – from the skate park, the ice rink, horse-riding, indoor rockwall-climbing, swinging a golf club and bowling.
✉ 23rd St & Hudson River, Chelsea ☎ 336-6000 🌐 www.chelsea piers.com 🚇 23rd St (C, E) 🚌 M14, M23 ⏰ Gym: Mon-Fri 6am-11pm, Sat 7am-8pm, Sun 8am-8pm ⓢ $26/day

Chelsea Piers driving range

Integral Yoga

This longstanding village yoga school has a variety of hatha yoga classes and welcomes drop-ins of all levels.
✉ 25 First Ave, E Village (3, E7) ☎ 473-0370 🚇 2nd Ave 🚌 M15 ⓢ $10/80min class

New York Integral Yoga Institute

Meditation programs and yoga classes for beginners through to advanced. The instructors request that you bring a towel, wear clean socks and don't eat for 2hrs before class. There's a great wholefood supermarket downstairs.
✉ 227 W 13th St, b/w Seventh & Eighth Aves, Greenwich Village (3, C3) ☎ 929-0586 🌐 integralyogaofnew york.org 🚇 14th St (1, 2, 3, 9, A, C, E), 8th Ave 🚌 M10, M14 ⓢ most classes $10/85min; $40/1 week unlimited classes

Prescriptive Fitness Gym

This well-equipped gym also has a steam room, masseurs and a cafe on site. It's a relaxed scene and you won't feel too weird if you're not the full 6-pack.
✉ 250 W 54th St, Midtown (2, J5); other locations ☎ 307-7760

Pier Back Through History

The Chelsea Piers are where anxious crowds waited for survivors of the Titanic to land in 1912 and also where happier sports fans welcomed Jesse Owens back from the 1936 Berlin Olympics.

🌐 www.prescriptive fitness.com 🚇 7th Ave (B, D, E), 57th St (N, R) 🚌 M10, M104 ⏰ Mon-Fri 5am-midnight, Sat-Sun 8am-10pm ⓢ $20/day

SoHo Sanctuary

A women-only day spa with massage (including reflexology and shiatsu), facials and aromatherapy and a variety of yoga and Alexander Technique sessions. Welcoming and pampering vibe.
✉ 119 Mercer St, SoHo (3, F5) ☎ 334-5550 🚇 Spring St (6) 🚌 M6 ⏰ Tues-Fri 10am-9pm, Sat 10am-6pm, Sun 12-6pm ⓢ drop-in yoga class $20, 1hr massage or facial $95

Tenth St Baths (3, C7)

These historic steam baths offer a traditional Russian-style massage followed by an ice-cold bath. It's become very much an 'in' place for younger local residents in recent years, much to the chagrin of the grizzled regulars. The baths recently became completely co-ed.
✉ 268 E Tenth St, E Village ☎ 674-9250 🚇 1st Ave 🚌 M14, M15 ⏰ 9am-10pm ⓢ $20, $45 with massage

Street Games

Playground basketball games are an important part of New York life and it isn't always just plain fun. For the kids, there's always the hope that a tarmac-prowling college scout will spot them; adult competitions are a focus for neighbourhood identity as well as a good way to let off some 9-to-5 steam. The W 4th St Courts, at Sixth Ave (3, D4) are a great spot to watch high-quality hoops.

out & about

WALKING TOURS
Central Park

From Columbus Circle **(1)**, go through Merchants' Gate **(2)** and up to Sheep Meadow **(3)**, a wide green favoured by sunbathers and frolickers. Turn right onto a pathway that runs along the southern side of the meadow to the Carousel **(4)**, and then the Dairy **(5)**, where the park's visitors' centre is located.

SIGHTS & HIGHLIGHTS

The Carousel
Park View at the Boathouse restaurant (p. 82)
Delacorte Theater (see Joseph Papp, p. 86)

Bobbing hire boats under Bow Bridge

Kim Grant

North of the Dairy, past the Christopher Columbus statue, is The Mall **(6)**, bordered by 150 American Elms. At the end of The Mall is Bethesda Fountain **(7)**, a hippie hang-out in the 1960s. Continue on the path to the left to

> **distance** 2.8 miles (5km)
> **duration** 2hrs
> **start** ⊕ Columbus Circle
> **end** ⊕ 72nd St (B, C)

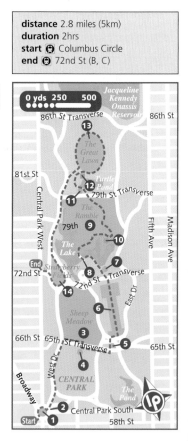

the Bow Bridge **(8)**. Cross the bridge to the Ramble **(9)**, a lush, wooded expanse that is a meeting place for dog owners. Turn right to stop for a meal or drink at the *Park View at the Boathouse* restaurant **(10)** overlooking The Lake.

The Ramble gives way to Belvedere Castle **(11)** and the Delacorte Theater **(12)**, where the Joseph Papp Public Theater gives free performances in summer. Immediately beyond is the Great Lawn **(13)**, a group of softball fields where the New York Philharmonic and Metropolitan Opera play each summer.

Turning left and walking down West Drive to 72nd St brings you to Strawberry Fields **(14)**, dedicated to John Lennon. For further Central Park information, see p. 15.

Chinatown

Start at Chatham Square **(1)**, where the goods of Irish debtors were auctioned off in the early 19th century. Walk up Doyers St, the oldest street in Chinatown, and turn left onto Pell St, an ancient road named for a butcher who worked here in the colonial period. Cross Mott St to the Church of the Transfiguration **(2)** at No 29. North on Mott St you'll pass the quenching *Saint's Alp Teahouse* **(3)** at No 51. Turn left on Bayard St to find the Museum of Chinese in the Americas **(4)** (on the corner of Mulberry St). The delicious *Pho Viet Huong* **(5)** is at 73 Mulberry St.

SIGHTS & HIGHLIGHTS

Church of the Transfiguration (p. 16)
Saint's Alp Teahouse (p. 72)
Museum of Chinese in the Americas (p. 31)
Pho Viet Huong (p. 72)

Double back to the corner of Bayard and Mott Sts and continue north on Mott. The Eastern States Buddhist Temple **(6)** is on the right (No 64) – stop to buy a $1 fortune. Turn left on Canal St and follow it all the way to Broadway, browsing at the food shops and the jewel-in-the-junk-heap variety stores like *Pearl River* **(7)** at No 277. You might like detour down desolate Cortlandt Alley to have a look at the gloomily photogenic factories and warehouses.

Chinatown is full of fun shopping opportunities (see p. 55).

Tom Smallman

distance 1 mile (1.5km) **duration** 1hr
start 🚍 M9, M15, M22
end 🚇 Canal St (N, R)

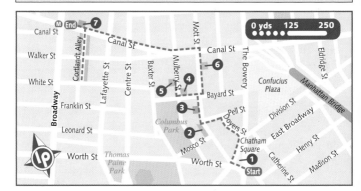

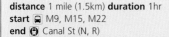

Greenwich Village

From Washington Square Park **(1)** head down Thompson St past the Judson Memorial Church **(2)**, designed by Stanford White. Cross W 3rd St and check out the chess shops **(3)** on the left. Turn right at Bleecker St and walk along to *Le Figaro* **(4)** at 184 (☎ 677-1100) where Jack Kerouac and Allen Ginsberg hung out, and *Cafe Borgia* **(5)** at 185 (☎ 674-9589), another 1950s beatnik haunt. Walk right up Macdougal St to No 115 at the cnr of Minetta Lane and pay homage at *Café Wha?* **(6)** (☎ 254-3706) – Jimi Hendrix once played here. Duck into Minetta Lane, then left into Minetta St. Cross sixth Ave back into Bleecker St.

SIGHTS & HIGHLIGHTS

Washington Square Park (p. 19)
Chumley's (p. 97)
Stonewall Place (p. 99)

Bubbles and tunes, Washington Square

Kim Grant

Browse along Bleecker as far as Seventh Ave, then make a hard left and cross over to Commerce St. Turning right at Bedford St brings you to New York's narrowest house **(7)** at No 75½, past the home of Edna St Vincent Millay and Cary Grant. Detour up Barrow St to see the Federal row houses **(8)** at Nos 49 & 51. Continue along Bedford St to *Chumley's* **(9)** at No 86 for good pub meals. Roll back out along Bedford and duck left on Grove St to see some lovely row houses **(10)**. Bedford St ends at raucous Christopher St, the artery of gay Village life. Turn right and walk up to Stonewall Place **(11)**, where you can catch the subway.

distance 2.2 miles (3.5km) **duration** 1½hrs
start ❹ W 4th St
end ❹ Christopher St

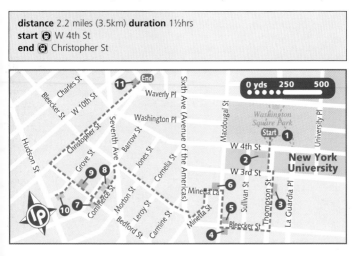

Lower Manhattan

Start early at City Hall **(1)** and walk north to the courthouses at Foley Square **(2)**. Directly in front of the Federal Courthouse head west along Duane St past the African Burial Ground **(3)**, then left down Broadway past the other side of City Hall. As you walk south you'll pass the Woolworth Building **(4)** and St Paul's Chapel **(5)** before you hit Liberty St where you can turn right to the World Trade Center **(6)**.

Double back to Broadway and continue south to Trinity Church **(7)**. Cross Broadway and walk down Wall St to Federal Hall **(8)**. Stop for a reviving meal or drink at *Mangia* **(9)** or turn down Broad St to the New York Stock Exchange **(10)**. Continue south on Broad St, turn right down Exchange Place and head back to Broadway, turn left and walk south to Bowling Green **(11)** and Customs House, which houses the National Museum of the American Indian **(12)**. Walk south along Whitehall St, turn right at Bridge St and cross State St to Battery Park **(13)**, where you can visit Castle Clinton **(14)** – an imposing fortress built in 1811 – or just grab a drink and gaze over the water.

distance 2.2 miles (3.5km)
duration 1½hrs
start 🚇 City Hall
end 🚇 Bowling Green or South Ferry

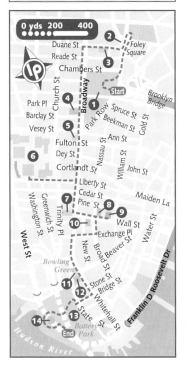

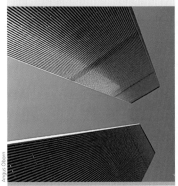

World Trade Center's vertiginous towers

EXCURSIONS
Cold Spring   (5, B2)

Cold Spring, on the eastern bank of the Hudson River, is a quaint little village 90 minutes north of New York, with charming antique shops, inns and restaurants. It's a lovely destination in itself and a good base for walks along the river and into the surrounding countryside. The steep Washburn Trail to the top of Mount Taurus is probably the best mix of challenge and terrific scenery.

Cold Spring is particularly enjoyable in autumn when the leaves are turning and the weather is mild. Ask at any of the stores about guided walking tours of the town itself or pick up a self-guided tour brochure.

INFORMATION

50 miles north of NYC

- 🚍 George Washington Bridge to Palisades Interstate Parkway N, Bear Mtn Bridge, Route 9D N along river
- 🚉 MetroNorth from Grand Central, to Cold Spring
- 🄴 www.hudsonvalley.org
- ⓘ Historic Hudson Valley (☎ 914-631-8200), 150 White Plains Rd, Tarrytown, NY 10591; New York State Travel Information Center (☎ 800-225-5697)
- ✕ Hudson House (☎ 914-265-9355; www.hudsonhouseinn.com); also provides lodgings

Cold Spring's main shopping strip

Angus Oborn

Coney Island   (4, E4)

This former summer playground was where sweating city dwellers came to enjoy the fun house, minor games of chance and bumper car rides in the Dreamland amusement park before WWI. In its heyday, 'amusements' included elephants on water slides and warm jets of air blown up from the walkways to raise women's skirts. These days, the island is a ghostly shadow of its former self but it's still worth the trip: the Cyclone roller coaster is truly terrifying (including a stomach-flapping 100ft plunge at almost 70mph), the aquarium (p. 41) is there and the beach is swimmable. Even from October to May, when everything's shut, the boardwalk stroll to Russified Brighton Beach is appealing.

INFORMATION

12.5 miles south of Manhattan

- 🚇 Stillwell Ave/Coney Island
- ✉ 1000 Surf Ave & W 10th St
- ☎ Dreamland: 718-372-5159
- ⓘ Aquarium (☎ 718-265-3400), Coney Island Sideshow (freak show; ☎ 718-372-5159)
- 🕐 Dreamland: mid-Apr to mid-Jun Sat-Sun noon-midnight; mid-Jun to mid-Sept noon-midnight
- 💲 free
- ✕ Caffe Volna (p. 70)

Jersey Shore   (5, D2)

The New Jersey coast stretches 130 miles from Sandy Hook in the north to Cape May in the south. Along the way are towns that range from beautiful to seedy – from quiet and Victorian Spring Lake to loud and youth-oriented Belmar. The quietest town on the Jersey Shore is Bay Head, the terminus of the North Jersey Coast train line. At Wildwood, there's a massive boardwalk, wide beaches and a fairground. Bear in mind that every oceanfront town in New Jersey shuts down for winter from mid-September to May.

Lower Manhattan view across the Hudson River from New Jersey.

INFORMATION

50 miles south of NYC

- 🚗 Lincoln Tunnel to NJ Turnpike, Woodbridge exit to Garden State Parkway S to last exit
- 🚆 New Jersey Transit from Penn station
- ⛴ NY Waterway ferry from W 38th St and Battery Park City to Sandy Hook
- 🚌 NJ Transit bus from Port Authority
- 🅴 www.nj.com/shore/beach_guide
- ⓘ New Jersey Tourism (☎ 609-292-2470, 800-537-7397); NY Waterway (☎ 800-533-3779) for ferry times
- 💲 Bay Head beach pass approx $5, from Bay Head Improvement Association (☎ 732-892-4179); ferry ticket $20 return
- ✕ Belmar: Havens & Hampton (☎ 732-681-1231); Spring Lake: Sandpiper Hotel (☎ 732-449-4700)

Princeton   (5, C2)

This attractive town is known throughout the world for its Ivy League university, which educates 6000 students each year within its wall-enclosed campus. Princeton is also a historic place, the site of an important Revolutionary battle on 3 January 1777, and an erstwhile national capital (4 months in 1783). The **Princeton Battlefield State Park**, site of the battle that ended in a decisive victory for George Washington, has remained virtually unchanged – an illustrated plan of the fighting stands next to the flagpole. **Albert Einstein's Home** at 112 Mercer St is not open to the public. Princeton has some lovely architecture, including the Gothic marvels of the university, and a nice array of shops and restaurants along Nassau St.

INFORMATION

62.5 miles south-west of NYC

- 🚗 NJ Turnpike to exit 9, Route 1 S, Route 571 W to Princeton
- 🚆 NE Corridor trains from Penn station to Princeton Junction, then transfer to the shuttle train
- 🅴 njht@sosgw.sos.state.nj.us (New Jersey Historic Trust) www.princetonol.com www.princeton.edu
- ⓘ Princeton Convention & Visitors Bureau (☎ 609-683-1760); Orange Key Guide Service university tours (☎ 609-258-3603); New Jersey Historic Trust (☎ 609-984-0473); New Jersey Transit (☎ 973-762-5100)
- ✕ Lahiere's (☎ 609-921-2798)

ORGANISED TOURS

Boat Tours

It's easy to forget what a tiny island you're on when you're lost among New York's bustle and skyscrapers. A boat trip is a great way to float yourself a sense of perspective. See also commuter ferry/boat information, page 113.

Bus Tours

Being driven around Manhattan – and even sitting in traffic – can be a good way to get your bearings. The slew of tours ranges from guided quick bursts to 2-day self-guided trawls.

Day Trips

Gray Lines offers trips to Atlantic City, the Hudson Valley and Washington DC by bus or train. If you're game, there's even a day (air) tour to Niagara Falls. New York Apple Tours has unescorted train trips and guided air tours to Washington DC as well as escorted or DIY air tours to Niagara Falls.

Helicopter Tours

A helicopter ride is thrilling in itself, but belting over one of the most spectacular cities in the world takes it to a whole new level of breathtaking.

Walking Tours

There's big money in being paid to lead people around New York, talking and pointing things out. The tours we've chosen are well-established or at least reputable, and put an interesting spin on the city.

Apple Tours
Loop Manhattan on a rumbling double-decker bus. A hop-on hop-off ticket is valid for 2 days and evenings of sightseeing along 5 routes.
✉ **depart from W 50th St & 7th Ave (2, K5)**
☎ **800-876-9868** 🅴
info@nyappletours.com;
www.nyappletours.com
⑤ **full city tour $39/22**

Arthur Marks
Tours in song by a colourful character who's tailored tours for 35 years. For a food tour of Chinatown, an anecdotal tour of Greenwich Village or an architectural tour through Tribeca, Arthur could be your man.
✉ **24 5th Ave, New York, NY 10011-8818**
☎ **673-0477** ⑤ **negotiable from $500/2½ hrs for 1-40 people**

Big Onion Walking Tours
Qualified historians with an interest in New York bordering on cheerful obsession lead tours to such places as the Jewish Lower East Side, Greenwich Village's gay sites and Irish New York.
✉ **PO Box 20561, Cherokee Stations, New York, NY 10021-0070** ☎ **439-1090**
🅴 **bowtnyc@aol.com;**
www.bigonion.com
⑤ **$10/8**

Circle Line
The Circle Lines runs a popular 3hr tour that circumnavigates Manhattan and cruises close to the

All aboard for magic views

Veronica Garbutt

Some Harlem kiddies can hardly wait for church.

Statue of Liberty. The sunset Harbor Lights tour is shorter, while The Beast ride puts wind in your hair.
✉ **tours depart from Pier 83 at W 42nd St (2, L2)** ☎ **563-3200** ⑤ **full island $22/12-19; Harbor Lights $18/10-16**

Gray Lines
Choose from 30 comfortable half and full day tours. The fact that lunch is served at 'the world's most elegant McDonald's' gives you an idea of the tone.
✉ **1740 Broadway (2, L5); Times Square visitors' centre (2, L4)** ☎ **397-2600** ❷ **www .graylinenewyork.com** ⑤ **$35/23 half day, $55/41 full day tour**

Harlem Spirituals
A variety of gospel church and food tours on Wednesday, Friday and Sunday. You could do it yourself (see p. 37), but if you'd rather not look at a map, these might be for you.
✉ **690 8th Ave b/w 43rd & 44th St (2, L4)** ☎ **391-0900** ❷ **hstours@pipeline.com; www.harlemspirituals .com** ⑤ **$35-65**

Helicopter Flight Services
HFS offers 2 tours: the New Yorker, which spins around the Statue of

Liberty and Manhattan as far as Central Park; and the more expensive Ultimate Tour, which includes the Yankee Stadium. Also flies up to 6 people to any NY airport for $595.
✉ **heliport E 34th St & First Ave (2, N8)** ☎ **355-0801** ⑤ **$99-139**

Howard Goldberg's Adventures on a Shoestring
Howard leads tours like Haunted Greenwich Village, Colourful Chinatown, Hell's Kitchen, Millionaire's Row and elegant Gramercy Park. The 90min walks emphasise talking with locals and getting off the tourist lemming trail.
☎ **265-2663** ⑤ **$5**

Joyce Gold History Tours of New York
This university history teacher leads a varied program of walking tours all over Manhattan. Good for serious history buffs and those interested in the quirky and scandalous.
✉ **141 W 17th St, New York, NY 10011** ☎ **242-5762** ❷ **nyctours@aol .com; www.nyctours .com** ⑤ **$12**

Kenny Kramer
If re-runs aren't enough, join the K-man for 3hrs of *Seinfeld* background, trivia, insight and gossip. This weekend-only bus tour is

hosted by the real-life inspiration for the TV character.
✉ **from Pulse Theater, 432 W 42nd St (2, L4)** ☎ **268-5525** ❷ **kram er@bway.net; www.ken-nykramer.com** ⑤ **$37.50**

NY Waterway
Though commuter ferries are good for a squizz at the Statue, there's nothing like a cruise for photo ops aplenty. NY Waterway will even drop you at a baseball game.
✉ **Pier 78, W 38th St & Twelfth Ave (2, M2)** ☎ **800-533-3779** ❷ **www.nywaterway.com** ⑤ **$18/9/90mins; prices vary depending on tour**

Radical Walking Tours
Bruce Kayton's alternative history tours (from March to December) include Greenwich Village, Harlem and Lower Manhattan. The 3hr walks focus on historical figures and neighbourhood characters.
☎ **718-492-0069** ⑤ **$10**

Tourguide?
Artsy, confronting, offbeat tours, treasure hunts, outings and aboutings in association with Deitch Projects (p. 33) and the Public Art Fund. Summer only.
✉ **76 Grand St (3, F5)** ☎ **802-7383** ❷ **thinkonyourfeet@ hotmail.com** ⑤ **$12**

World Yacht
Well-regarded year-round culinary cruises around Manhattan. Reservations and proper dress required.
✉ **depart from Pier 81 & W 41st St (2, M2)** ☎ **630-8100** ⑤ **$40/2hr brunch; $79/3hr dinner**

shopping

People come to New York just to shop – from world famous stores to quirky backstreet shops, there's no beating it for range and quality. And while it may not be strictly true that you can find 'anything' in the Apple, it is pleasingly difficult to come up with an acquisitive craving that can't be satisfied. Tibetan fur-rimmed hat? Absolutely. Boots in the right shade of orange? Dozens to choose from. Worm-studded lollypops? Thought you'd never ask!

In fact, the shopping is so good, you might find yourself hunting for something you only realise you need when it's time to depart: extra luggage to transport your goodies home.

Shopping Areas

Midtown is the place for department stores, chain clothing and theme stores attracting tourists, middle America and uptown darlings picking their way through the dross. **Madison Ave** tends to be more upmarket than **Fifth Ave**, though there are exceptions. Certainly, farther north into the Upper East Side, Madison becomes more exclusive, with designer boutiques and ritzy department stores giving way to numerous antiques emporiums. The **Garment District** (Seventh Ave between 34th & 42nd Sts) is full of clothing wholesalers. This is the place to nose out sample sales and sell-offs of label clothes at under-the-counter prices.

SoHo is mirroring a lot of the Upper East Side stores these days, perhaps with a bit more black and a bit more attitude. Broadway below Houston is a bustling string of chain stores and mid-range clothiers. **NoLIta** is where the up-and-coming designers and couturiers are clustering – Mott, Mulberry and Elizabeth Sts are buzzing. Over east, 7th, 8th and 9th Sts between Ave A and Third Ave dotted with funky little stores selling new and used clothes, gifts, crafts and oddities.

Greenwich Village has cult stores, bad thrift stores, a shoe and leather strip (8th St between Fifth & Sixth Aves) and a chess shop strip (Thompson St near Washington Square Park). **Lower Manhattan** is a mishmash of shops; Fulton St and Nassau St are worth a crawl for their discount and clearance clothing stores.

Orchard St is the spot for low to mid-range luggage and leather clothing. The T-shirt, underwear, watches and sunglasses are no great shakes,

Open Sesame

Most retail stores are open 7 days a week. Weekday and Saturday hours tend to be from 10am to 6pm, with late night closing on Thursday, when stores are open until at least 7pm. On Sunday stores are open from around noon to 6pm, except along Madison Ave, where a lot of the high fashion places remain closed. Many shops in Lower Manhattan open earlier, usually by 8am, to give downtowners a pre-work retail window. SoHo, Greenwich Village and East Village stores are later openers, often starting up around noon and mooching through to mid-evening. Book, music and food shops tend to stay open later than their clothing counterparts.

and it isn't much chop in the people-watching stakes, but whatever happens you can finish off with a meal at *Katz's Deli* (p. 73). As many of these businesses are owned by religious Jews, most are closed on Friday afternoon and all day Saturday. Sunday is the big day – there's live music, and the merchants association (☎ 226-9010) runs a free shopping tour (April to December only – meet outside *Katz's*, on the corner of Ludlow and E Houston Sts, at 11am).

Wandering around **Chinatown** is an assault on the senses – you can buy a bucket of fresh frogs, a gorgeous silk waistcoat, cheap kitchenware, some medicinal bark and a crispy duck without even hunting. Grand, Canal and Mulberry Sts probably have the most interesting shops. One of the best is *Pearl River*, which has everything from dollar novelties that fall apart as soon as you pay for them to carefully tended bonsai. There's one at 277 Canal St (☎ 431-4770) and another at 200 Grand St (☎ 966-1010), open 10am-7.30pm.

Get the Wind in Your Sales

Sales are a New York ritual, followed obsessively and played aggressively. The biggest sale seasons are late January and July – just about every retail enterprise offers true markdowns. Smaller but still significant sales occur before Christmas (beginning the Friday after Thanksgiving) and directly after Christmas. The Memorial Day long weekend (end of May) is another bargain bonanza, while August midsummer clearances are a good bet for summer clothes.

Elysa Lazar is New York's shopping tsar – her *Sales & Bargain Report* (www.lazarshopping.com) is only available by subscription, though you can order just one issue.

Flea Markets

Most flea markets are weekend affairs. The easy browsing zone is Sixth Ave in the 20s: the Annex Antiques Fair & Flea Market is at W 26th St (2, O6) and the Chelsea Antiques Building at W 25th St. The Grand St Antiques Fair (3, F5) on Broadway includes clothing, homewares, LPs, CDs and furniture. Big 'Greenflea' markets are held on school grounds at 67th St, b/w First & York Aves, Upper East Side (Saturday only; 2, G8), and on Columbus Ave, between 76th & 77th Sts, (Sunday only; 2, E4). There's a casual local weekend market at Ave A & 11th St, East Village (3, C7), with second-hand clothes, books, furniture, kitchenware and assorted junk.

Bored mannequins, Greenwich Village

Paying With Plastic

It's a rare store that doesn't accept credit cards: even the lowliest deli will usually oblige, though some may require a minimum purchase of $15-20 before they'll let you charge it. Occasionally shops will waive sales tax if you pay in cash, especially if you're buying second-hand goods; it's worth asking if you're spending up big.

DEPARTMENT STORES

Barney's
The flagship of the hip and haughty chain store that's famous for treating potential customers as too fat, too poor and, in the menswear department, too straight. Fred's, the swanky basement eatery, is the place to hide out b/w bothering the cashiers.
✉ **660 Madison Ave & 61st St, Upper E Side (2, H6) ☎ 826-8900 🚇 59th St (4, 5, 6), Lexington Ave (N, R) 🚌 M1 to M4 ⏲ Mon-Fri 10am-8pm, Sat 10am-7pm, Sun 12-6pm**

Bergdorf Goodman
Still a favourite stop for out-of-towners looking for classy gifts in prestige wrapping to take home. Terrific jewellery and couture collections (the menswear range is growing), attentive staff and great sales.
✉ **754 Fifth Ave & 58th St, Midtown (2, J6) ☎ 753-7300 🚇 5th Ave (N, R), 59th St (4, 5, 6) 🚌 M1 to M5, M31, M57 ⏲ 10am-7pm (to 8pm Thurs, to 6pm Sat)**

Bloomingdale's (2, H7)
Bloomie's is a cramped, crowded but well-loved New York institution. The clothing range has been reinvigorated in recent years by the addition of snappy young designers.
✉ **E 59th St & Lexington Ave, Midtown ☎ 705-2000 🚇 59th St (4, 5, 6), Lexington Ave (N, R) 🚌 M101 to M103 ⏲ 10am-10pm (to 8.30pm Mon, to 8pm Sat, to 7pm Sun)**

Century 21
A discount department store with a large, if unreliable, selection of men's and women's wear. Whatever it is, it will always be marked down. Shopping here is a ritual for downtown office workers and people waiting out jury duty at the nearby courthouses.
✉ **22 Cortlandt St, Lwr Manhattan (3, K5) ☎ 227-9092 🚇 Cortlandt St, Fulton St 🚌 M1, M5, M15 ⏲ Mon-Fri 7.45am-8pm (to 8.30pm Thurs), Sat 10am-7.30pm, Sun 11am-6pm**

Hip on Fifth Avenue – Henri Bendel

Henri Bendel
Curious, fun clothing, cosmetics and accessories from newly established and flavour-of-the-moment designers. A warning: the fashion here tends to be so 'now' that it becomes 'yesterday' very easily.
✉ **712 Fifth Ave & 56th St, Midtown (2, J6) ☎ 247-1100 🚇 5th Ave (E, F, N, R), 57th St (B, Q) 🚌 M1 to M5 ⏲ Mon-Wed & Fri-Sat 10am-7pm, Thurs 10am-8pm, Sun 12-6pm**

Lord & Taylor
Ten floors of fashion, with a tendency to conservative American daywear for the ladies. Swimsuits are also a strong point. The sales assistants are pleasantly non-threatening, even in the cosmetics department.
✉ **424 Fifth Ave & 40th St, Midtown (2, M6) ☎ 391-3344 🚇 42nd St 🚌 M1 to M5, M27, M50 ⏲ Mon-Tues & Sat 10am-7pm, Wed-Fri 10am-8.30pm, Sun 11am-7pm**

Department Store Concierge
Every department store has a customer service centre able to provide all sorts of help to those who spend under its roof. Stores will certainly free your arms for more shopping by delivering purchases to your hotel, or even shipping them home for you. If you need help putting together an outfit, assistants will crawl the store with you, showing you what's where and advising you on suitable items. You can even ask for advice on eating and other shopping in the area. Of course, you're expected to buy more than a pair of socks if you do take advantage of such services.

Macy's (2, N5)

Though its claim to be the world's largest store is dubious, Macy's is certainly massive. Even so, it's quite easy to manage except during the floor-packing sales. The store is regarded affectionately by New Yorkers because it sponsors Fourth of July fireworks and the Thanksgiving Day parade. Eatzi's (p. 78) has the best on-site nosh.

Macy's mercantile marvel

✉ 151 W 34th St, Herald Sq, Midtown ☎ 695-4400 🚇 Herald Sq 🚌 M5 to M7, M15 ⏱ Mon & Thurs-Sat 10am-8.30pm, Tues 9am-8.30pm, Wed 9am-10pm, Sun 11am-7pm

Saks Fifth Ave (2, K6)

Famous for its January sale, Saks has a vast ground-floor selling space with

No sacks here, it's Saks

pleasantly arranged stock and helpful staff.
✉ 611 Fifth Ave & 50th St, Midtown ☎ 753-4000 🚇 Rockefeller Center 🚌 M1 to M4, M27, M50 ⏱ Mon-Sat 10am-7pm, (to 8pm Thurs, to 6.30pm Sat), Sun 12-6pm

Takashimaya

A stunning Japanese-owned store that sells goods from all over the world with an emphasis on style, craftsmanship and gorgeous packaging. Great travel gear, and the ground floor florist is a treat. Escape the bustle by taking 'east-west afternoon tea' in *The Teabox* in the basement.
✉ 693 Fifth Ave & 55th St, Midtown (2, J6) ☎ 350-0100 🚇 5th Ave (E, F, N, R) 🚌 M1 to M4 ⏱ Mon-Sat 10am-7pm

CLOTHING & ACCESSORIES

Amy Chan

'Where did you get your bag?' kind of bags that you could base a whole outfit on. Bum bags, tool belts, whimsical ballroom clutches and purses, both pretty and practical.
✉ 247 Mulberry St, NoLIta (3, F6) ☎ 966-3417 🚇 Broadway/Lafayette St, Spring St (6), 2nd Ave 🚌 M21 ⏱ Mon-Sat 12-7pm, Sun 12-5pm

Armani Exchange

Muted well-cut coordinates and accessories with the name but not the whole price tag. Clever twists on classics with dash rather than splash.
✉ 568 Broadway &

Prince St, SoHo (3, E5) ☎ 431-6000 🚇 Prince St (N, R) 🚌 M6, M21 ⏱ Mon-Thurs 10am-8pm, Fri-Sat 10am-9pm, Sun 11am-8pm

Brooks Brothers

A legendary store selling conservative clothing and formal wear, largely for men, though there is a small, immaculate women's range. The fitting rooms are as big as some Manhattan apartments.
✉ 346 Madison Ave & 43rd St, Midtown (2, L6); also at Fifth Ave & 53rd St (2, J6) ☎ 682-8800 🚇 42nd St 🚌 M1 to M5 ⏱ Mon-Wed & Fri-Sat 9am-7pm, Thurs 9am-8pm, Sun 12-6pm

Calvin Klein

The media savvy designer's flagship store is a study in elegance. Clothes hang arm's length from each other, swinging lazily in a subtle air-con breeze, and sales staff waft around with perfect skin.
✉ 654 Madison Ave & 60th St, Upper E Side (2, H6) ☎ 292-9000 🚇 59th St (4, 5, 6), 5th Ave (N R) 🚌 M1 to M4 ⏱ Mon-Sat 10am-6pm (to 8pm Thurs), Sun 12-6pm

Calypso

The NoLIta pioneer has become something of a mini-empire but the clothes are as stylish as ever. From slinky to cute and flouncy to cosy, Calypso clothes are always

special. Parents can dress their kids at Calypso Enfants (284 Mulberry St; 3, F6).
⊠ **280 Mott St, NoLIta (3, F6)** ☎ **965-0990** 🚇 **Broadway/Lafayette St, Spring St (6), 2nd Ave** 🚌 **M21** ⏰ **Mon-Thurs 12-8pm, Fri-Sat 11am-8pm, Sun 12-7pm**

Canal Jeans
A massive store with vintage in the bargain basement and brand casual wear up top. A one stop shop for easy living at easy prices.
⊠ **504 Broadway, b/w Spring & Broome Sts, SoHo (3, F5)** ☎ **226-1130** 🚇 **Spring St (6)** 🚌 **M6** ⏰ **9.30am-9pm**

Cartier
When the darlings of the diamond world first opened up shop in the United States, they bought their Fifth Ave site in exchange for a pearl necklace. Rocks to knock your socks off and watches, glasses, bags and brooches all dying to become your new best friend.
⊠ **653 Fifth Ave & 52nd St, Midtown (2, K6)** ☎ **446-3460** 🚇 **5th Ave (E, F)** 🚌 **M1 to M4** ⏰ **Mon-Sat 10am-6pm**

Fashion Weeks
There are 2 major fashion weeks in New York: early autumn (fall, ie mid-September) and early spring (ie mid-March). Bryant Park is the site of most of the parades and primping – mostly trade only – but keep your eyes open for events and model sightings around town.

Giorgio Armani
Massive 4 floor flagship store where you can browse in peace among gorgeous clothes, many of them unencumbered by the vulgarity of price tags.
⊠ **E 65th St & Madison Ave, Upper E Side (2, G6)** ☎ **988-9191** 🚇 **68th St, Lexington Ave (B, Q)** 🚌 **M1 to M4, M66, M72** ⏰ **10am-6pm (to 7pm Thurs)**

Joseph
French designs with English accents: sleek apparel for young, slender men and women with hot dates at cool places.
⊠ **804 Madison Ave, b/w 67th & 68th Sts, Upper E Side (2, G6)** ☎ **570-0077** 🚇 **68th St** 🚌 **M1 to M4, M66, M72** ⏰ **Mon-Sat 10am-6.30pm (to 7pm Thurs), Sun 1-6pm**

Kenneth Cole
Reliably chic men's clothing, including especially good leather coats and dress shirts. Among accessories sold here are smart shoes (for women too), bags and luggage.
⊠ **597 Broadway, near Houston St, SoHo (3, E5)** ☎ **965-0283** 🚇 **Prince St (N, R), Broadway/Lafayette St** 🚌 **M6, M21** ⏰ **Mon-Sat 10am-9pm, Sun 12-7pm**

Nicole Miller
She's credited with reinventing the little black dress but there's more to her repertoire than that. Expect well made glam garb with kooky twists – an evening gown held together with Velcro, a swish jacket with comic buttons.
⊠ **134 Prince St, SoHo (3, E5)** ☎ **343-1362**

🚇 **Prince St (N, R), Broadway/Lafayette St** 🚌 **M6** ⏰ **Mon-Sat 11am-7pm, Sun 12-6pm**

Polo/Ralph Lauren
A fragrant mansion decorated with portraits of establishment youths and their ponies. The clothes are crisp and understated, the customers handsome and recently shampooed.
⊠ **Madison Ave & 72nd St, Upper E Side (2, F6)** ☎ **606-2100** 🚇 **68th St** 🚌 **M1 to M4, M66, M72** ⏰ **Mon-Sat 10am-6pm**

Stuart Weitzman
When your travel shoes bore you to tears, stride to Stuart for treads crazy or classy. They're not quite jogging shoes, but they are made with more than a curt nod to comfort.
⊠ **625 Madison Ave & 58th, Midtown (2, J6)** ☎ **750-2555** 🚇 **59th St (4, 5, 6), Lexington Ave (N, R)** 🚌 **M1 to M4** ⏰ **Mon-Fri 10am-6.30pm, Sat 10am-6pm, Sun 12-5pm**

Tiffany's
Not as snooty as you might expect, and if you look hard enough, you can take home a reasonably priced small item and get the impressive Tiffany's box.
⊠ **727 Fifth Ave & 57th St, Midtown (2, J6)** ☎ **755-8000** 🚇 **57th St (B, Q), 5th Ave (N, R)** 🚌 **M1 to M4, M31, M57** ⏰ **Mon-Sat 10am-6pm (to 7pm Thurs)**

Tracy Feith
A large-for-its-location emporium with urban angel/country sophisticated clothing. Precious dresses and coordinates, some of them period

Many a temptation awaits at Tiffany & Co.

inspired, all of them alluring.
✉ **209 Mulberry St, NoLIta (3, F6)** ☎ **334-3097** Ⓢ **Spring St (6)** 🚌 **M6** ⏲ **11am-7pm (from 12pm Sun)**

Valentino
One of the world's best-known couture designers stocks its classy store with men's and ladies' fashion and a small selection of gifts and homewares.
✉ **823 Madison Ave &**

65th St, Upper E Side (2, G6) ☎ **772-6969** Ⓢ **Lexington Ave (B, Q), 68th St** 🚌 **M1 to M4, M66, M72** ⏲ **Mon-Sat 10am-6pm**

Versace
Despite Gianni's tragic end, his Italian high-fashion label lives on. Muster up attitude before you venture into the store.
✉ **815 Madison Ave, Upper E Side (2, G6)** ☎ **744-6868** Ⓢ **68th St** 🚌 **M1 to M4, M66, M72** ⏲ **Mon-Sat 10am-6pm**

Vivienne Westwood
Punk's grand dame turns out a varied wardrobe of men's and women's wear. There's

still a decent dose of loopy fashion but some of the garments are sheer classic. The store is always fun for a gander at the grandeur.
✉ **71 Greene St, SoHo (3, F5)** ☎ **334-5200** Ⓢ **Spring St (6)** 🚌 **M6** ⏲ **Mon-Sat 11am-7pm, Sun 12-6pm**

XLarge
Easywear for guys from Beastie Boy Mike D. Gals can fit into the Mini by XLarge range. A good bet for cool – but not crazy – street clothes.
✉ **267 Lafayette St & Prince St, SoHo (3, F6)** ☎ **334-4480** Ⓢ **Prince St (N, R), Broadway/ Lafayette St** 🚌 **M21** ⏲ **12-7pm**

Not Too Taxing
Until March 2000, all clothing sold in the state of New York was subject to an 8.25% sales tax. Now that tax has been waived on all clothing items under $500. This won't help out with your Armani wedding dress, but it makes most apparel odysseys just that little bit easier.

SECOND-HAND & RETRO CLOTHES

Center For The Dull
The jeans, suits, jackets and shirts piled up, hung up and filling up the 'Center' are dead stock culled from warehouses, ie it's retro but not pre-worn … and not even dull.
✉ **216 Lafayette St, near Broome St, SoHo (3, F6)** ☎ **925-9699** Ⓢ **Spring St (6)** 🚌 **M6, M103** ⏲ **12-7pm**

Rags A Go Go
A second-hand clothing empire. These stores are good for not-too-expensive but never-crappy trend-

chasing threads.
✉ **73 E 7th St, b/w First & Second Aves, E Village (3, C3); also at at 119 St Marks Pl (3, D7) & 218W 14th St, (3, D7)** ☎ **254-4771** Ⓢ **1st Ave** 🚌 **M8, M14, M15** ⏲ **1-9pm (to 8pm Sun)**

The Stella Dallas Look
Well-preserved vintage frocks, strides and accessories mostly from the 50s and 60s. Stella doesn't sell cheap but she has good seasonal sales.
✉ **218 Thompson St,**

Greenwich Village (3, E5) ☎ **674-0447** Ⓢ **W 4th St, B'way/ Lafayette St** 🚌 **M5, M21** ⏲ **1-8pm (approx – call ahead)**

The Village Scandal
A cluttered shop with jewel-in-the-junk-heap dresses, shirts, suits and accessories that make you feel like dressing up every day.
✉ **19 E 7th St, E Village (3, D6)** ☎ **460-9358** Ⓢ **3rd Ave, Astor Pl** 🚌 **M8, M15, M101 to M103** ⏲ **1pm-midnight**

ART & ANTIQUES

Annex Antiques Fair & Flea Market (2, O6)
See p. 55.

Antiquarium
Museum quality classical, Egyptian and Near Eastern antiquities with an emphasis on wearable ancient jewellery and modern gold pieces set with ancient coins. If you've been eyeing an Egyptian sarcophagus at the Met, this is the place to buy one.
✉ **948 Madison Ave, near 75th St, Upper E Side (2, F6)** ☎ 734-9776 🚇 77th St 🚌 M1 to M4 ⏲ Tues-Sat 10am-5.30pm

Bernd Goeckler Antiques
Italian and French furniture from 18th century neoclassical through Art Nouveau to Art Deco. Chandeliers and mirrors a speciality.
✉ **30 E 10th St, Greenwich Village (3, C5)** ☎ 777-8209 🚇 8th St/NYU 🚌 M1, M3, M5, M6 ⏲ Mon-Fri 9am-6pm, Sat 10am-5pm

Bernhard & S Dean Levy
Five floors of American antiques from the 17th century to the early 19th century. The furniture is sublime but there are also paintings, silver,

Sidewalk antique sale, Greenwich Village

Kim Grant

art and porcelain. This impeccable store has been in the same family for 100 years.
✉ **24 E 84th St, Upper E Side (2, D6)** ☎ 628-7088 🚇 86th St (4, 5, 6) 🚌 M1 to M4, M86 ⏲ Apr-Sept: Mon-Fri 9.30am-5.30pm; Oct-Apr: Tues-Sat 9.30am-5.30pm

Chelsea Antiques Building
The most concentrated selection of antiques in the city, with 100 stores over 12 floors selling serious (18th century mahogany tables) and fun (cookie jars from the 1950s) goods to serious collectors and haphazard browsers.
✉ **110 W 25th St, Chelsea (2, O6)** ☎ 929-0909 🚇 23rd St (F) 🚌 M5 to M7, M23 ⏲ Mon-Fri 10am-6pm, Sat-Sun 8.30am-6pm

Dalva Brothers
The 5 storey showroom/town house would be worth a visit

even if it didn't contain the US's biggest collection of European (particularly French) 18th century furniture, porcelain, paintings and sculpture.
✉ **44 E57th St, Midtown (2, J7)** ☎ 758-2297 🚇 5th Ave (N, E), 59th St (4, 5, 6) 🚌 M1 to M5, M31, M57 ⏲ Mon-Sat 9.30am-5.30pm

Guild Antiques II
English 18th and 19th century antiques, mostly lovely mahogany and walnut pieces (also smaller boxes, book stands, pedestals and trays). There's also a fine selection of Chinese porcelain, lamps and glassware.
✉ **1089 & 1095 Madison Ave & 82nd St, Upper E Side (2, D6)** ☎ 472-0830 🚇 86th St (4, 5, 6) 🚌 M1 to M4 ⏲ Mon-Sat 10am-5pm

Manhattan Art & Antiques Center
Over 100 different stores on 3 levels, with everything from Japanese curios to Art Deco Americana. A good place to come if you're not particularly focused and want to see what's out there.
✉ **1050 Second Ave & 55th St, Midtown (2, J8)** ☎ 355-4400 🚇 59th St (4, 5, 6), Lexington Ave (N, R) 🚌 M15, M31, M57 ⏲ Mon-Sat 10.30am-6pm, Sun 12-6pm

Going, Gong, Gone
There are frequent art and antique auctions in Manhattan, most of them free and open to the public. Check Friday's *New York Times* for listings or contact the houses directly: Sotheby's (☎ 606-7010), 1334 York Ave (2, F8); William Doyle Galleries (☎ 427-2730), 175 E 87th St (2, C6); Tepper (☎ 677-5300), 110 E 25th St (2, O7); Christie's (☎ 636-2000), Rockefeller Plaza & 49th St (2, K6).

MUSIC

New York is a good town to tune into the latest, greatest and spaciest and to hunt down personal classics that no-one back home ever heard of. Below 14th St is the place for quirky, specialist shops. Uptown music stores are mostly chains stocking an acceptable range of mainstream CDs. Along Broadway and in Midtown, street vendors sell $5 pirated CDs – mostly rap and R&B: it's buyer beware. Legitimate second-hand CDs and vinyl can be almost as cheap.

Academy Records & CDs

A large selection of classical, jazz, rock and pretty much whatever else you can think of, both new and used.
⊠ 12 W 18th St & Fifth Ave, Union Sq (3, B5) ☎ 242-3000 ⊕ Union Sq, 23rd St ⊟ M2, M3, M5 to M7 ⊘ Mon-Sat 9.30am-9pm, Sun 11am-7pm

Bleecker Bob's

Second-hand desirables and trash (mostly rock, R&B and folk) – stuff you've been looking for since you were 15 and stuff you never wanted to see again. Rock T-shirts too.
⊠ 118 W3rd St near Macdougal St, Greenwich Village (3, D4) ☎ 475-9677 ⊕ W 4th St ⊟ M5, M6 ⊘ noon-1am (to 3am Fri-Sat)

Etherea

A small shop that somehow manages to have every dance, electronic or indie CD or LP you're looking for. There's new and second-hand stock, often at snap-uppable prices.
⊠ 66 Ave A & 5th, E Village (3, D7) ☎ 358-1126 ⊕ 2nd Ave ⊟ M14 ⊘ noon-10.30pm (to 11.30pm Fri-Sat)

Footlight Records

Magnificent collection of out-of-print albums, show music, Sinatra bootlegs and movie soundtracks on CD and LP.
⊠ 113 E12th St & Third Ave, E Village (3, C6) ☎ 533-1572 ⊕ Union Sq, 3rd Ave ⊟ M1, M9, M14, M101 to M103 ⊘ Mon-Fri 11am-7pm, Sat 10am-6pm, Sun 11am-5pm

Gimme Gimme

Used and mostly collectible vinyl; a labour-of-love grab-bag of soul, folk, rock, 12 inches and whatever else turns up in the hunt.
⊠ 325 E 5th St, b/w First & Second Aves, E Village (3, D7) ☎ 475-2955 ⊕ 1st Ave ⊟ M8, M14 ⊘ Thurs 8-11pm, Fri-Sat 1-10pm, Sun 1-7pm

Other Music

Electronic, experimental, indie and fusion with a smattering of lounge and world. New and used, vinyl and CD.
⊠ 15 E 4th St & Lafayette St, E Village (3, D6) ☎ 477-8150 ⊕ Astor Pl ⊟ M1, M5, M6 ⊘ 12-9pm (to 10pm Fri, to 7pm Sun)

Rocks in Your Head

New and used CDs, LPs and books. The emphasis is on indie rock and imports but there's a decent selection of radio rock, country and blues.
⊠ 157 Prince St & W Broadway, SoHo (3, F5) ☎ 475-6729 ⊕ Prince St ⊟ M5, M6, M21 ⊘ 12-9pm

Shrine

Lucky dip mix of second-hand CDs and vinyl. Pop, jazz, country, reggae, indie, German electronica: this place does it.
⊠ 441 E 9th St & Ave A, E Village (3, C7) ☎ 529-6646 ⊕ 1st Ave (L) ⊟ M8, M14 ⊘ 12-10pm (to 11pm Fri-Sat)

Tower Records

Wide selection of music in a huge store. It's best for rock/pop and soul (classical, jazz and country are tucked away upstairs). There's a Ticketmaster outlet on site and a massive Tower Books & Video store one block east on Lafayette St.
⊠ 692 Broadway & W 4th St, E (3, D6) ☎ 505-1500 ⊕ Astor Pl, 8th St ⊟ M5, M6 ⊘ 9am-midnight

Virgin Megastore

The aim seems to be to please most of the people most of the time. Sure, there's everything mainstream but it's mega enough to house a decent selection of dance, jazz, classical and progressive music.
⊠ W 45th St & Broadway, Midtown (2, L5); also Union Sq, Chelsea (3, B5) ☎ 921-1020 ⊕ Times Sq ⊟ M6, M7, M10, M27, M104 ⊘ 9am-1am (to 2am Fri-Sat)

BOOKS

New York is just pipped by London as the best city in the world to buy books in English. The choice here is staggering and, for the bookish, truly exciting. Despite the rise and rise of chain superstores with the buying power to discount new books, independent stores are holding their own. For information on books for children, see p. 66.

Barnes & Noble
Each of the many superstores features over 200,000 titles, comfortable seating and a cafe where you can read magazines and muse over potential purchases.
✉ 33 E17th St at Union Sq, Chelsea (3, B5); also at Astor Pl, 600 Fifth Ave & 48th St, Midtown (2, K6) and other locations ☎ 253-0810 Ⓜ Union Sq 🚌 M1 to M3, M6, M7 ◷ 10am-10pm

Corner Bookstore
A small-but-select shop with a focus on art books, fiction and children's literature. A comfortable place to browse through and listen to periodic author readings.
✉ 1313 Madison Ave & 93rd St, Upper E Side (2, B6) ☎ 831-3554 Ⓜ 96th St (6) 🚌 M1 to M4 ◷ Mon-Fri 10am-8pm (to 7pm Fri) Sat-Sun 11am-6pm

Gotham Book Mart
(2, K6) One of the city's premier stand-alone shops, this cluttered store is a real treasure. In business since 1920, its trademark shingle declares that 'wise men fish here'; WH Auden, Marianne Moore and Delmore Schwartz have all dangled a line.
✉ 41 W 47th St, b/w Fifth & Sixth Aves, Midtown (2, K6) ☎ 719-4448 Ⓜ Rockefeller Center 🚌 M1 to M4, M27, M50 ◷ Mon-Fri 9.30am-6.30pm, Sat 9.30am-6pm

Rizzoli Bookstore
It's impossible not to swoon at the great art, architecture and design books in this beautiful store. The comfortable layout makes it easy to tip from subject to subject and delightfully hard to leave. Also 31 W 57th St, Midtown
✉ 454 W Broadway, SoHo (3, F5) ☎ 674-

1616 Ⓜ Spring St (C, E) 🚌 M6, M21 ◷ Mon-Sat 10.30am-8pm, Sun 12-7pm

Shakespeare & Co
Pleasant store with a large selection of theatre and film books and scripts. The downstairs section has more academic texts. This is the biggest of the 4 Shakespeare & Co stores in Manhattan.
✉ 716 Broadway, Greenwich Village; also at 939 Lexington Ave, 1 Whitehall St & 137 E 23rd St ☎ 529-1330 Ⓜ Astor Pl, 8th St 🚌 M5, M6 ◷ 10am-11pm (to midnight Fri-Sat)

St Marks Book Shop
A lovely big bookshop with a neighbourhood identity and an international outlook. It's strong on political work, literature, poetry and academic journals.
✉ 31 Third Ave, E Village (3, C6) ☎ 260-7853 Ⓜ Astor Pl 🚌 M8, M103 ◷ 10am-midnight (from 11am Sun)

SECOND-HAND BOOKS
Alabaster Bookshop
Small, select used store with a good range of fiction, art and photography books.
✉ 122 Fourth Ave, Greenwich Village (3, C6) ☎ 982-3550 Ⓜ Union Sq 🚌 M1, M3 ◷ 10am-8pm (from 11am Sun)

Suggested Readings
You could spend the rest of your life reading books about New York – another 1 is published every 3 days. Personal favourites include the warm, witty stories of O Henry, written in early last century; Paul Auster's *New York Trilogy*, spooky neo-Kafkan anti-spy tales; and *Low Life* by Luc Sante, a pithy history of poor and downtrodden 19th century New Yorkers. EB White's 1949 essay *Here is New York* is light, bright and absolutely right. For splashy, somewhat trashy tales of the modern city pick up anything by Jay McInerney or Tama Janowitz. If you want a sense of what's bubbling while you're here, grab *Open City*, a local literary journal.

Archivia

Breathlessly beautiful books on the decorative arts, architecture, gardening and interiors, many of them rare, out-of-print or otherwise hard to find. The store itself is a masterpiece of interior design.
✉ **944 Madison Ave, Upper E Side (2, F6)** ☎ **439-9194** Ⓜ **77th St** 🚌 **M1 to M4** 🕐 **Mon-Fri 10am-6pm, Sat-Sun 12-5pm**

The Argosy

Estate sales, rare prints, autographs, old maps, art books, classics and other eclectic books on all topics. Bargain tables start at $1.
✉ **116 E 59th St, Midtown (2, H7)** ☎ **753-4455** Ⓜ **59th St (4, 5, 6), Lexington Ave (N, R)** 🚌 **M101 to M103** 🕐 **Mon-Fri 10am-6pm, call for Saturday hours**

Coliseum Books

Huge selection of paperback fiction and out-of-print titles.
✉ **1771 Broadway, Midtown (2, J4)** ☎ **757-8381** Ⓜ **59th St (A, B, C, D, 1, 9)** 🚌 **M5, M7, M10, M104** 🕐 **Mon 8am-10pm, Tues-Thurs 8am-11pm, Sat 10am-11.30pm, Sun 12-8pm**

The Strand

Eight miles of used books and review copies; the kind of shop that either inspires or crushes the aspiring writer.
The Strand Book Annex (☎ 732-6070), cnr Fulton and Gold Sts (3, J6), has discounted, out-of-print and review copies of bestsellers, business titles and more.
✉ **828 Broadway & 12th St, Greenwich Village (3, C5)** ☎ **473-1452** Ⓜ **Union Sq** 🚌 **M1 to M3, M6, M7** 🕐 **9.30am-10.30pm (from 11am Sun)**

SPECIALIST BOOKS

Bluestockings

Words for, by and about women in a comfy space that used to be a crack house. Regular installations, performances and readings on-site.
✉ **172 Allen St & Stanton St, Lower E Side (3, E7)** ☎ **777-6028** Ⓜ **2nd Ave** 🚌 **M15** 🕐 **Tues-Sun 12-8pm**

A Different Light Bookstore

Stocks 15,000 gay & lesbian titles and has a small cafe, several author readings a week and a free Sunday night movie series.
✉ **151 W 19th St, Chelsea (2, P5)** ☎ **989-4850** Ⓜ **18th St** 🚌 **M10** 🕐 **11am-11pm**

Incommunicado

Small-but-lovely showcase of independent books from Incommunicado Press, other small presses and whatever the owner likes – 'techno-eavesdroppers, urban agitators and severe literature'. Open evenings for bookworms out after dark.
✉ **Tonic, 107 Norfolk, b/w Rivington & Delancey, Lower E Side (3, F8)** ☎ **473-9350** Ⓜ **Delancey/Essex Sts** 🚌 **M9, M14, M21** 🕐 **Tues-Sun 6pm-midnight**

A Photographers Place

Everything for lens lovers from dreamy art books to down-and-dirty technical tomes.
✉ **133 Mercer St, SoHo (3, F5)** ☎ **966-2356** Ⓜ **Prince St** 🚌 **M6** 🕐 **Mon-Sat 11am-7pm, Sun 12-8pm**

Printed Matter

A stimulating not-for-profit arts space dedicated to artists' publications ('that is, book or book-like objects'). A wonderful place to browse through bent and beautiful offerings from all over the world.
✉ **77 Wooster St, SoHo (3, F5)** ☎ **925-0325** Ⓜ **Spring St (C, E)** 🚌 **M6** 🕐 **Tues-Fri 10am-6pm, Sat 11am-7pm**

Traveler's Choice Bookstore

Guides, phrasebooks, dictionaries, language learning packs, maps, travel accessories – everything to inspire you to stay on the road.
✉ **2 Wooster St & Canal St, SoHo (3, G5)** ☎ **941-1535** Ⓜ **Canal St (A, C, E)** 🚌 **M6** 🕐 **Mon-Wed & Fri-Sat 9am-6pm, Thurs 9am-8pm**

The longest strand of books you're ever likely to see.

FOOD & DRINK

For a bunch of people that seem to eat out all the time, New Yorkers still stock their pantries with all sorts of edibles. If you're self-catering or just picnicking, there is a plethora of food stores with a wonderful range. And because this is New York, and we're all very busy, just about all of these stores will make you a meal to eat on the run.

Balducci
Great for fresh produce – in season, choose from a dozen sorts of tomatoes, lose yourself in 'mushroom corner' or swoon before the cheese display.
✉ Sixth Ave & 9th St, Greenwich Village (3, C4) ☎ 673-2600 🚇 6th Ave 🚌 M5, M6, M8 ⏲ 7am-8.30pm

Butterfield Market
Long-standing house of delectables. The premises aren't huge so the emphasis is on well-selected necessities and gourmet treats in a pleasant store with informed staff.
✉ 1114 Lexington Ave & 77th St, Upper E Side (2, E7) ☎ 288-7800 🚇 77th St 🚌 M101 to M103 ⏲ Mon-Sat 7.30am-8pm (Sat to 5.30pm), Sun 8am-5pm

Chelsea Market
Big food complex in an old cookie factory where you can shop for breads, soups, bagels, cheese, wine, kitchen supplies and more.
✉ 75 Ninth Ave, b/w 15th & 16th Sts, Chelsea (3, B2) ☎ 243-6005 🚇 8th Ave, 14th St (A, C, E) 🚌 M11, M14 ⏲ 10am-6pm (from noon Sun)

Dom's
An Italian food store with an on-site butcher who specialises in spicy sausages and salamis. There's also a

good selection of fruit, vegetables and coffee beans.
✉ 202 Lafayette St & Broome St, SoHo (3, F6) ☎ 226-1963 🚇 Spring St (6) 🚌 M1 (part-time service), M6 ⏲ 8am-8.30pm

Dowel Quality Products
An Indian grocery worth ducking into just to soak up the smell. The spices, lentils, rice and curry wherewithal are wonderful; there's a small selection of fresh vegetables and meat as well as a promised 400 varieties of beer.
✉ 91 First Ave & 6th St, E Village (3, D7) ☎ 979-6045 🚇 1st Ave 🚌 M15 ⏲ 11am-midnight

Economy Candy
A big discount candy store that also sells chocolates, nuts, coffee and dried fruit from around the world. It's the town's sweetest spot to soothe your inner zit.
✉ 108 Rivington St & Essex St, Lower E Side (3, E8) ☎ 254-1531 🚇 Delancey/Essex Sts 🚌 M9, M14 ⏲ Mon-Fri & Sun 8.30am-6pm, Sat 10am-5pm

Gourmet Garage
A treasury of fine foods for cooking or eating right away. Head to the back of the shop for free olive tastings.
✉ 453 Broome St & Mercer St (3, F5) ☎ 941-5850 🚇 Spring St (6) 🚌 M6 ⏲ 7am-9pm

Sherry-Lehman
A world-class wine and spirit store that also has reasonable prices and staff who can help you pick the right wine for the occasion.
✉ 679 Madison Ave & 61st St, Upper E Side (2, H6) ☎ 838-7500 🚇 5th Ave (N, R) 🚌 M1 to M4 ⏲ Mon-Sat 9am-7pm

Zabar's
The city's most popular food emporium is cluttered in just the right way – it's a feast of sights and smells, both packaged and fresh. There's a great selection of house-made soups and an attached cafeteria serving drinks and pastries.
✉ Broadway & 80th St, Upper W Side (2, E3) ☎ 787-2000 🚇 79th St 🚌 M104 ⏲ Mon-Fri 8am-7.30pm, Sat 8am-8pm, Sun 9am-6pm

Squeezing in a healthy snack

COMPUTERS & ELECTRONICS

New York (and, for foreign visitors, the US generally) is a good place to buy electronics, especially since the upsurge in sales over the Internet has forced retailers to keep prices down and extras (bonus gifts, extra service) up.

Bang & Olufson
The most expensive and best-designed electronic equipment in the world. If you don't want to kit out the whole lounge, consider the desk consoles, which are slimline, sexy and somewhat affordable.
✉ 952 Madison Ave & 75th St, Upper E Side (2, F6) ☎ 879-6161 🚇 77th St 🚌 M1 to M4 ⊘ Mon-Sat 10am-6.30pm, Sun 12-5pm

CompUSA
Aisles of computers, printers, scanners, software and accessories make this a good place to browse through a range of products. Don't count on expert advice though: if you're a whizz, you might know more than the staff.
✉ 420 Fifth Ave & 37th St, Midtown (2, M6) ☎ 764-6224 🚇 42nd St (4, 5, 6, 7) 🚌 M1 to M4 ⊘ Mon-Fri 8.30am-8pm, Sat 10am-7pm, Sun 10am-6pm

J&R Computer World
Massive store with a good reputation for selection and price, but the level of service depends on the salesperson you encounter. Avoid shopping on busy weekends.
✉ 15 Park Row, Lwr Manhattan (3, J5) ☎ 238-9100 🚇 City Hall 🚌 M1, M6, M9, M15, M22, M101, M102 ⊘ Mon-Sat 9am-7pm (to 7.30pm Thurs), Sun 10.30am-6.30pm

RCS
A decent selection of PC desktops, laptops, handhelds and software. The rushed staff are mostly well-informed and helpful.
✉ 575 Madison Ave & 56th St, Midtown (2, J6) ☎ 949-6935 🚇 5th Ave (E, F, N, R), 59th St (4, 5, 6) 🚌 M1 to M4, M31, M57 ⊘ Mon-Fri 9am-7pm, Sat 10am-6pm, Sun 11am-5pm

Sony Style
Play with flash new Sony products in the main showroom and be blown away by the home entertainment systems downstairs.
✉ 550 Madison Ave & 56th St, Midtown (2, J6) ☎ 833-8000 🚇 51st St (6), 5th Ave (E, F), 59th St (4, 5,6) 🚌 M1 to M5, M57 ⊘ Mon-Sat 10am-7pm, Sun 12-6pm

The Wiz
Chain of electronics and appliances at good prices but varying levels of service and staff expertise.
✉ 212 E 57th St & Lexington Ave, Midtown (2, J7) ☎ 754-1600 🚇 59th St (4, 5, 6) 🚌 M101 to M103 ⊘ 10am-9.30pm (to 6pm Sun)

Warning
Beware of discount electronics stores dotted around Times Square and along Fifth Ave in Midtown. The sales assistants are often smarmy, badgering and belligerent, making shopping in these stores unpleasant at best and sometimes downright scary.

In all cases, remain calm and do not be hassled into buying something you're not sure about. If you know exactly what you want and know what the regular retail price is in the US, you can sometimes wangle a good deal but make sure you get a new, boxed product with proper documentation.

Contact the Department of Consumer Affairs (☎ 487-4444; www.ci.nyc.ny.us/consumers) if you get ripped off. Ways to avoid rip offs include:

- knowing the store's refund policy before you buy (in the case of no posted policy, you have the right to a full refund if you return the item within 20 days)
- obtaining a receipt with the name and address of the store and a full product description
- knowing the Manufacturer's Suggested Retail Price (stores must tell you the MSRP if they are charging above it)

FOR CHILDREN

The image of over-involved New York parents taking their offspring to a psychiatrist, to tai chi classes and to the Hamptons doesn't really fit ... well, except on the Upper East Side. Most locals appreciate, and many stores stock, sturdy, good value clothing and safe, fun, educational toys for kids

Books of Wonder
Children's titles and young adult fiction (to about 15 years old) both new and old, rare and collectible.
✉ 16 W 18th St, b/w Fifth & Sixth Aves, Chelsea (3, B4) ☎ 989-3270 🚇 Union Sq 🚌 M2, M3, M5 to M7 🕐 Mon-Sat 11am-7pm, Sun 12-6pm

Disney Store
Merchandise and meet-the-characters over 3 floors. If that's not enough Disney, you can get help planning your family's theme park vacation here.
✉ Fifth Ave & 55th St, Midtown (2, J6) ☎ 702-0702 🚇 5th Ave (E, F) 🚌 M1 to M5 🕐 10am-8pm (to 7pm Sun)

The Enchanted Forest
A delightful store with wonderful books, teddy bears, hand puppets and games. There's hardly anything that needs batteries and almost nothing to plug in. The emphasis is on play for pleasure rather than education.
✉ 85 Mercer St & Spring St, SoHo (3, F5) ☎ 925-6677 🚇 Spring St (6) 🚌 M6 🕐 Mon-Sat 11am-7pm, Sun 12-6pm

FAO Schwarz
The most crowded, expensive and elaborate toy store in New York City, with a wildly popular Barbie salon. There's even a 'schweetz' store to keep the kids hyper.
✉ 767 Fifth Ave & 58th St, Midtown (2, J6) ☎ 644-9400 🚇 5th Ave (N, R) 🚌 M1 to M5 🕐 Mon-Wed 10am-7pm, Thurs-Sat 10am-8pm, Sun 11am-6pm

Gymboree
A big chain (call ☎ 1-800-558-9885 for locations) with colourful, durable, reasonably priced casual clothing for newborns to 7-year-olds. The emphasis is on good materials, thoughtful manufacture and easy mix-and-matching.
✉ 1120 Madison Ave & 83rd St, Upper E Side (2, D6) ☎ 717-6702 🚇 86th St (4, 5, 6) 🚌 M1 to M4 🕐 Mon-Fri 10am-7pm, Sat 10am-6pm, Sun 12-5pm

Infinity
A rumble-tumble store with piles, racks and packed nooks of good value clothing for boys and girls. There's practical playground and classroom wear and a sensible range of party and formal wear.
✉ 1116 Madison Ave & 83rd St, Upper E Side (2, D6) ☎ 517-4232 🚇 86th St (4, 5, 6) 🚌 M1 to M4 🕐 10am-6pm

Little Eric
Shoes for little feet walk-don't-run out of this well-stocked store. From little man to homeboy, baby ballerina to party doll, Eric's got boots to suit. The gumboots (galoshes) are the most super sloshers around.
✉ 1118 Madison Ave & 83rd St, Upper E Side (2, D6) ☎ 717-1513 🚇 86th St (4, 5, 6) 🚌 M1 to M4 🕐 Mon-Sat 10am-6pm (Mon & Thurs to 7pm, Sun 12-5pm)

Noodle Kidoodle
Games, videos and computerised gadgets for learning and fun. A relaxed store with play areas where kids can try toys out.
✉ 2407 Broadway & 89th St, Upper W Side (2, C3) ☎ 917-441-2066 🚇 86th St (1, 9) 🚌 M86, M104 🕐 Mon-Sat 9.30am-9pm, Sun 11am-6pm

Warner Bros Studio Store
In addition to Sylvester staplers and Bugs Bunny coffee mugs there are animation cels for upwards of $2500.
✉ 1 E 57th St & Fifth Ave, Midtown (2, J6) ☎ 754-0300 🚇 5th Ave (E, F), 57th St (B, Q) 🚌 M1, M2, M3, M4, M5 🕐 10am-8pm (from noon Sun)

Zittles
A cluttered lucky dip of a toy store. There are all the old faves – costumes, masks, jigsaws – and a smart selection of silicon chipped toys with an educational emphasis.
✉ 3rd fl, 969 Madison Ave & 75th St, Upper E Side (2, F6) ☎ 644-9400 🚇 77th St 🚌 M1 to M4 🕐 Mon-Fri 9am-8pm, Sat 9am-7pm, Sun 10am-6pm

SPECIALIST STORES

Davidoff of Geneva
Cigars, pipes, tobacco, cologne, ashtrays, ties: in fact, everything smokable except Cuban cigars.
✉ Madison Ave & 54th St, Midtown (2, J6) ☎ 751-9060 ⓜ 5th Ave (E, F) 🚌 M1 to M5 🕐 Mon-Fri 10am-6.30pm, Sat 10am-6pm

Dö Kham
This store is best known for its gorgeous Tibetan fur-rimmed hats, but it's full of exquisite gifts and wear-ables, many of them made by Tibetan refugees.
✉ 51 Prince St & Mulberry St, SoHo (3, E6) ☎ 966-2404 ⓜ Prince St 🚌 M21 🕐 10am-8pm

Flynn's School of Herbology
A 'medicine shoppe' where you'll find herbs, potions, oils and lotions in a tiny, fragrant store. Colon thera-py is also available.
✉ 60 E4th St & The Bowery, E Village (3, D6) ☎ 677-8140 ⓜ Blee-cker St 🚌 M15, M103 🕐 Thurs-Sat 12-7pm

Gruen Optika
Lolly eyes to grave frames - this is the best store in the city for stand-out eyewear. Call for other locations.
✉ 740 Madison Ave & 64th St, Upper E Side (2, G6) ☎ 988-5832 ⓜ Lexington Ave (B, Q) 🚌 M1 to M4 🕐 Mon-Fri 9am-6.30pm, Sat 10am-5pm, Sun 12-5pm

Hammacher Schlemmer
Amazing, kooky and sud-denly necessary gadgets, gizmos and gifts. Everything, from the water-proof shower radio to the one-person helium balloon, has been rigorously tested.
✉ 147 E 57th St, b/w Lexington & Third Aves, Midtown (2, J7) ☎ 421-9000 ⓜ Lexington Ave (N, R), 59th St (4, 5, 6) 🚌 M31, M57, M101 to M103 🕐 Mon-Sat 10am-6pm

Kiehl's
Quirky pharmacy that's been selling organic skin-care products since 1851. This precursor to the Body Shop has a very loyal clientele, and celebrities such as Richard Gere can be spotted in the place buying products and admiring the late owner's Harley-Davidson collection.
✉ 109 Third Ave & 13th St, E Village (2, C6) ☎ 475-3400 ⓜ 3rd Ave 🚌 M9, M14, M101 to M103 🕐 Mon-Fri 10am-6.30pm (to 7.30pm Thurs), Sat 10am-6pm

Mackenzie-Childs
This overwhelming store is absolutely packed with country cottage homeware and furniture. See the miniature mansion on the top level and have a cake in the Butler's Pantry Cafe.
✉ 824 Madison Ave & 69th St, Upper E Side (2, G6) ☎ 570-6050 ⓜ 68th St 🚌 M1 to M4, M30, M66, M72 🕐 Mon-Sat 10am-6pm

Paragon Athletic Goods
Excellent selection of sports merchandise at prices that regularly beat those of the chain stores. Best selection of in-line skates in the city.
✉ 867 Broadway & 18th St, Union Sq, Chelsea (3, B5) ☎ 255-8036 ⓜ Union Sq 🚌 M6, M7 🕐 Mon-Sat 10am-8pm, Sun 11am-6.30pm

Toys in Babeland
A sweet-smelling unsleazy sex shop where men and women are both welcome. Along with toys, sex aids, books and videos, there's a celebratory atmosphere ("August is anal sex month!") plus workshops ('Sex Toys 101'), readings and performances.
✉ 94 Rivington St & Ludlow St, Lower E Side (3, E7) ☎ 375-1701 ⓜ Delancey/Essex Sts 🚌 M9, M14 🕐 Tues-Sat 12-10pm, Sun 12-8pm

Universal Cafe & News
Magazines (7000 of them) from the US and Europe, including a good selection of literary periodicals. There's also a cafe with a pretty good salad bar.
✉ 977 Eighth Ave & 58th St, Midtown (2, J4) ☎ 586-7205 ⓜ Columbus Circle 🚌 M5, M7, M10, M104 🕐 5am-midnight

Go ahead – take that girl home!

places to eat

If you're hungry in New York, you're just not trying – it's a fabulous town for food. With around 20,000 places to eat, the possibilities are effectively endless: you could have dinner at a different restaurant every night for 50 years, running the gourmet gamut from hot dog to top notch noshery and back again.

New York Cuisine

The immigrant nature of New York is expressed nowhere better than in its

Meal Costs

$ under $10
$$ main course $10-19
$$$ main course $20-35
$$$$ main course $35+

Look out for prix fixe offers – some expensive restaurants have reasonable lunch deals.

food. You can eat by neighbourhood – Chinese in Chinatown, Italian in Little Italy – or wander a little wider and wilder. Not only are there restaurants serving just about every ethnic cuisine imaginable, but the melting pot has moved beyond Tex-Mex to such unlikely-sounding cultural fusions as Cuban-Chinese and Indian-French. It seems to be only French restaurants that make it hard to eat vegetarian; most New York eateries are conscious of the need to offer herbivorous meals – see p. 76 for vegetarian recommendations.

Drinks

Keep an eye on your alcohol intake as restaurants savagely mark-up drinks. If you want to sip sedately, house wine by the glass is usually pretty good. Tap water is perfectly drinkable (p. 118) and ice water is offered with most meals.

Tipping & Tax

The standard tip for meals is 15 to 20%; double the 8% sales tax listed on your bill and you'll be leaving a reasonable gratuity. Many places add a 'service charge' for groups of 6 or more – you're not required to tip on top. In casual eateries where you order your meal at the counter, tipping is optional.

Reservations

To avoid queues and disappointment, make reservations for restaurants above diner level. Individual restaurant reviews indicate when booking is advised.

Best Brunches

New York's pick of the crop include:

Sarabeth's (p. 82), **The Grange Hall** (p. 75), **EJ's Luncheonette** (p. 82) and **Odessa** (p. 69). Harlem's **Copeland's** (p. 90) does a great gospel brunch.

Opening Hours

The majority of eateries open daily, but if they take a day off, it's likely to be Monday. See the following breakfast, lunch and dinner sections for usual meal times; specific restaurant opening hours are provided with reviews in this chapter.

Breakfast & Brunch

New Yorkers never seem to eat breakfast at home, preferring to head out from 7am to one of the city's hundreds of cafes and diners for that cooked breakfast special, bagels (p. 71) or for that 'cawfee' on the run (p. 83).

It's bizarre that people as impatient as New Yorkers don't mind queuing up for weekend brunch (almost always eaten over a copy of the *New York Times*). Most cafes and a good number of restaurants have special brunch offerings, served from 11am to 4pm-ish. The classics are eggs, waffles, French toast and pancakes but most places also have cereals, fruit and pastries. Bloody Marys and Mimosas are standard brunch beverages – you'd be surprised how smoothly they segue with a fry-up.

Lunch

Generally, lunch is served from 11am to 2.30pm. Midtown restaurants may not serve lunch on weekends, while Lower Manhattan restaurants often close altogether over the weekend. The business lunch is alive and well in New York City, see Taking care of Business below for some of the best.

Eating around the Clock
Our pick of 24hr dining options:
Odessa (☎ 253-1470), 119 Ave A, near E 7th St (3, D7; $) – great omelettes and French toast but steer clear of the main meals
Empire (☎ 243-2736), 210 10th Ave & 22nd St (2, P3; $) – classic boxcar diner where celebrities go for fries
Gray Papaya (☎ 260-3532), 402 6th Ave & W 8th St (3, D4; $) – lash out on the perennial 'recession special' (2 franks and a drink: $1.95)
Bereket (☎ 475-5500), 187 E Houston & Orchard St (3, E7; $) – for Turkish kebabs and good vegetarian felafel

Also try Veselka (p.73) and Florent (p. 75)

Angus Oborn

Tom's – a major Seinfeld shrine – setting of much 'yada yada' about nothing

Taking Care of Business
If you want to fête your clients with your lavish expense account, try **La Côte Basque** (p. 79) or the **Four Seasons** (p. 78). For something less formal, consider the seafood restaurant **City Crab** (☎ 529-3800), 235 Park Ave & E 19th St (3, B5) or the **Wall St Kitchen & Bar** (p. 98) for finger food, classy pastas and 50 wines by the glass. **Fraunces Tavern** and **Bridge Cafe** (both p. 77) are good places to charm the seal-it handshake from potential associates.

Dinner & Beyond

The evening meal is usually taken between 5 and 10pm, with most restaurants finishing later on Friday and Saturday nights. Later, when it is coming up for dawn, you're clubbed out and the tummy is rumbling, there's no need to go hungry. New York understands how a midnight snack can suddenly seem as distant as yesterday's breakfast (see our picks above).

BROOKLYN

Caffe Volna   S-$$
Russian
Along the boardwalk, a 15min stroll from Coney Is, this is one of a string of Russian cafes serving blintzes, herring, kebabs, stroganoff, sturgeon and borscht. Just like a real Russian restaurant, it may or may not have what you ask for, and if it does, staff may or may not serve you with a smile.
✉ 3145 Brighton 4th St, Brighton Beach (4, E4)
☎ 718-332-0501
🚇 Aquarium 🚌 B1, B68
🕐 11am-11pm ⚥ yes

Grimaldi's   S
Pizza
The jukebox is stacked with Sinatra, the pizzas are stacked with toppings, the bases are crispy and the customers are regulars. There isn't anything fancy about the food or the restaurant but the coal brick oven makes the humble pizza taste divine. Cash only.
✉ 19 Old Fulton St (3, K9) ☎ 718-858-4300 🚇 Clark St, York St 🚌 B25, B51 🕐 Mon-Fri 11.30am-11pm (to midnight Fri), Sat noon-midnight, Sun 12-11pm ⚥ yes V

Henry's End $$-$$$
New American
Walk over the Brooklyn Bridge to this pleasant bistro with a fine eye for matching mostly American wines (by the bottle or glass) with mostly meaty foods. The duckling – boned, crisped and braised – is a speciality, but it's all creative and tantalising. Bookings, which are recom-

mended, are only accepted for parties of 3 or more.
✉ 44 Henry St (3, K9)
☎ 718-834-1776
🚇 Clark St 🚌 B25, B51
🕐 5.30-10.30pm (to 11.30pm Fri-Sat) ⚥ yes

Plan-Eat
Thailand   S-$$
Thai/Japanese
Massive industrial Thai-Japanese food theme park with a good Thai menu (noodles, sautés, salads and seafood with ginger, coconut and chilli accents) plus a hibachi grill, a sushi bar and normal old drinking bars. Despite the scale of the hub-bub and clatter, the food is tasty and service is brisk.
✉ 141 N 7th St (4, D3)
☎ 718-599-5758 🚇 L to Bedford Ave 🚌 B39, B61 🕐 11.30am-1am (to 2am Thurs-Sat) ⚥ yes V

CHELSEA/UNION SQUARE

Centro Español $$
Spanish
Dim dungeon with a stumbled-on-a-secret entrance, full of Spanish people (from Spain) eating authentic tapas, home-style chicken, seafood and paella and more than likely singing something sweet and loving or crying into their sangria.
✉ 239 W 14th St (3, C3) ☎ 243-9308
🚇 8th Ave 🚌 M14
🕐 11am-11pm ⚥ yes

The Dish   S
Diner
Unpretentious new-style diner with gourmet sandwiches, pita melts and classic breakfasts. It's a cruisy place to sit and read the paper on a weekday;

weekends it's a good spot to see who's pulled up how from the night before.
✉ 201 Eighth Ave (2, P4) ☎ 352-9800 🚇 23rd St (C, E) 🚌 M10, M23 🕐 Mon-Thurs 7am-1am, Fri-Sat 8am-2am, Sun 8am-1am ⚥ yes V

El Cid $$
Spanish
Smallish rollicking tapas place with tight-knit tables, a long bar and queues out the door. Consider your choices over complimentary potato salad – the grilled prawns are good, so is the chorizo al vino – and you've got to wash it down with El Cid's sangria. Bookings are recommended.
✉ 322 W 15th St

(3, B3) ☎ 929-9332
🚇 8th Ave 🚌 M10, M11, M14 🕐 5-11pm (to 11.30pm Fri-Sat), closed Mon ⚥ yes

Le Gamin $$
French Cafe
Pencil on a moustache, practice saying 'mais oui' with an arch smile and you're ready for Gamin ('urchin') café au lait, crepes, salads and air kisses. The Chelsea branch is the loveliest of the 4 downtown sites, with reliable food, pressed tin ceilings and a parade of composed and attractive customers (including your good self). Also at 50 Macdougal St (3, E4), 536 E 5th St (3, D7) & 170 Waverly Pl (3, D4).
✉ Ninth Ave & 21st St

(2, P4) ☎ 243-8864 🚇 23rd St (C, E) 🚌 M11, M23 ⏰ 8am-midnight ♿ yes **V**

Trois Canards $$
French

A jazzy joint with a chatty-meets-romantic mood and delectable food. 'Three Ducks' finds the line between classy and trendy with old fashioned French classics and new fangled seafood, salads and pasta. There are reasonably priced French wines and the butter for your crispy roll comes in a duckling shape – a gimmick that quacks.
✉ 184 Eighth Ave (3, B3) ☎ 929-4320 🚇 23rd St (C, E) 🚌 M10 ⏰ lunch Mon-Fri 12-3pm, Sat-Sun 11am-4pm; dinner Sun-Thurs 5-11pm, Fri-Sat 5pm-midnight ♿ yes

Union Square Coffee Shop $$
American/Brazilian

A big trendy restaurant/bar with reasonable food. The menu is honest New American (including a raw bar) with Brazilian specials like Moqueca Stew (with seafood). It's often noisy (rising to cacophonic when busy); the reliably gorgeous waiting staff (cross-dressers late at night) provide just about adequate service. Bookings are recommended Thurs-Sun.

> ### Roll With a Hole
> Bagels are as New York as yellow cabs and subway evangelists – if you're not eating at least one a day, you're just not getting it, pal. When you're shopping for bagels, you want them hand-rolled, boiled and fresh. The classic bagel is bald and shiny, but there's also sesame, poppyseed, whole wheat, onion and 'everything' bagels, along with various vegetable and smoked fish 'shmears' (cream cheese spreads). Here's some of our favourite bagelries:
> **Ess-a-Bagel** 831 Third Ave, b/w 50th & 51st St (2, K7) & 359 First Ave (3, A7) – classic Jewish deli and bakery
> **Murray's** 500 Sixth Ave, b/w 12th & 13th Sts (3, C4) – for sun-dried tomato bagels and lots of spreads
> **Barney Greengrass** 541 Amsterdam Ave, near 86th St (2, D3) – expensive, amazing smoked salmon bagels
> **H&H Bagels** 2239 Broadway & 80th St (2, E3) – sugary, addictive bagels also sold around town

✉ 29 Union Sq W (3, B5) ☎ 243-7969 🚇 Union Sq 🚌 M1 to M3, M6, M7 ⏰ 7am-6am ♿ yes

Zen Palate $-$$
Vegetarian

Multi-culti vegetarian food with an Asian emphasis but a lot of pasta, mashed potato and 'vegiloaf' on the menu. Downstairs is casual, upstairs is more formal, but it's light and fresh throughout. Bookings are recommended for the upstairs restaurant.
✉ 34 E Union Sq (3, B5); call for details of other locations ☎ 614-9345 🚇 Union

Sq 🚌 M1 to M3, M6, M9, M14 ⏰ Mon-Sat 11am-11.30pm (Fri-Sat to midnight), Sun 12-10.30pm ♿ yes **V**

Zen for vegetarians

CHINATOWN

Goody's $
Chinese

A cheap choice with lunch specials including the 'Spicy Eight Treasure Delight' and good noodle soups. The duck is a specialty as is fish braised in seaweed batter. The 'Little

Bit of Everything' is for the indecisive and the brave.
✉ 1 E Broadway at Chatham Sq (3, H7) ☎ 577-2922 🚇 Canal St (J, M, Z) 🚌 M9, M15, M22 ⏰ 11.30am-10.30pm (from 11am Sat-Sun) ♿ yes **V**

Marco Polo Noodle Shop $
Chinese

Forget about the queues at the nearby restaurants and turn to this cheap, bright restaurant where they make their own lovely noodles (you can see them being

churned out on the hand-driven pasta machine in the kitchen).
✉ 94 Baxter St (3, G6) ☎ 941-6679 🚇 Canal St (N, R, S, 6, J, M, Z) 🚌 M103 🕐 11am-11pm ♿ yes V

Pho Viet Huong $
Vietnamese
The smell of fresh herbs hits you as you walk into this large restaurant with a dinky bamboo courtyard theme and a menu that overwhelms with choice. The soups are great, the clay-pot curries and fondues arrive burbling and the vegetables are crispy and glistening. It's easy, casual and not at all greasy.
✉ 73 Mulberry St (3, G6) ☎ 233-8988 🚇 Canal St (N, R, S, 6, J, M, Z) 🚌 M1 (part time), M6 🕐 12-10pm ♿ yes V

Saint's Alp Teahouse $
Chinese Teahouse
Hong Kong style teahouse which has green tea and an iced tea selection described as 'exhilarating', 'charming' and 'luring'. Tea with tapioca balls comes with a fat straw so you can suck up the spheres. Snacks include hotcakes with coconut butter, cuttlefish balls and toast with condensed milk.
✉ 51 Mott St (3, G6) ☎ 766-9889 🚇 Canal St (N, R, S, 6, J, M, Z) 🚌 M1 (p/time), M6 🕐 Sun-Thurs 11am-11.30pm, Fri-Sat 11.30am-midnight ♿ yes V

EAST VILLAGE

Cafe Mogador $-$$
Moroccan
Cut out of the main St Marks drag and eat at Mogador, a dipped down Moroccan cafe with excellent couscous, *merguez* (spicy beef sausage) and *harissa* (the hot sauce for the new millennium). A good place to split dips with a buddy or to eat a solo sandwich with the newspaper. Weekend evenings it hots up with music and lotsa chatter.
✉ 101 St Marks Place (3, D7) ☎ 677-2226 🚇 1st Ave 🚌 M8, M14 🕐 9am-12.30am (to 1.30am Fri-Sat) ♿ yes V

Rockin' Moroccan Mogador
Michelle Bennett

Esashi $$
Japanese
A local favourite with brilliant sushi and sashimi platters (don't miss yellowtail if it's on the menu) and an eel roll (with avocado and studded with flying fish roe) that's worth the visit on its own merits. If you're game, order cold sake served in a square wooden box. Finish up with a trio of ginger, green tea and red bean ice cream. Bookings are advisable on Friday and Saturday evenings.
✉ 32 Ave A (3, D7) ☎ 505-8726 🚇 2nd Ave 🚌 M14 🕐 5-11.30pm (to 11pm Sun) ♿ yes

Habib's Palace $
Middle Eastern
Follow the sweet music to Habib's, a mostly takeaway joint where the falafel is fine and the jazz is always a-calling. Ask Habib what's good, order it without question, take it to the park or hang out in-house and ask Habib about the old days when Alphabet City was a jungle.
✉ 438 E9th St (3, C7) ☎ 979-2243 🚇 1st Ave 🚌 M9, M14 🕐 11am-11pm approx ♿ yes V

La Paella $$
Spanish
A lively tavern with good tapas, sangria and, of course, paella. The big daddy Español comes with the whole barnyard and aquarium: chorizo, chicken, clams, mussels, squid and prawns. The mixed veg verdura services the less carnivorous. Low-talkers and the long-legged note: as soon as it's crowded – which is most nights – it gets noisy and cramped. Nab an outside table if you want to whisper or stretch.
✉ 214 E 9th St (3, C6) ☎ 598-4321 🚇 Astor Pl 🚌 M8, M101 to M103 🕐 5-10.30pm ♿ yes V

Mama's $
Home Cooking
Where the East Village goes for eat-yo-greens fare. Point and get plated: fried, grilled or roasted chicken, grilled fish and luscious vegie sides (try the soggy sweet potato in honey glaze). It's casual

Angus Oborn

Jewish Delis

The East Village is the place to get skyscraper sandwiches and kissable knishes. **Katz's**, E Houston & Ludlow Sts (3, E7; $), has been serving up pastrami on rye since 1888. The **Second Ave Deli**, 156 Second Ave & E 10th St (3, C7; $), does a mean matzo ball soup. **Veselka**, 144 Second Ave & E 9th St (3, C7; $), has brilliant borsht and perfect piroshkis and pancakes. **Yonah Shimmel Knish Bakery**, 137 E Houston St, b/w First & Second Aves (3, E7; $), has sweet and savoury knishes, latkes and blintzes.

(you heat your own pie in the microwave). An associated juicery next door has goodness you can suck up with a straw.
✉ **200 E Third St (3, D8)** ☎ **777-4425** Ⓟ **2nd Ave** 🚌 **M9, M14, M21** ⏲ **Mon-Sat 11am-11pm** ♿ **yes** **V**

Panna II $-$$
Indian
The North Indian food is just okay but the interior must be seen to be believed: the profusion of lights, glitter and baubles hanging from the ceiling means that the waiters serve the food hunched double. It's hard not to have a good time here. Bring Indian beer from *Dowel* (p. 64) next door.
✉ **93 First Ave (3, D7)** ☎ **598-4610** Ⓟ **2nd Ave** 🚌 **M15** ⏲ **noon-midnight** ♿ **good** **V**

Radio Perfecto $$
New American
Tune in for fabulous flame

roasted rotisserie chicken, a herb-sauced skirt steak, the best fish in the market and (save room) dreamy desserts. This is food for the relaxed gourmand, hearty with a pleasing attention to detail but a complete lack of fuss. The garden out back is the only place to eat in summer, especially with a perfecto pitcher of sangria.
✉ **190 Ave B (3, C8)** ☎ **477-3366** Ⓟ **1st Ave** 🚌 **M9, M14** ⏲ **6pm-midnight (to 1am Fri-Sat)** ♿ **yes**

Raga $$
Indian
When you feel more like 'darling!' than dhal-ing, this 'Indian inspired cuisine' might hit the right spot. Think tandoori steak or swordfish over basmati served in a stylin' but friendly neighbourhood restaurant with an enthusiastic outlook. There's a nice wine list, and beer on tap; early evening prix fixe

meals are available. Bookings recommended Fri and Sat evenings.
✉ **433 E Sixth St (3, D7)** ☎ **388-0957** Ⓟ **1st Ave** 🚌 **M14** ⏲ **6-11pm (to midnight Fri-Sun); call for weekend brunch hrs** ♿ **yes**

The Sanctuary $
Vegetarian
All vegetarian, organic and largely dairy and karma-free cafe with a calm atmosphere, ethereal light and tasty food. Choose from lighter sandwiches with 'chicknone', 'faking bacon', 'harmless ham' and 'un-turkey' or more substantial Asian accented vegie dishes. Quench with juices and smoothies, chat with fake and real coffee.
✉ **25 First Ave (3, E7)** ☎ **780-9786** Ⓟ **2nd Ave** 🚌 **M15, M21** ⏲ **11.30am-9pm (to 11pm Wed-Fri), closed Mon** ♿ **yes** **V**

Telephone Bar & Grill $-$$
Pub/Restaurant/Bar
A roomy bar and eatery that wears its English pub theme lightly – you can get HP sauce and Branston Pickle with your shepherd's pie but no-one's going to call you 'Guv'. Come when the tummy's really rumbling

Michelle Bennett

Mama says: 'eat-yo-greens'

and fill up on fish & chips, burgers, big sandwiches, salads and a weird assortment of beer cocktails.
✉ 149 2nd Ave (3, C7) ☎ 529-5000 Ⓜ 1st Ave ☒ M15 ⏰ 11.30am-midnight (to 1.30am Sat) ♿ yes **V**

Three of Cups   S-SS
Italian
It's dim, red and cavernous but the vague goth overtones don't quite stretch to spookiness, especially once the cheery antipasti start rolling out. Wood-fired pizzas are winners, but the Sicilian spaghetti hits some faux pasta troughs. A good place for late-night eats after Lower East Side bar hopping; if you want more crawl, there's a bustling bar downstairs.
✉ 83 First Ave (3, D7) ☎ 388-0059

Ⓜ 2nd Ave ☒ M15 ⏰ 6pm-4am (from noon Sat-Sun) ♿ no **V**

Two Boots Pizzeria   S
Pizza
Super slices and pies made to order. Sit down in glossy red booths or at the tables outside or grab your feisty pizza to go. *The Den of Cin* performance space and video screening room is next door – call ☎ 777-2668 to find out what's going on.
✉ 42 Ave A & 3rd St (3, D7) ☎ 254-1919 Ⓜ 2nd Ave ☒ M14 ⏰ 11.30am-1am (to 2am Fri-Sat) ♿ yes **V**

Veniero's   S
Cakes
A cake shop and bakery that has been sugaring up the East Village for more than a

Veniero's for a sweet fix
Michelle Bennett

century. Take a number and wait at the counter or line up to sit down in the glowing dining room. The cheesecakes are sensational and the miniature eclairs, custard tarts and biscotti make great gifts or instant scoff fodder.
✉ 342 E 11th St (3, C7) ☎ 674-7070 Ⓜ 1st Ave ☒ M15 ⏰ 8am-midnight (to 1am Fri-Sat) ♿ yes **V**

GREENWICH VILLAGE

Bessie's   S
Home Cooking
This tiny eatery serves up ready-made home-style and Southern food for travellers who miss their mothers. Chicken soup, meatloaf and fried chicken are all good and it's easy to make a meal of the delicious veggie side dishes. The garlic mashed potatoes and macaroni and cheese are kissable. Batten down for choc-chip cookies, cakes and pies.
✉ 70 Greenwich Ave (3, C4) ☎ 929-7878 Ⓜ 14th St (1, 2, 3, 9) ☒ M10, M14 ⏰ 11.30am-10pm (Sat-Sun from 5pm) ♿ yes **V**

Bleecker St Pastry and Cafe   S
Cakes
The lip-smacking window display is as much review as you

need. When the cookie monster strikes, come for Italian cakes and biscuits. Sit down with a coffee or supply yourself for a walking munch.
✉ 245 Bleecker St (3, E4) ☎ 242-4959 Ⓜ W 4th St ☒ M5, M6, M10, M21 ⏰ 7.30am-midnight ♿ yes **V**

Cornelia Street Cafe   SS
New American
A sizable restaurant with great food, accommodating service and jazz on weekends. The menu hovers around modern classics like perky soups, squid ink ravioli and salmon steaks; there's a nice wine list with a good swathe by the glass. Bookings are recommended for dinner (Thurs to Sat).
✉ 29 Cornelia St (3, D4) ☎ 989-9319

Ⓜ W 4th St ☒ M5, M6 ⏰ 10am-10.45pm ♿ yes

Corner Bistro   S
Burgers
My notes about this legendary burger bar are slurred, sloppy and stained. I quote: 'forhet about yr met eating compainions – m burgwr whichn is ruined just yby putting it down a majoir burger fauxb oas'. Summation: come here late at night when you're drunk. It's great.
✉ 331 W 4th St & Jane St (3, C3) ☎ 242-9502 Ⓜ 14th St, 8th Ave ☒ M10, M11, M14 ⏰ 11.30am-4am (from noon Sun) ♿ no

Espresso Bar   S
Cafe
A veritable temple to caffeine that excels in your basic espresso but also does

iced double mochachinos, yogi teas and the like. Food to sop up the 5-cup jitters includes mostly organic salads, sandwiches and homemade soups and delicious cakes. There's a summer garden with a troppo vibe.
✉ **82 Christopher St (3, D3)** ☎ **627-3870** Ⓧ **Christopher St** 🚌 **M8, M10** ⏱ **8am-7pm** ♿ **yes** Ⓥ

Espresso at Espresso

Florent $$
French/American
Meatpacking pioneer which keeps hauling them in because it's just great! Pre, post or tween club, it's tuff, cheeky and friendly, with a diner setting but a mod-ish vibe. The *boudin noir* (blood sausage), pork chops and mussels are justly lauded. Cakes and breakfasts are good too. Bookings are recommended and it's cash only.
✉ **69 Gansevoort St (3, C2)** ☎ **989-5779** Ⓧ **14th St (A, C, E), 8th Ave** 🚌 **M10, M11, M14** ⏱ **Mon-Thurs 9am-5am, Fri-Sun 24hrs** ♿ **yes** Ⓥ

The Grange Hall $$
American Classic
An airy restored speakeasy with a big harvest mural, Amish potatoes and a

renowned weekend brunch. The hearty main dishes (mostly roasted, baked or grilled meats) come 'simple' (with vegetable or salad accompaniment) or 'complete' (with soup or salad as well). The menu celebrates seasonal ingredients, many of them organic. Bookings recommended for dinner Thurs-Sat and weekend brunch.
✉ **50 Commerce St (3, E3)** ☎ **924-5246** Ⓧ **Houston St** 🚌 **M8, M10** ⏱ **Mon-Fri 12-3pm & 5.30-11pm (Fri-Sat till midnight), Sat 11am-3pm, Sun 10.30am-4pm** ♿ **yes** Ⓥ

Joe Jr Diner $
Diner
A very normal diner with good coffee, a chip fryer that sounds like applause and a local vibe that makes walking in feel a bit like interrupting an extended family's good natured brawl. Crowded on weekends for brunch.
✉ **482 Sixth Ave (3, C4)** ☎ **924-5220** Ⓧ **14th St (F), 6th Ave** 🚌 **M5, M6, M14** ⏱ **6am-1am** ♿ **yes**

Little Havana $$
Cuban
A tiny village gem serving earthy and filling but still delicate dishes in a cosy muralled room. The tamales are tops, the roast pork is bitey but tempered with a green tomato sauce. It's

low-key and leisurely and everything goes well with a Cuban (made in Florida) Hatuey beer. Bookings are recommended.
✉ **30 Cornelia St (3, D4)** ☎ **255-2212** Ⓧ **W 4th St** 🚌 **M5, M6** ⏱ **Tues-Sun 5-11pm** ♿ **no**

Moustache $
Middle Eastern
Style your own mo – make it as light or as banquettish as you like. Filo concoctions run from classic spinach and cheese to more substantial chicken and pilaf. Create your own 'pitza' or pick and mix a selection of salads: everything is fresh and herby. A handlebar branch is at 265 E 10th St, E Village.
✉ **90 Bedford St (3, D3)** ☎ **229-2220** Ⓧ **Christopher St, Houston St** 🚌 **M8, M10, M21** ⏱ **noon-11.30pm** ♿ **no** Ⓥ

Trattoria $$
Italian
An amiable bistro with pressed tin ceilings, a wooden floor and plenty of panache. The food is Main St Italian with straight up appetisers, honest pasta and a litany of fish staples and specials reeled off rapid fire by your waiter.
✉ **262 Bleecker St (3, E4)** ☎ **645-2993** Ⓧ **W 4th St** 🚌 **M5, M6, M10, M21** ⏱ **noon-midnight** ♿ **yes** Ⓥ

Restaurant Reading
The most comprehensive restaurant guide is the **Zagat Survey**, available at bookstores all over the city, though its critical assessments tend to be overly enthusiastic about the city's more famous restaurants. Restaurant reviews also appear weekly in the **New York Press** and **Time Out** magazine and in the Friday **New York Times**.

HARLEM

El Paso Taqueria $
Mexican
Sparse Mexican joint on the edge of Spanish Harlem where English talkers turn heads and it's hard to spend more than $5 on a meal. The tostadas, *flautas* (stuffed tortillas), burritos and tacos can be made with chorizo, *lengua* (beef tongue), and marinated spicy pork as well as regular rice and beans.
✉ **141 Lexington Ave & 103rd St (1, E7)**
☎ 831-9831 ⊖ 103rd St (6) 🚌 M101 to M103 ⊘ **7am-midnight (to 11pm Sun)** ♿ yes

Pan Pan $
Diner
A terrific diner for breakfast – eggs, grits, pancakes and such – or dinner with southern accents. Sunday it's packed with post-church noshers –

consider your brunch while you wait for a stool at one of the semicircular benches.
✉ **500 Lenox Ave (1, A5)**
☎ 926-4900 ⊖ 135th St (2, 3) 🚌 M7, M102 ⊘ **7am-10pm** ♿ yes

Sisters $
Caribbean
An unprepossessing eatery where you sit down to eat in the glow of the fridge,

the TV and family photos. The rotis and curries are delicious (and huge), the side dishes (collard greens and plantain) are yummy and the breakfasts (sautéed codfish, eggs 'n' grits) are as downhome as you get.
✉ **47 E 124th St (1, A6)** ☎ 410-3000
⊖ 125th St (4, 5, 6)
🚌 M35, M101, M103
⊘ **8am-9pm** ♿ yes **V**

Flesh-Free & Fabulous

New York City makes for relatively easy vegetarian eating, but there are a few stand-out places where you can be spoiled for vegetarian choice. **The Herban Kitchen** (☎ 627-2257), 290 Hudson St, near Spring St (3, F4; $$), is organic, ambient and creative. Chinatown options include the **House of Vegetarian** (☎ 226-6572), 68 Mott St (3, H6; $) and **Vegetarian Paradise 3** (☎ 406-6988), 33 Mott St (3, H6; $). **Spring Street Natural** (p. 80), **Zen Palate** branches (p. 71) and **The Sanctuary** (p. 73) are also recommended.

LITTLE ITALY/NOLITA

Cafe Gitane $$
Italian
A very smart, arty cafe that tends to attract a beautiful French clientele kissing left, right and centre, and some beautiful Australians who go lighter on the smooching. Gitane's food

is elegant and delicious rather than hearty. It's a fabulous place for breakfast, salads, coffee and eyeing off.
✉ **242 Mott St (3, F6)**
☎ 334-9552 ⊖ Bowery 🚌 M103 ⊘ **7am-midnight** ♿ yes **V**

Caffe Roma $
Cafe
Longstanding Little Italy hang-out with atmosphere aplenty and an unhurried vibe. A good place to watch passers-by from an outdoor table or to huddle indoors with granita, coffee or canolli. Seat yourself at a bench-style table and converse with a fellow cake eater.
✉ **385 Broome St (3, F6)** ☎ 226-8413
⊖ Bowery 🚌 M103 ⊘ **8am-midnight** ♿ yes **V**

Housingworks Used Books Cafe $
Cafe
A great airy space with preloved books that you can read while enjoying coffee, pie, pasta or soup in the

Butts Out

Regulations forbid smoking in restaurants unless the management can satisfactorily separate smoke from nonsmokers – this means that smoking is banned in most restaurants. In warmer months, smokers can take advantage of New York's love affair with outdoor eating; in winter, see if it's OK to smoke at the bar.

Perversely, as smoking has been shunned, cigar bars have become more popular. The **Fifty Seven Fifty Seven Bar** at the Four Seasons Hotel (p. 103) has cigars fresh from the humidor and magic martinis.

knowledge that all profits go to benefit people living with HIV and AIDS. As well as being a relaxing place to sit and page-turn, it has periodic readings and jazz sessions.
✉ **126 Crosby St (3, E6)** ☎ **334-3324** ⊕ **Broadway/Lafayette St** 🚍 **M21** ⏲ **Mon-Fri 10am-8pm (to 9pm, Thurs-Fri) Sat 12-9pm, Sun 12-7pm ♿ yes** **V**

Nyonya $$
Malaysian
A festive place with adventurous dishes like sautéed frog and stingray plus a wide selection of more accessible

choices. The seafood dishes are generally excellent – the speciality of the house is jumbo prawns – and the noodle soups will fill you up all the way to tomorrow.
✉ **194 Grand St (3, F6)** ☎ **334-3669** ⊕ **Grand St** 🚍 **M103** ⏲ **11am-11.30pm ♿ yes** **V**

Rice $-$$
Multicultural Rice
Tiny restaurant with adjoining takeaway cafe where just about everything has something to do with rice. It's best to share a selection of small dishes – the eggplant maki is clean and bright, the coconut

curry is good, and you get a choice of fancy rices.
✉ **227 Mott St (3, F6)** ☎ **226-5775** ⊕ **Broadway/Lafayette St** 🚍 **M21** ⏲ **noon-midnight ♿ yes** **V**

Faster pasta or linguini awhile

LOWER EAST SIDE

El Nuevo Amanecer $
Mexican/Dominican
A late nighter with fake roses, honest Mex and downhome Dominican fare. The jukebox has a giggly mix of hopping Latin hits and the frozen margaritas are big enough to drown in. The food isn't going to have you fêting the chef, but it's reasonable.
✉ **117 Stanton St**

(3, E8) ☎ **387-9115** ⊕ **2nd Ave** 🚍 **M9, M14** ⏲ **8am-4am ♿ yes** **V**

Time Cafe $$
Eclectic Restaurant/Bar
Though it looks like it might couple pretentious decor with mediocre food, Time actually clocks in a winner. The menu is varied, running from soup to tapas, seafood to steak and

pizza to quesadilla, and chances are your meal will be really good. Eat outside under umbrellas or join the chattery indoor hubbub.
✉ **380 Lafayette St & Great Jones St (3, E6)** ☎ **533-7000** ⊕ **Bleecker St** 🚍 **M1, M5, M6** ⏲ **Mon-Fri 8am-midnight (to 1am Fri), Sat 10.30am-1am, Sun 10.30am-midnight ♿ yes**

LOWER MANHATTAN

Bridge Cafe $$
New American
Duck under the Brooklyn Bridge to find this exceedingly congenial dining room in a red-slatted homey haven. Good for a long business lunch especially if there are delicate matters to discuss or for a romantic dinner. The fare is fine pasta, steak and seafood and the wine list is excellent. Bookings are recommended.
✉ **279 Water St (3, J7)** ☎ **227-3344** ⊕ **City Hall**

🚍 **M22** ⏲ **Sun-Fri 11.45am-10pm (to midnight Tue-Fri), Sat 5pm-midnight ♿ yes**

Fraunces Tavern (3, L6) $$
Pub/Restaurant
This clubby place, attached to the museum (p. 30), is full of suited brokers, low-talking deal-makers and serious wall-mounted animal heads. The Tap Room serves cheaper food all day (the club sandwiches are

pretty good) and big comfy chairs. Otherwise, you're up for reliable seafood, burgers and steaks (early birds can plug for the fancy breakfast). Lunch bookings are recommended for groups of 4 plus.
✉ **54 Pearl St** ☎ **269-0144** ⊕ **Bowling Green, South Ferry, Whitehall St** 🚍 **M1, M6, M15** ⏲ **tavern: Mon-Fri 7-10am, 11.30am-4pm & 5-9.30pm; tap room: 11.30am-9.30pm ♿ yes**

Mangia $
Deli
Possibly the classiest lunch-eonette in the city, featuring salads with star appeal, great soups (ask for a taste) and tasty sandwiches. Take it back to the trading floor or snag a munching seat in a comfortable banquette. Despite all the suits, it's not outrageously expensive.
✉ **40 Wall St (3, K6)**
☎ **425-4040** Ⓜ **Wall St, Rector St** 🚌 **M6**
🕐 **7am-6pm** ♿ **yes** Ⓥ

Paris Cafe $$
Pub
Since 1873, this handsome bar has hosted seamen, fisherfolk and the famous and notorious, including Annie Oakley, Butch Cassidy and the Sundance

Kid, Teddy Roosevelt and members of the Murder Inc crime gang of the 1930s. Today it's an untouristy bar and restaurant with decent food, heated foot rails and

plenty of atmosphere.
✉ **119 South St (3, K7)**
☎ **240-9797** Ⓜ **Fulton St** 🚌 **M15** 🕐 **noon-4am (kitchen closes 2am)** ♿ **yes**

Chew On That View
The obvious place to munch and gawp is at the top of 1 World Trade Center (2, J5), where your eating options on the 107th floor include the **Greatest Bar on Earth** (☎ 524-7011; views south and east; $$; dress smart), **Wild Blue** (☎ 524-7107; views south and west; $$-$$$$) and **Windows on the World** (☎ 524-7000; northern view, $$$$; jacket required). Before going up for the view, check that you can see the top of the tower – if it's lost in cloud, there won't be much of an outlook.

For a ground level vista across Central Park, head for the **Park View at the Boathouse** (p. 82). The **River Cafe** (☎ 718-522-5200), 1 Water St, Brooklyn (3, J9; $$-$$$$) has an unparalleled view over the East River to Lower Manhattan from under the Brooklyn Bridge.

MIDTOWN

Carnegie Deli $$
Deli
Maybe it's the star endorsements all over the walls or the stream of film crews shooting on site: whatever it is, the Carnegie keeps packing them in even though it's tired and often complacent. Sure, you can get a pastrami sandwich bigger than your head but it's going to cost you a lazy $15 (and there's a nasty $3 slug on sharing).
✉ **54 Seventh Ave (2, J5)** ☎ **757-2245** Ⓜ **57th St (N, R)** 🚌 **M6, M7**
🕐 **6.30am-4am** ♿ **yes**

Eatzi's $
Deli/Cafe
In this reworking of the department store cafeteria you can buy food to take home or order it to eat in the reasonably pleasant

attached eating area. It's not perfect – plastic cutlery is a drag and $8 sandwiches are standard, but hey, it tastes mighty fine.
✉ **Cellar, Macy's, 151 W 34st St (2, N5)** ☎ **216-9660** Ⓜ **34th St/Herald Sq** 🚌 **M5 to M7, M15**
🕐 **Mon-Sat 10am-9pm, Sun 9am-8pm** ♿ **yes** Ⓥ

Four Seasons $$$$
New American/French
Retro and eclectic superbly food and Philip Johnson/Miles van der Rohe designed dining rooms that make you feel like you're either Sean Connery or a Bond girl, classy as can be. The menu and mood changes each season; the art by Picasso, Miro and Larry Rivers stays up all year. Bookings are essential, as are jacket and tie attire.

✉ **99 E 52nd St (2, K7)**
☎ **754-9494** Ⓜ **59th St (4, 5, 6), Lexington Ave (N, R)** 🚌 **M101 to M103** 🕐 **lunch Mon-Fri 12-2.30pm; dinner Mon-Fri 5-9.30pm, Sat 5-11.30pm** ♿ **no**

Fred's $$
New American
The snooty basement bar/restaurant at Barney's (geddit?) complements the fashion upstairs. Fortify yourself for another assault on the racks with pasta, salad, melt or dainty pizza. Or, if you've already shopped and are about to drop, Fred's is the perfect venue at which to road-test your Barney's purchases. Bookings are recommended.
✉ **10 E 61st St (2, H6)**
☎ **833-2200** Ⓜ **59th St (4, 5, 6), Lexington Ave (N, R)** 🚌 **M1 to M4**

⏲ **Mon-Sat 11.30am-5pm & 5.30-8.30pm, Sun 12-6pm** ♿ yes **V**

Kom Tang Kalbi House $$
Korean

This Little Korea stayer is popular enough to need its 3 floors. If you're a DIY type you can poke around in the table top charcoal pits. Take advantage of the cheap lunch specials or slide in after a late night in Midtown (Kom Tang stays up later than you).
✉ **32 W 32nd St (2, N6)** ☎ **947-8482** Ⓜ **34th St/Herald Sq, 33rd St** 🚌 **M2 to M5, M16, M34** ⏲ **24hrs from Mon 9am-Sun 7am** ♿ yes

La Côte Basque $$$
French

Opened in 1957 on different premises, this is still one of the city's finest dining experiences. The food is exquisite and it's served in luxurious setting by knowledgeable and amiable hosts. The fixed price menu sticks to the French classics but is no less delightful for that. Bookings are essential

and a jacket is required.
✉ **60 W 55 St (2, J6)** ☎ **688-6525** Ⓜ **5th Ave (E, F), 51st St** 🚌 **M1 to M5** ⏲ **12-2.15pm & 5.30-10.30 (to 11.30pm Fri-Sun)** ♿ no

Reuben's $
Diner

Old style diner with winning orange vinyl benches and a fine choice of roasts, cold cuts and sandwiches. The choice naturally includes the famous invented-on-site Reuben sandwich: corned beef, sauerkraut and Swiss cheese on rye. There's a top bunch of triple decker celebrity sandwiches; we like the 'Billy Joel' (with tongue).
✉ **244 Madison Ave (2, M6)** ☎ **867-7800** Ⓜ **Grand Central** 🚌 **M3, M4** ⏲ **Mon-Fri 6am-10pm, Sat-Sun 7am-4pm** ♿ yes

Simply Caviar $$$
Caviar

Sometimes eggs for breakfast just aren't enough eggs to get you through till bedtime. On these difficult days, consider power

lunching with a Beluga sandwich or holding off till dinnertime to order Caspian Sea caviar by the ounce or folded into blini. Bookings are advisable.
✉ **350 Park Ave (2, K7)** ☎ **838-3900** Ⓜ **51st St, Lexington Ave (E, F)** 🚌 **M1 to M4, M27, M50** ⏲ **Mon-Sat 12-5pm & 6-10pm (hrs may vary in summer)** ♿ yes

Soup Kitchen International $
Soup

New York's soup-for-lunch craze seems to be dying down of late but this place will probably survive because the soup is darned delicious. The restaurant's proprietor was made famous as *Seinfeld's* (it was a TV comedy, dear) Soup Nazi, and that show was telling it like it really is: you'd better know exactly what you want by the time you reach the head of the queue.
✉ **259A W 55th St (2, J4)** ☎ **757-7730** Ⓜ **7th Ave (B, D, E)** 🚌 **M10, M104** ⏲ **vary; closed right through summer** ♿ yes **V**

SOHO

Abyssinia $
Ethiopian

The service resembles coma, but the food is mushily excellent. *Atakilt* (vegetables sautéed in spicy herbs), *shuro* (chick pea and vegetable puree) and *ye'beg tibs* (juicy lamb fried with rosemary and black pepper) are all great, and come with *injera* (Ethiopian pancake bread with a tripe texture). Dress down – the stools are more cute than comfortable.
✉ **35 Thompson St**

(3, F5) ☎ **226-5959** Ⓜ **Canal St (A, C, E)** 🚌 **M6** ⏲ **5-11pm (to midnight Fri-Sun)** ♿ yes **V**

Cafe Borgia II $
Cafe

Dim heart-of-SoHo cafe where you can canoodle over a strudel, some good coffee and decent toasted sandwiches, quiches and omelettes. There are a few sidewalk tables if you want fresh air and a parade of gallery trawlers.

✉ **161 Prince St (3, E5)** ☎ **677-1850** Ⓜ **Prince St (N, R), B'way/Lafayette St** 🚌 **M6** ⏲ **10am-midnight (to 2am Fri-Sat)** ♿ yes

Cafe Noir $$
Moroccan

Louche and loud in summer, den-like in winter, Noir has a Moroccanish menu featuring huge couscous platters (consider sharing), wraps, salad, lots of seafood and paella. There are tapas too if

you're in the mood for nibbling rather than noshing.
✉ 32 Grand St (3, F5)
☎ 431-7910 ⊕ Canal St (A, C, E) 🚊 M6
🕐 noon-4am ♿ yes Ⓥ

CUB Room $$
Cafe/Restaurant/Bar
A large restaurant, bar and lounge comfortable for a slow brunch, a light lunch, a big dinner or a nightcap. It's zoned so you can hang with Armani barflies, families or art-buying bankers. Everything is organic, from the peanut butter and honey sandwich on the kids' menu to the obligatory crusted salmon on the grown-ups' rap sheet.
✉ 183 Prince St (3, E5)
☎ 777-0030 ⊕ Prince St (N, R), Broadway/Lafayette St 🚊 M6
🕐 Mon-Fri 12-10.30pm (to 12.30am Fri), Sat 11am-12.30am, Sun 11am-10pm ♿ kids (up to 10) pay their age in $s for kids' menu food

Fanelli $-$$
Pub
One of Manhattan's oldest eateries, this bar is an unhurried haven during the day but it slinks into a speakeasy vibe late at night. It's an easy place to strike up a conversation or bite unbothered on bar snacks, sandwiches, pasta, fish or a burger (last food orders 1½-2hrs before

closing time). Remind yourself you're in SoHo before you step back outside.
✉ 94 Prince St (3, E5)
☎ 226-9412 ⊕ Prince St 🚊 M5, M6, M21
🕐 Mon-Thurs 10am-2am, Fri-Sat 10am-3am, Sun 11am-2am ♿ no Ⓥ

Moondance Diner $
Diner
Dinky boxcar diner which sneaks in hummus and frittata while staying trendoid free. This is a good place to slurp on a shake or order your eggs over easy and pretend you're in a movie. The food is good, the portions are big and there's a minimal outdoor area if you wanna get offa the train.
✉ 80 Sixth Ave, near Grand St (3, F5) ☎ 226 1191 ⊕ Canal St (A, C, E) 🚊 M6 🕐 Mon-Wed 8.30am-midnight, Thurs 8.30am-4am, Fri 8am-Sun midnight ♿ yes Ⓥ

Palachinka $
Cafe
SoHo fringe cafe where you can linger over crepe, ciabatta, salad or a drink (great coffee!) at a chrome table or in the comfy anti-sidewalk-watching window bench. It's classy down to the details – even the toilet paper is groovy – but you get the feeling it's pure aesthetic delight rather than purposeful trendiness.

Deeply cool, Palachinka

✉ 28 Grand St (3, F5)
☎ 625-0362 ⊕ Canal St (A, C, E) 🚊 M6
🕐 10am-10pm ♿ yes Ⓥ

Spring Street Natural $-$$
Health/Vegetarian/Bar
Unprocessed, mostly organic ingredients turned into excitingly but not preachingly healthy cuisine of the noodle, stir fry, sauté and salad variety. It's mostly vegetarian but ventures into chicken and fish, and – horrors! – there's a decent wine list. The large space has a slight clattery cafeteria feel but the service is attentive and the food is above par.
✉ 62 Spring St (3, F6)
☎ 966-0290 ⊕ Spring St (6) 🚊 M1 (part time), M6 🕐 11.30am-midnight (to 1am Fri-Sat) ♿ yes Ⓥ

TRIBECA

Bubby's $$
American
Big, breezy kid-friendly eatery with alarmingly popular weekend brunches. A good bet for salads, sandwiches (also served in realistic half portions), pastas and New York's best burger

(they say so – watch the 'wup-ass' sauce). Kids get crayons and balloons; under 8s eat free, weekends from 6 to 10pm.
✉ 120 Hudson St (3, G4) ☎ 219-0666 ⊕ Franklin St 🚊 M10
🕐 Mon-Tues 8am-mid-

night, Wed-Fri 8am-3am, Sat 9am-3am, Sun 9am-midnight ♿ excellent Ⓥ

Chanterelle $$$$
French
A romantic French restaurant with a downtown edge and seriously good food.

Extravagant prix fixe meals more or less take care of your eating choices so you can concentrate on wooing your dinner partner. Seafood scarpers through the menu – the grilled seafood sausage is a perennial favourite. The cheese platters are sublime. Unsurprisingly, bookings are essential.
✉ **2 Harrison St (3, H4)**
☎ 966-6960
Ⓖ Franklin St 🚇 M10
🕐 lunch Tues-Sat 12-2.30pm, dinner Mon-Sat 5.30-11pm ♿ no

Odeon $$-$$$
New American
A fab, fancy diner buzzing with a smart, happy crowd eating legs of this and slabs of that, or pasta and risotto with designer dabs (truffle oil, wild mushrooms, tomatoes dehydrated in the latest style). Lunch sees businessfolk tucking in, mid-evening it's

downtown families. Indoors you get Deco details, outdoors you get a cool World Trade Center view. Bookings are recommended from Thursday to Saturday.
✉ **145 W Broadway (3, H5)** ☎ 233-0507
Ⓖ Chambers St (1, 2, 3, 9, C) 🚇 M10 🕐 Mon-Thurs noon-2am, Fri noon-3am, Sat 11.30am-3am, Sun 11.30am-2am ♿ good, special menu for kids under 12 Ⓥ

Walker's $$-$$$
Pub
A welcoming pub with 3 dining rooms, poems taped up in the bathrooms, jazz on Sunday and really good food. The menu is straightforward, running from burgers and beers to more elaborate grills, and the specials are always worth a look.
✉ **16 N Moore St (3, G5)** ☎ 941-0142
Ⓖ Franklin St 🚇 M10
🕐 noon-1am ♿ yes

UPPER EAST SIDE

Brother Jimmy's $-$$
Southern Food/Bar
BBQ ribs and wings, prawns by the bucket and lashings of beer in a sports bar that welcomes kids (they eat free). Lots of specials and all-you-can-eat and drink evenings – it ain't classy but it's easy-going.
✉ **1644 Third Ave (2, C7)** ☎ 426-2020
Ⓖ 96th St (4, 5, 6)
🚇 M101 to M103
🕐 5pm-4am (from noon Sat-Sun); kitchen closes 11pm (1am Fri-Sat) ♿ kids' menu

Butterfield 81 $$
New American
Book ahead for New American instant classics

served up to locals and foodies in the cosy, clubby dining room. The collar loosens a little for Sunday brunch, but at all times this is a restaurant serious about seriously delicious food.
✉ **170 E 81st St (2, E7)** ☎ 288-2700 Ⓖ 77th St 🚇 M79, M101 to M103 🕐 Mon-Sat 5.30-10pm (Fri-Sat to 11pm), Sun lunch 11am-2pm, dinner 5.30-9pm ♿ yes

Comfort Diner $$
Diner
Self-consciously retro diner (check the glowing 1950s-family images on the wall) serving comfort food from an imaginary past, eg 'Mom's Meatloaf (on her

best day)'. Packed for weekend brunches – the challah French toast is enough to have you fondly recalling a Jewish grandmother, even if you never had one.
✉ **142 E 86th St (2, D7)** ☎ 426-8600 Ⓖ 86th St (4, 5, 6) 🚇 M86, M101 to M103
🕐 8am-10pm (to midnight Thurs, to 2am Fri-Sat) ♿ good menu Ⓥ

Daniel $$$$
French
The exquisite food and service and the lavish setting (ancient mosaics and frescoes always make food taste better, don't you find?) keep Daniel Boulud's restaurant at the top of the heavily

laden Manhattan tree. If you stretch belly and budget to the tasting menus you'll get a feel for the all round culinary genius of the man. It's essential to book well in advance and don a jacket.
✉ **Mayfair Hotel, 60 E 65th St (2, G7) ☎ 288-0033 ✪ Lexington Ave (B, Q), 68th St 🚇 M1 to M4 ⏰ Mon-Sat lunch from noon, dinner from 5.45pm ♿ no**

Lexington Candy Shop $
Diner
Don't pass this classic diner by. School kids soak up their curfews with malteds and gossip; neighbourhood folk nurse a coffee or a famed fresh lemonade; wannabes soak up the Robert Redford vibe (*Three Days of the Condor* was filmed here) and visitors try to look local by talking baseball over their burgers.
✉ **1226 Lexington Ave (2, D7) ☎ 288-0057 ✪ 86th St (4, 5, 6) 🚇 M101 to M103 ⏰ Mon-Sat 7am-7pm, Sun 9am-6pm ♿ good** **V**

Park View at the Boathouse (2, F5) $$$
New American
Most alluring in the sunny months when you can nibble outdoors with half an eye on the boaters on the lake. But winter, when the dining room crackles with a wood fire, is no mean alternative. The food is interesting, varied and often outstanding, and bookings are recommended.
✉ **The Boathouse in Central Park, 72nd St & East Dr ☎ 517-2233 ✪ 77th St 🚇 M1 to M4 ⏰ lunch Mon-Fri 12-4pm, Sat-Sun 11am-3.45pm; dinner Mon-Thurs 5.30-10pm, Fri-Sat 6-11pm, Sun 6-10pm ♿ yes**

Sarabeth's $$-$$$
American
Comfy haven famous for pastries and weekend brunches but just as lovely for lunch, afternoon tea or dinner. At brunch go for Goldie Lox (scrambled eggs with salmon and cream cheese) paired with a killer Bloody Mary. High tea (served 3.30-5.30pm

weekdays) is an opportunity for elegant chitchat (until you start chugging back the cakes). Bookings are recommended for dinner; no bookings are taken for lunch. A branch also at the Whitney Museum (p. 32).
✉ **1295 Madison Ave & 92nd St (2, C6) ☎ 410-7335 ✪ 96th St (6) 🚇 M1 to M4 ⏰ 8am-10.30pm (to 9.30pm Sun) ♿ yes**

Wu Liang Ye $$
Chinese
This uptown gem rescues New York's Sichuan cuisine from home delivery hell. Start with cold noodles or dumplings then move onto seafood (conch and prawn dishes are good) or the tea-smoked duck. If you're looking for something lean, there are $5 lunch specials and low fat steamed dishes.
✉ **215 E 86th St (2, D7) ☎ 534-8899 ✪ 86th St (4, 5, 6) 🚇 M86, M98, M101 to M103 ⏰ Mon-Fri 11.30am-11pm (to 11.30am Fri), Sat 12-11.30pm, Sun 12-11pm ♿ yes** **V**

UPPER WEST SIDE

Blockheads $
Mexican
This streamlined Mexican place surprises with fresh and tasty burritos, tacos and wraps. And don't get us started on the frozen margaritas! An easy place to eat fast and efficient, but no-one will look askance if you want to linger longer – there are even candles on the laminex tables. Other branches in Midtown and the Upper East Side.
✉ **424 Amsterdam Ave (2, E3) ☎ 787-5445 ✪ 79th St, 81st St 🚇 M7, M11, M79**

⏰ **12-11pm (to midnight Fri-Sat) ♿ good** **V**

Cafe con Leche $-$$
Creole
An easy-going all-day neighbourhood place with fast service and a spicy menu dominated by eggy breakfasts, chicken and seafood dishes. There's a feisty paella (for 1 or 2) and a good variety of vegetarian dishes. This is a comfortable place to eat solo and a convivial place to eat with a group.
✉ **424 Amsterdam Ave (2, E3) ☎ 595-7000**

✪ **79th St, 81st St 🚇 M7, M11, M79 ⏰ 8am-11pm (to midnight Thurs) ♿ yes** **V**

EJ's Luncheonette $-$$
Diner
A contrived 'classic' diner with excellent food, dreamy shakes, friendly service and queues out the door for weekend brunches. The Crunchy French Toast (with almonds and cornflakes) is a spooky-sounding winner. The Blue Plate dinner specials are the ones to go for

if dining at the other end of the day. Branches at 1271 Third Ave & 432 Sixth Ave.
✉ **447 Amsterdam Ave (2, E3)** ☎ 873-3444 Ⓜ 79th St, 81st St 🚌 M7, M11, M79 🕐 11.30am-12.30am (from 11am Sat, 10.30am Sun) ♿ **excellent (high chairs)** Ⓥ

Isabella's $$-$$$
New American
Self-consciously classy restaurant that does brunches, lunches, sunset snacks and dinners stacked with the seafood, grills, omelettes and salads that satisfy uptown's 6-pack tummies. Settle in the pleasant, spacious indoor area (there's a bar too) or go for the shady sidewalk seating. Bookings recommended (Fri-Sun pm). No brunch bookings taken.
✉ **359 Columbus Ave (2, E4)** ☎ 724-2100 Ⓜ 81st St 🚌 M7, M11 🕐 11.30am-12.30am (from 11am Sat, 10.30am Sun) ♿ yes

La Caridad $
Cuban-Chinese
This great cuisine mix means you get Chop Suey

de Pollo and Egg Foo Young de Jamon plus bean soup and sweet and sour plantain. Don't come for the atmosphere – it's a canteen setup with brutal lighting and over-enthusiastic climate control. Do come for the food – it's simply good and conducive to sharing.
✉ **2199 Broadway (2, E3)** ☎ 874-2780 Ⓜ 79th St 🚌 M79, M104 🕐 11.30am-1am (to 10.30pm Sun) ♿ yes Ⓥ

Ollie's $-$$
Chinese
Diner-style Chinese eating modified for the discerning western (as in Upper West Side) palate. Highlights of the huge menu are the dumplings and meal-sized soups. A fine place to bring the kids or for a pre-movie (unromantic) date. Bookings advisable for mid-evening meals.
✉ **2315 Broadway (2, D3)** ☎ 362-3111 Ⓜ 86th St (1, 9) 🚌 M104 🕐 11.30am-midnight (to 1am Fri-Sat) ♿ yes

Ruby Foo's $$-$$$
Asian
A swish 400 seater with a

dim sum-meets-sushi menu, a pan-Asian melange of decors and a lot of stylish clatter and blather. The food is top notch – even unlikely combinations usually shine – and the service is attentive. The restaurant's namesake drink is the perfect (potent) accompaniment to its fresh, flouncy food. Bookings are recommended.
✉ **1782 Broadway (2, E3)** ☎ 724-6700 Ⓜ 79th St 🚌 M104 🕐 11.30am-12.30am (to 1am Fri-Sat) ♿ yes Ⓥ

Saigon Grill $$
Vietnamese
This tasty and popular neighbourhood eatery has a large menu that starts at savoury crystal dumplings and doesn't take a breath till 'Grandma's Sweet Rice Dumplings'. The stand-outs along the way are seafood bouillabaisse and curry okra but everything is made with top produce and a dollop of care. Bookings on Friday and Saturday.
✉ **2381 Broadway (2, C3)** ☎ 875-9072 Ⓜ 86th St (1, 9) 🚌 M86, M104 🕐 11am-midnight ♿ good Ⓥ

INTERNET CAFES

Cybercafe
A large pleasant space with good coffee and pastries and up-to-date though expensive computer facilities.
✉ **273 Lafayette St (3, E6)** ☎ 334-5140 Ⓜ Prince St (N, R), B'way/Lafayette St 🚌 M21 🕐 8.30am-10pm (from 11am Sat-Sun)

Internet Cafe
Beer, snacks, jazz and the Internet might not be an obvious mix but they've got them melded well at this dim

and slightly poky cafe/bar.
✉ **82 E3rd St (3, D7)** ☎ 614-0747 Ⓜ 2nd Ave 🚌 M15 🕐 11am-2am (to midnight Sun)

The Village Escape
Cheaper than most of the downtown Internetteries, with a tasty T1 connection and enough computers to ensure you rarely have to wait.
✉ **277 Bleecker St (3, D4)** ☎ 488-8811 Ⓜ Christopher St, W 4th St 🚌 M5, M6, M10 🕐 8am-4am

Getting It Straight
Asking for a 'regular' coffee in Midtown means you'll get it with milk and a bit of sugar. The same request at a Wall St area shop will immediately lead the server to throw 3 heaped spoonfuls of the sweet stuff in the cup, because that's the way the hyper stock brokers and lawyers like it served.

entertainment

New York's novella-length weekly entertainment listings tend to include a favourite performer you never dared dream you'd see live, half a dozen legendary ensembles, at least one musician you thought was dead, and hundreds of acts that you haven't heard of but which sound fascinating. In all, a tantalising mixture, encompassing just about every form of performance imaginable, from splashy Broadway shows to unannounced street art.

There are also thousands of venues, from poky bars to pulsating nightclubs, where you can create your own party. Broadly speaking, SoHo is the place for trendy lounges and bar/restaurants while Greenwich Village has the best concentration of live music, student hang-outs and gay bars. Chelsea is a volatile mix of mainstream and hardcore gay/straight clubs and lounges. The East Village has a residue of grungy bars and a top layer of fashionable hide-outs. Midtown has an upmarket after-work and visitor scene, the Upper West Side has a sprinkling of student and ritzy lounges and Harlem has a mix of dive, jazz and gospel venues.

Information Lines

NYC On Stage ☎ 768-1818 – has comprehensive theatre, music and dance listings

Clubfone ☎ 777-2582 – selective dance clubs, live music and cabaret lists

Culture Finder www.culturefinder.com – a good resource for all sorts of goings on

To find out about high culture happenings, see the Sunday and Friday *New York Times* and the weekly *New Yorker*. For clubs and live music listings see the free weekly *Village Voice* and *New York Press*. The Voice and the weekly *Time Out* magazine both have extensive gay listings; *Homo Xtra*, *LGNY* and *Next* are gay street papers available in bars, clubs and bookshops. The monthly magazine *Paper* is good for the ever-changing dance club scene. *Free Time* is an excellent monthly guide to free or cheap goings on around town.

Once you know what shows you want to see, book tickets as far in advance as possible. Though New Yorkers are shockingly lackadaisical about the bounty available, many shows do sell out. The *Yellow Pages* has some handy theatre and sporting arena maps that will enable you to assess the relative worth of seats before you buy tickets.

The whole world loves the stage – queues outside TKTS, Times Square (see p. 86)

What's On

January *Three Kings Parade* – 5 January; children parade along Fifth Ave to Spanish Harlem
Winter Antiques Show – mid-January at the Armory
Chinese New Year – fireworks and parades in and around Chinatown

February *Black History Month* – African-American history and culture events

March *St Patrick's Day Parade* – 17 March; huge Irish march down Fifth Ave

April *Avignon-New York Film Festival* – harbinger of summer cultural events

May *Fleet Week* – annual convocation of sailors, naval ships and air rescue teams
Carnaval – celebration of Hispanic culture on Memorial Day weekend

June *Museum Mile Festival* – 2nd Tuesday; upper Fifth Ave museums free
Jazz Festival – all concert halls in town jump with the top names in jazz
Comedy Festival – comedians take to the stage of Carnegie Hall and a host of clubs
NY Shakespeare Festival – 3 months of free performances in Central Park
Lesbian & Gay Pride Week – parade down Fifth Ave and many other events in Greenwich Village

July *Independence Day* – 4 July; celebrations throughout the city
Lincoln Center Festival – features international actors, singers and acrobats, and includes free events
Central Park Summerstage – free musical performances and author readings continuing into August
Classic Movies in Bryant Park – open-air screenings Monday evenings till August
Central Park Concerts – under the stars performances by the New York Philharmonic and the Metropolitan Opera

August *Harlem Week* – a 'week' that takes the whole month to celebrate Harlem's history and culture
Village Jazz Festival – club and outdoor performances in Greenwich Village
Fringe NYC – Lower East Side mishmash of theatrical events

September *US Open Tennis Tournament* – grand slam in Flushing Meadows
Downtown Arts Festival – Chelsea and SoHo-based visual and performing arts events over 3 weeks
Fall Festival – celebration of the Arts that runs until November
Caribbean Day – Huge Brooklyn Parade
San Gennaro – Little Italy festa with a parade lead by the effigy of San Gennaro, Patron Saint of Naples
New York Film Festival – a major event at the Lincoln Center
Jazz at Lincoln Center – headed up by trumpeter Wynton Marsalis

October *Halloween Parade* – wild and colourful march down Sixth Ave in Greenwich Village with a street party
New York Marathon – road race through all 5 boroughs

November *Macy's Thanksgiving Day Parade* – balloons and floats paraded down Broadway from W 72nd St to Herald Square

December *Rockefeller Center Christmas Tree Lighting* – start of the Christmas season with celebrity performances and the Radio City Music Hall Rockettes
Radio City Christmas Spectacular – featuring, of course, The Rockettes
New Year's Eve – Times Square festivities, 5 mile midnight run in Central Park, fireworks at South Street Seaport

THEATRE & COMEDY

The centre of the theatre district, Times Square is dominated by overblown spectaculars. The so-called Broadway shows are those in the large theatres around Time Square. 'Off-Broadway' refers to dramas in smaller spaces (200 seats or fewer) elsewhere in town – still big business. 'Off-off-Broadway' events are fringe or experimental pieces in spaces with less than 100 seats.

New York's strong comedy scene is a mostly southern Manhattan phenomenon but mainstream performers tend to gravitate to the Times Square giggle palaces.

Circle in the Square Theatre

Off-Broadway nonprofit theatre that staged ground-breaking productions, such as Eugene O'Neill's *The Iceman Cometh*, at its original 159 Bleecker St premises (which now hosts performances by New School students). The company is actively involved in New York's thespian scene, not least through its theatre school.
✉ **1633 Broadway & 50th St, Times Sq (2, K5)** ☎ **307-2705, Telecharge 239-6200** ☻ the-atre school: www.circle square.org ⊕ **50th St (1, 9)** 🚌 **M6, M7, M10, M27, M50, M104** ⚥ **yes**

Comedy Cellar

Long-running comedy club with high-profile comics well known (in the US, at least) from TV chat shows and cable comedy specials. The Cellar has a history of surprise guests like Robin Williams, Steven Wright and Jerry Seinfeld.
✉ **117 Macdougal St, b/n Third & Bleecker Sts, Greenwich Village (3, E4)** ☎ **254-3480** ☻ **www.comedycellar.com** ⊕ **W 4th St** 🚌 **M5, M6, M21** ☼ **9pm-2.30am** ⑤ **free tix Mon-Thurs – call & say you saw them online**

Eugene O'Neill Theater (2, K5)

Pleasant 1100-seat theatre

with a fine history of top theatrical productions like Neil Simon's *A Thousand Clowns* and *Prisoner of Second Avenue* and Arthur Miller's *All My Sons*. A recent production of *Death of a Salesman* got rave reviews.
✉ **230 W 49th St, b/n Broadway & Eighth Ave, Times Sq (2, K5)** ☎ **Telecharge 239-6200** ⊕ **49th St, 50th St (1, 9)** 🚌 **M10, M27, M49, M104** ⚥ **yes**

Joseph Papp Public Theater (3, D6)

Founded in 1954, this is one of the city's most important cultural centres. Meryl Streep, Robert de Niro and Kevin Kline and many other stars have performed here. The theatre hosts the New York Shakespeare Festival at Central Park's Delacorte Theater. It also runs Joe's Pub, a plush cabaret hall next door which hosts music, comedy and dance.
✉ **425 Lafayette St, E Village** ☎ **539-8500, box office 260-2400** ☻ **www.publictheater .org** ⊕ **Astor Pl** 🚌 **M1 to M3, M8** ⑤ **free Shakespeare in Central Park tickets** ⚥ **yes**

The Kitchen

Artists of everything-but-the-sink creativity featured over

Discount & Rush Tickets

The **TKTS** booth in Times Square (☎ 768-1818), at Broadway & W 47th St, sells same-day tickets to many productions at up to 75% off (evening tickets: Mon-Sat from 3pm, Sun 11am-8pm; matinee tickets Wed & Sat 10am-2pm). The less crowded TKTS outlet at mezzanine level, 2 World Trade Center, opens Mon-Fri 11am-5.30pm, Sat 11am-3.30pm; matinee tickets sold the day before the performance. Neither accept credit cards and queues can start 1 hour before booths open.

Visit box offices for rush, student rush and standing room tickets, usually released on the day of performance only. At about 6pm, ask if there are any unclaimed VIP, press or cast tickets available (these mightn't be discounted, but you may score the best seats in the house).

30 years have included Philip Glass, Laurie Anderson, David Byrne, Peter Greenaway, Brian Eno, Robert Mapplethorpe and Cindy Sherman. Expect to see anything from new wave trapeze to video installations.
✉ **512 W 19th St, b/n Tenth & Eleventh Ave, Chelsea (3, B2)** ☎ **255-5793** 🌐 **www.thekitchen .org** Ⓜ **14th St (A, C, E), 8th Ave, 23rd St (C, E)** 🚌 **M11, M14** ♿ **yes**

Majestic Theater

(2, L5) Probably Broadway's best theatre, with a history of blockbuster musicals like *Carousel*, *South Pacific*, and *Camelot* with Julie Andrews and Richard Burton. It's now hosting *The Phantom of the Opera*, probably until the sky falls down. Most of its 1600 seats offer good views.
✉ **247 W 44th St, near Eighth Ave, Times Sq** ☎ **Telecharge 239-6200** Ⓜ **42nd St/Times Sq** 🚌 **M10, M27, M104** ♿ **yes**

New Amsterdam Theatre (2, L5)

This 1771-seat jewel has been rescued from decrepitude by the Disney corporation, which stages upbeat kid-friendly productions like *The Lion King* here. The lobby, restrooms and auditorium are extremely lavish but the seating is a bit cramped.
✉ **214 W 42nd St, near Seventh Ave, Times Sq** ☎ **282-2900, Ticketmaster 307-4100** 🌐 **disney.go.com/disney onbroadway/index.htm** Ⓜ **42nd St/Times Sq** 🚌 **M6, M7, M10, M27, M42, M104** ♿ **yes**

New Victory Theater

(2, L5) Home to high energy family-friendly theatre productions from all round the world such as Australia's *Flying Fruit Fly Circus*, and The Netherlands' *Runt*, featuring 28 dog-puppets.
✉ **209 W 42nd St & Broadway, Times Sq** ☎ **382-4000, Telecharge 239-6200** 🌐 **www.newvictory.org** Ⓜ **42nd St/Times Sq** 🚌 **M6, M7, M10, M27, M104** ♿ **yes**

Performing Garage

Off-Broadway theatre founded in 1967 and still one of the most consistent of the avant-garde performance spaces. Home to the Wooster Group whose members have included Willem Dafoe, Spalding Gray and Steve Buscemi.
✉ **33 Wooster St, b/n Broome & Grand Sts, SoHo (3, F5)** ☎ **966-3651** Ⓜ **Canal St (A, C, E, 1, 9)** 🚌 **M6** ♿ **yes**

PS 122

Off-off-Broadway dance and theatre space which, since its 1979 inception, has been committed to fostering new artists and their way out ideas. Performers on its 2 stages have included Blue Man Group, Eric Bogosian, Meredith Monk

Off-off at PS 122

and Penny Arcade.
✉ **150 First Ave & E 9th St, E Village (3, C7)** ☎ **477-5829, box office 477-5288** 🌐 **www.ps122 .org; tickets: www.ticket web.com** Ⓜ **Astor Pl** 🚌 **M8, M15** ♿ **yes**

Samuel Beckett Theater

Nice off-Broadway theatre with good views and comfy seats. Tends to hold small-scale productions of mainstream new plays and high quality revivals such as Gregory Murphy's 1939 play *The Countess*.
✉ **410 W 42nd St & Ninth Ave, Times Sq (2, L4)** ☎ **594-2826** Ⓜ **Port Auth/42nd St** 🚌 **M11, M16, M42** ♿ **yes**

Surf Reality

Eclectic, alternative and cutting-edge comedy, theatre and vaudeville space. Sunday nights open mic attracts young comedians with attitude. Surf Reality is part of a Lower East Side comedy festival in early May.
✉ **172 Allen St, b/n Stanton & Rivington Sts, Lower E Side (3, E7)** ☎ **673-4182** 🌐 **www.surfreality.org** Ⓜ **Delancey/Essex Sts** 🚌 **M15** 🕐 **Wed-Sun 7pm-midnight** ♿ **yes**

Todo con Nada

Alternative storefront space that produces underground drama, vaudeville, comedy and unclassifiable performance on-site and at other venues around town. Shows are usually original works with a comic bent staged by local performers.
✉ **67 Ludlow St, Lower E Side (3, E7)** ☎ **420-1466** Ⓜ **Delancey/Essex Sts** 🚌 **M9, M15, M21**

Angus Oborn

CLASSICAL MUSIC, OPERA & DANCE

Amato Opera Theater

This small but tenacious company has been going for more than 50 years and is just as ambitious as ever. The auditorium is small – it seats just over 100 – and the stage tiny – 6m wide – but 70 performers have been crammed onto it. One of the city's prime proving grounds for up-and-coming singers.
⊠ **319 The Bowery & Second St, E Village (3, E6)** ☎ **228-8200** 🄮 **www .amato.org** 🄶 **2nd Ave** 🚌 **M21, M103** ⚇ **yes**

Brooklyn Academy of Music

An excellent complex that hosts popular artists and experimental performers who nudge the main-stream, like Philip Glass, Laurie Anderson and the Kronos Quartet. There are 3 spaces: the Opera House, which seats 2100, the Playhouse (1100) and the Leperq Space (500).
⊠ **30 Lafayette Ave, cnr Flatbush & Atlantic Ave, Brooklyn (4, D3)** ☎ **718-636-4100** 🄮 **www .bam.org** 🄶 **Atlantic Ave, Pacific St, Fulton St** 🚌 **BAMbus from 120 Park Ave & 42nd St 1hr prior to most perform-ances** Ⓢ **free offers via Web site; $7.50 cash-only student rush tickets (2hrs**

before showtime) ⚇ no under 5s

Café Forty-One

Fun Saturday night tap shows with great talent and an amiable bar room set-ting. Sit down for eats from the American menu or drinks (2 drink minimum) or perch at the bar and tap those toes. Call about come-dy and other entertainment.
⊠ **41 Clark St & Hicks St, Brooklyn Heights (3, L9)** ☎ **718-222-4488** 🄶 **Clark St** 🚌 **B25, B51** ⊘ **bar open 4pm-midnight (Sat shows at 8 & 10pm)** ⚇ **yes**

Carnegie Hall (2, J5)

Since it opened in 1891, *everyone* has appeared here: Tchaikovsky conducted the opening festival, Mahler and Prokofiev performed their own works, Fats Waller, Woody Guthrie, Miles Davis, the Beatles and the Rolling Stones have all played here. The stellar line-ups continue – see the schedule of monthly events in the lobby.
⊠ **154 W 57th St & Seventh Ave, Times Sq** ☎ **CarnegieCharge 247-7800** 🄮 **www.carnegie hall.org** 🄶 **57th St (N, R), 7th Ave (B, D, E)** 🚌 **M6, M7, M57** Ⓢ **as cheap as $12 for nonsub-scription events; cheap student tickets from box**

Street classic

office 2hrs before some concerts ⚇ yes

Chamber Music Society of Lincoln Center

Directed by clarinetist David Shifrin, the Society is the foremost chamber music company in the US. The main concert series is in early autumn. Alice Tully Hall also holds seasons of the New York Chamber Symphony.
⊠ **Alice Tully Hall, Lincoln Center, Upper W Side (2, G3)** ☎ **875-5050, CenterCharge 721-6500** 🄮 **www.chamber-music society.org** 🄶 **66th St/Lincoln Center** 🚌 **M5, M7, M66, M104** ⚇ **yes**

City Center of Music & Dance (2, J5)

Landmark theatre that seats around 2750 people in its main hall and hosts the Alvin Ailey American Dance Theatre every December, and engage-ments by the American Ballet Theatre and foreign companies. The Manhattan Theatre Club performs in

Juilliard School

The Juilliard School is one of America's foremost training academies for classical performance artists. When it was founded in 1905, it was the only classi-cal music college in the country. Most of the 500 annual performances staged by students are free. Call ☎ 799-7406 to find out where and when.

Bargemusic

It sounds more like the name of an underground warehouse party, but Bargemusic is actually chamber music performed on a boat at the Fulton Ferry Landing, Brooklyn. Call ☎ 718-624-4061 for a program and tickets.

smaller auditoriums on site.
✉ W 55th St, b/n Sixth & Seventh Aves, Midtown ☎ 247-0430, box office 581-1212 ❻ www.city center.org ❼ 57th St (N, R), 7th Ave (B, D, E) 🚌 M6, M7, M57 ♿ yes

Dance Theater of Harlem

A neoclassical company founded in 1969 by Arthur Mitchell and Karel Shook and now recognised as one of the world's best. The mostly black company's oft reprised classics include *Firebird*, *South African Suite* and *The Prodigal Son*. Performances also at City Center of Music & Dance.
✉ 466 W 152nd St, Harlem (north of 1, A3) ☎ 690-2800 ❼ 157th St 🚌 M3, M18, M100, M101 ♿ yes

Joyce Theater

This offbeat dance venue seats 470 in a renovated cinema. The foundation subsidises most seasons at the theatre, enabling non-commercial troupes to bring their work to an audience. The Erick Hawkins and Merce Cunningham dance companies are among those to have performed here.
✉ 175 Eighth Ave & W 19th St, Chelsea (3, B3)

☎ 242-0800 ❻ www .joyce.org ❼ 18th St 🚌 M10 ♿ yes; family programs

Metropolitan Opera

(2, H3) Uniformly spectacular mixture of classics and premieres. It's nearly impossible to get into the first few performances of operas that feature big stars (season runs September to April). Once the B team takes over, tickets become available.
✉ Lincoln Center, Upper W Side ☎ 362-6000 ❻ www.metopera.org ❼ 66th St/Lincoln Center 🚌 M5, M7, M66, M104 ♿ yes

New York City Ballet

Established by Lincoln Kirstein and George Balanchine in 1948, the company's varied program of premieres and revivals always includes a Christmas season of *The Nutcracker*. Twyla Tharp was recently commissioned to choreograph a work for the group.
✉ New York State Theatre, Lincoln Center, Upper W Side (2, H4) ☎ 870-5570, Center-Charge 721-6500, student hotline 870-7766 ❻ www.nycballet.com ❼ 66th St/Lincoln Center 🚌 M5, M7, M66, M104

New York City Opera

Daring and affordable performances of new works, neglected operas and revitalised standard repertory by emerging, enthusiastic singers (perhaps the Met stars of tomorrow). The split season runs for a few weeks in early autumn and again in late spring.
✉ New York State Theatre, Lincoln Center, Upper W Side (2, H4) ☎ 870-5570, box office 362-6000, Ticketmaster 307-4100 ❻ www.nycopera.com ❼ 66th St/Lincoln Center 🚌 M5, M7, M66, M104 ♿ yes

New York Philharmonic

The orchestra has been getting rave reviews under the direction of German-born conductor Kurt Masur, though the ageing and conservative Philharmonic audience still resists programs that deviate from the standard repertory.
✉ Avery Fisher Hall, Lincoln Center, Upper W Side (2, G4) ☎ Center-Charge 721-6500, call 875-5656 for discount ticket information ❻ www.newyorkphil harmonic.org ❼ 66th St/Lincoln Center 🚌 M5, M7, M66, M104 ♿ yes

Ticket Agencies & Brokers

Ticketmaster (☎ 307-4100; www.ticketmaster.com) and **Telecharge** (☎ 239-6200; www.telecharge.com) – most major concerts and sporting events
CenterCharge (☎ 721-6500) – Lincoln Center events
Ticket Central (☎ 279-4200), 416 W 42nd St (2, L4) – Broadway and off-Broadway theatre tickets
The Broadway Ticket Center, Times Square Visitors' Center, 1560 Broadway, b/n 46th & 47th Sts (2, L5); Mon-Sat 9am-7pm, Sun 10am-6pm

JAZZ & BLUES

Arthur's Tavern

A tiny bar with a minuscule stage (a horn player may suddenly stand up beside you and blow your ear off). There's jazz and blues every night and sing-along classics on the weekends. No cover charge but a one drink minimum per set.

✉ 57 Grove St & Seventh Ave, Greenwich Village (3, D4) ☎ 675-6879 🚇 Christopher St 🚌 M8, M10 ⏱ Sun-Mon 8pm-3am, Tues-Thurs 6.30pm-3am, Fri-Sat 6.30pm-3.30am

Back Fence

A long-standing bluesy, folksy bar that kicks into classic rock mode on weekends.

✉ 155 Bleecker St & Sullivan St, Greenwich Village (3, E5) ☎ 475-9221 🚇 Bleecker St, B'way/Lafayette St 🚌 M5, M6 ⏱ Sun-Thurs 4pm-4am, Fri-Sat 1pm-4am ⑤ free (Sat: $5)

Blue Note

New York's most famous (and expensive) jazz club, where big stars play short sets. Tourists are thick on the ground, but some great music gets played here. Blue Note members get special offers (join via Web site).

✉ 131 W 3rd St & Sixth Ave, Greenwich Village (3, D4) ☎ 475-0049, reservations 475-8592 🌐 www.bluenote.net 🚇 W 4th St 🚌 M5, M6 ⏱ 7pm-late ⑤ 'Music charges' (up to $60); Fri & Sat only $5

Chicago Blues

Blues masters and up-and-coming baton carriers play 7 nights a week in this none-too-flashy club. If you've got a harmonica in your pocket, you can jump in for Monday night's blues jam.

✉ 73 Eighth Ave & 14th St, Greenwich Village (3, C3) ☎ 924-9755 🚇 8th Ave 🚌 M14 ⏱ 5pm-2am (to 3am Fri-Sat)

Copeland's

Snaffle the soul food buffet every Sunday and enjoy a gospel choir. From Tuesday to Sunday evenings there's dinner and a show, with a varied jazz program and a mostly southern menu. Touristy scene but decent food and performances.

✉ 547 W 145th St, b/n Broadway & Amsterdam Ave, Harlem (4, A2) ☎ 234-2356 🌐 www.copelandsrestaurant.com 🚇 145th St (1, 9) 🚌 M4, M5, M101, M102 ⏱ Tues-Thurs 4.30-11pm, Fri-Sat 4.30pm-midnight, Sun 12-9pm

Fez

Hosts the wildly popular Mingus Big Band every Thursday. On other nights you can catch drag queen shows, readings of novels in progress, lounge music concerts and rock. Also at Great Jones St, under Time Cafe (3, D6).

✉ 380 Lafayette St, Greenwich Village (3, E6) ☎ 533-2680, reservations 533-7000 🌐 www.feznyc.com 🚇 Bleecker St 🚌 M1, M5, M6 ⏱ 6pm-2am (to 4am Fri-Sat) ⑤ some student discounts

55 Bar

Authentic smoky jazz, blues and fusion joint with live music 7 nights from about 10pm. Excellent residencies plus guest spots by the grand and unplanned when in town. Cover charges run from minimal up to about $15 but you get a couple of drinks with that.

✉ 55 Christopher St, Greenwich Village (3, C4) ☎ 929-9883 🚇 Christopher St 🚌 M10 ⏱ 8am-4am

Hudson Bar & Books

A meeting place with food, cigars and free jazz Friday and Saturday until 2am.

✉ 636 Hudson St & Horatio St, Greenwich Village (3, C3)

The Big Apple

It was long thought that New York City was dubbed 'The Big Apple' by jazz musicians who regarded a gig in Harlem as a sure sign that they had made it to the top. But the term first appeared in the 1920s when it was used by a journalist, John FitzGerald, who covered horse races for the *Morning Telegraph*. Apparently stable hands at a New Orleans racetrack called a trip to a New York racetrack 'the Big Apple' – or greatest reward – for any talented thoroughbred. The slang stayed in popular usage long after the newspaper – and FitzGerald – disappeared.

☎ 229-2642 🚇 14th St
(1, 2, 3, 9) 🚍 M10, M11,
M14 🕐 Sun-Thurs 5pm-
2am, Fri-Sat 6pm-4am

Iridium

A splashy club with way-out
decor and good acoustics. It
features quality trad jazz acts
2 sets a night from Sunday
to Thursday and a cooking 3
sets on weekends. There's a
Sunday jazz brunch, and the
irrepressible Les Paul appears
every Monday.
✉ 44 W 63rd St, b/n
Broadway & Columbus
Ave, Upper W Side
(2, H4) ☎ 582-2121
🚇 66th St/Lincoln
Center 🚍 M5, M7, M66,
M104 🕐 7pm-late

Showman's Cafe

Features jazz combos and
R&B vocalists. Food is
available if you want to tap
and chew.
✉ 375 W 125th St, b/n
St Nicholas & Morning-
side Aves, Harlem (3, A3)
☎ 864-8941 🚇 125th
St (A, B, C, D) 🚍 M3,
M18, M100, M101
🕐 Mon-Sat noon-late
💲 free (2 drink min)

Small's

Unique place without a
liquor licence that hosts a
10hr jazz marathon every
night from 10pm attracting
top talent. After 2am it's
'jam house' till dawn.
✉ 183 W 10th St &
Seventh Ave, Greenwich
Village (3, C4) ☎ 929-
7565 🚇 Christopher St
🚍 M8, M10 🕐 10pm-
8am (from 6.30pm Fri-
Sun) 💲 jazz marathon
$10, sodas free

Sweet Basil

New and used jazz every
night, mostly ensembles
and touring artists. Monday

is the uplifting Spirit of
Life; Saturday and Sunday
there's a tasty jazz brunch.
✉ 88 Seventh Ave S &
Grove St, Greenwich
Village (3, D4)
☎ 242-1785
🌐 www.sweet basil.com
🚇 Christopher St 🚍
M8, M10 🕐 noon-2am

Tonic

An interesting venue with a
fine ear for new music (jazz,
electronic, songwriter
nights, radical klezmer and
more) plus films, chats, slide
nights and other eclectica.
Food – from brunch to late
night snacks – too.
Incommunicado (p. 63) is
the attached bookshop.
✉ 107 Norfolk St,
Lower E Side (3, F8)
☎ 358-7501 🚇 Del-
ancey/Essex Sts 🚍 M9,
M14, M21 🕐 noon-late

Village Vanguard

This basement-level venue
may be the world's most

prestigious jazz club; it has
hosted literally every major
star of the past 50 years.
The cover charges aren't as
hefty as those at the Blue
Note but the crowds can
be a little less respectful.
✉ 178 Seventh Ave S &
11th St, Greenwich
Village (3, C4) ☎ 255-
4037 🌐 www.village
vanguard.net 🚇 Chris-
topher St 🚍 M10
🕐 8.30pm-late

Wells Restaurant

Progressive jazz combos on
Fri, Sat and Mon evenings
and a relaxed jazz Sunday
brunch. Most folks take in
dinner and show, but you
can just prop yourself at
the bar and listen to the
music.
✉ 2247 Adam Clayton
Powell Blvd & 133rd St,
Harlem (north of 1, A5)
☎ 234-0700 🚇 135th
St (2, 3) 🚍 M2
🕐 11am-midnight (to
4am Fri-Sat)

Small's – for an alcohol-free big night out

Jazz 'n' Blues Floater

Circle Line (☎ 630-8888) hosts jazz, blues and funk
music cruises from May to September, with top artists
and twinkling harbour lights. Clarence 'Gatemouth'
Brown, Irma Thomas, Chuck Mangione and Jon Lucien
have all performed recently. Call to see who's been
snagged for the current season; tickets are $25-35.

ROCK, HIP-HOP, FOLK & WORLD MUSIC

Apollo Theater
(1, A4) Harlem's leading space for political rallies and concerts since 1914. Virtually every major black artist of note in the 1930s and 40s performed here, including Duke Ellington, Bessie Smith, Billie Holiday and Charlie Parker. These days it's mostly hip-hop and R&B. Wednesday is amateur night, a pale imitation of the contests that launched Ella Fitzgerald and James Brown but still great fun.
✉ 253 W 125th St, Harlem ☎ 749-5838, box office 531-5305 Ⓜ 125th St (A, B, C, D) 🚌 M2, M7, M10, M100, M102 ♿ yes

Arlene Grocery
A one room hothouse of local music (live every night), student sagas and cheap bottled beer. It's often great; look out for hilarious punk rock karaoke.
✉ 95 Stanton St & Orchard St, Lower E Side (3, E7) ☎ 358-1633

CBGB
CBGB (OMFUG) stands for Country, Bluegrass, Blues and Other Music for Uplifting Gourmandizers. The country only lasted for the first year – by 1974, the emphasis was rock. Deborah Harry, David Byrne, the B52s and Joey Ramone are among the rock luminaries who sweated and styled here.

The Apollo – Harlem's major drawcard

Ⓜ 2nd Ave 🚌 M15, M21 🕐 6pm-4am 💲 free

Bottom Line
Large cabaret-style music hall with all sorts of live acts. Each night a single artist or group usually performs 2 sets (7.30pm and 10.30pm). Waiter service and food (pizzas and burgers) are available.
✉ 15 W Fourth St & Mercer St, Greenwich Village (3, D5) ☎ 228-6300, concert line 228-7880 🚌 Bleecker St 🚌 M5, M6 🕐 show nights 6pm-late

Bowery Ballroom
Big clubby venue with a dungeonesque bar and a large gig hall with balcony and make-out room. Hosts popular indie touring acts, both American and international.
✉ 6 Delancey St & The Bowery, Lower E Side (3, F6) ☎ 533-2111, tickets 269-4849 🌐 tickets: www.ticketweb.com Ⓜ Grand St, Bowery 🚌 M103

CBGB
The prototypical punk club, incubator of such famous acts as the Talking Heads and the Ramones, is still going strong after nearly 3 decades. It's one of the few places in New York that looks, feels and smells *exactly* like you imagined it would. CB's 313 Gallery (☎ 677-0455) next door presents acoustic music every night.
✉ 315 The Bowery, opp Bleecker St, E Village (3, E6) ☎ 982-4052 🌐 www.cbgb.com Ⓜ Bleecker St, 2nd Ave 🚌 M103 🕐 7pm-2am (to 4am Fri-Sat)

The Cooler
Live music in an old meat fridge with an electronic emphasis and DJs spinning on stage through the evening. There are 2 bar areas and a number of secluded hideaways for meaningful conversation.
✉ 416 W 14th St, b/n Ninth Ave & Washington St, Greenwich Village (3, C2) ☎ 229-0785, tickets 334-4480 (from Xlarge, 267 Lafayette St & Prince St) 🌐 www.thecooler.com Ⓜ 14th St (A, C, E), 8th Ave 🚌 M11, M14

Elbow Room
Mostly undiscovered local rock in a boomy, roomy

venue. Wednesday night karaoke can be fun.
✉ **144 Bleecker St, b/n Thompson & La Guardia Sts, Greenwich Village (3, E5)** ☎ 979-8434 @ www.elbowroomnyc .com ⊕ Bleecker St 🚇 M5, M6, M21 ⏲ 7.30pm-late

Eureka Joe
Coffee shop and bar that throws the stage over to undiscovered talent with its open mic session on Monday night. Varied local bands from play Thursday to Saturday evenings.
✉ **168 Fifth Ave & 22nd St, Flatiron (2, P6)** ☎ 741-7500, recorded info 741-7504 ⊕ 23rd St (N, R, F) 🚇 M2, M3, M5, M23 ⏲ Mon-Fri 7am-9pm (to 11pm Mon & Thurs, midnight Fri); Sat 9am-midnight, Sun 10am-6pm ⑤ free

Irving Plaza
A popular venue for well-known foreign acts (Tricky, Everything But the Girl, Pavement, Luscious Jackson). Its presence in a formerly sleepy neighbourhood has inspired the opening of many new bars on 15th St that attract an NYU undergraduate crowd.
✉ **17 Irving Pl & 15th St, Union Sq, Chelsea (3, B6)** ☎ 777-6817, concert hotline 777-1224, Ticketmaster 307-4100 @ www .irvingplaza.com ⊕ Union Sq 🚇 M1 to M3, M9, M14

Knitting Factory
A noise art space that features alt-jazz, rock, hip-hop, hasidic new wave, cosmic space jazz (ie whatever is out there on the fringe).

There are 4 performance spaces: Alterknit, Old Office Lounge, the main space and a tap bar that has free music every night from 11pm.
✉ **74 Leonard St, near Church St, Tribeca (3, H5)** ☎ 219-3006 @ www.knittingfactory .com ⊕ Franklin St 🚇 M6 ⏲ 4.30pm-late

Latin Quarter
Mostly merengue and salsa and a mature Latin crowd. There are live bands from Thursday to Saturday and at least one room playing hip-shaking favourites every night. Thursday is free for ladies, while Sunday attracts a younger party crowd with hip-hop and R&B. Dress elegantly – no jeans or sneakers.
✉ **Broadway & 95th St, Upper W Side (2, B3)** ☎ 864-7600 ⊕ 96th St (1, 2, 3, 9) 🚇 M96, M104 ⏲ Thurs-Sun 9pm-4.30am

Luna Lounge
A hang-out bar with a small room in the back for garage bands, local musicians and up and coming indie darlings. It's always free so it never hurts to poke your head in and see what's cooking.
✉ **171 Ludlow St, Lower E Side (3, E7)** ☎ 260-2323 ⊕ 2nd Ave 🚇 M9, M14, M15, M21 ⏲ 7.30pm-4am ⑤ free

Mercury Lounge
Smallish but comfortable venue blasting local and touring indie and rock music through its quality sound system every night. Jeff Buckley, Lou Reed and Bikini Kill have all played here.
✉ **217 E Houston St & Allen St, Lower E Side (3, E7)** ☎ 260-4700, tickets 269-4849 @ www.mercurylounge nyc.com; tickets: www.ticketweb.com ⊕ 2nd Ave 🚇 M15, M21 ⏲ 7pm-late

SOB's
Afro-Cuban sounds, salsa and reggae, both live and on the turntable. There are dinner shows nightly but the place really starts jumping after 2am.
✉ **204 Varick St & W Houston St, Greenwich Village (3, E4)** ☎ 243-4940 @ www.sobs.com ⊕ Houston St 🚇 M10, M21 ⏲ 7pm-late

Wetlands Preserve
Concert venue with a history of reformed big-hair bands and nostalgic covers outfits. These days there's a happening diet of hip-hop, live DJs, reggae, a smattering of rock and a social conscience.
✉ **161 Hudson St & Laight St, Tribeca (3, G4)** ☎ 386-3600, 966-8864 @ www.wet lands-preserve.org ⊕ Canal St (1, 9) 🚇 M10

World Music Institute
This organisation (☎ 545-7536; www.heartheworld .org) books about 90 concerts a year at various venues including Town Hall and Washington Square Church. There are usually 2 shows each weekend and you can expect anything from an Algerian folk singer to Zairean congo players.

CINEMAS

Angelika Film Center
Specialises in 'films, not movies'; and is always crowded on weekends. It's situated in the Old Cable Building, which housed cables for trolley cars.
✉ 18 W Houston St & Mercer St, E Village (3, E5) ☎ 995-2000, 777-FILM #531 🌐 www.citycinemas.com ⊖ B'way /Lafayette St, Prince St, Spring St (6) 🚇 M21

Anthology Film Archives
The archive features far-out fringe and foreign films, works by local film-makers and otherwise unreleased fare.
✉ 32 Second Ave & E 2nd St, E Village (3, E7) ☎ 505-5110
🌐 www.anthologyfilmarchives.org ⊖ 2nd Ave 🚇 M15, M21

Cinema Classics
Mostly screens 60s to early 90s 16mm classics in a loungey theatrette. Your $5 ticket includes 2 features most nights – a real East Village bargain. Movie rental and cafe on site too.
✉ 332 E 11th St, b/n First & Second Aves, E Village (3, C7) ☎ 971-1015 🌐 www.cinemaclassics.com ⊖ 1st Ave, Astor Pl 🚇 M8, M15

Film Forum
Three screens of revivals and alternative releases very popular with the Village set and NYU students. Bring something to read while you stand in a line down the block.
✉ 209 W Houston St & Varick St, SoHo (3, E4) ☎ 727-8110 🌐 www.filmforum.com ⊖ Houston St 🚇 M10, M21

Screening Room
A recent season included a disco-porn movie. Not impressed? What about we tell you it was in 3-D. Regular fare isn't always so out there, but it's usually alternative enough to please the local loft-dwellers. There's a good restaurant on site and prix fixe dinner-and-movie deals. There are midnight shows on Fri and Sat.
✉ 54 Varick St & Canal St, SoHo (3, F4) ☎ 334-2100 🌐 www.thescreeningroom.com ⊖ Canal St (1, 9, A, C, E), 3rd Ave 🚇 M10

Sony Theatres Lincoln Square
Super-dooper multiplex with 12 large-screen theatres and a 3-D IMAX hall.
✉ Broadway & W 68th St, Upper W Side (2, G3) ☎ 336-5000 🌐 www.sonyimax.com ⊖ 66th St/Lincoln Center 🚇 M5, M7, M66, M104

Walter Reade Theatre at the Lincoln Center
(2, G3) Shows independent films, career retrospectives and themed series, and hosts screenings of the New York Film Festival every September.
✉ 165 W 65th St, Lincoln Center, Upper W Side ☎ 875-5600 🌐 www.filmlinc.com ⊖ 66th St/Lincoln Center 🚇 M5, M7, M66, M104

The Small Screen Scene
Free tickets are available for a number of TV show tapings. Tickets for many shows are sold months in advance but standby tickets are often available on the day of filming. **NBC** (☎ 664-3056) distributes tickets from its premises at 30 Rockefeller Plaza on 49th St. Stand in line for *Rosie O'Donnell* at 7.30am, *Conan O'Brien* Tuesday to Friday at 9am and *Saturday Night Live* at 9.15am on the day of the show. **CBS** (☎ 247-6497) sometimes has standby tickets for *David Letterman*: call the network at 11am. If you do get a ticket, take something warm to wear to the taping – the studios are freezing.

Heeeeeeeeeerrrrres David Letterman!

Richard l'Anson

CABARET

Cotton Club

One of old Harlem's humdingers rides again as a buffet-dinner (southern food) and show venue. There's a changing program of swing, blues and jazz shows but you can count on a sausage-and-grits gospel brunch on Saturday and Sunday.
✉ **656 125th St & West Side Hwy, Harlem (1, A2)** ☎ 663-7980 **ⓔ** www .cottonclub-newyork.com **ⓟ** 125th St (1, 9) 🚍 M4, M5, M104 ◷ Mon, Thurs & Fri 8pm, Sat 12, 2.30, 6 & 9pm, Sun 12, 2.30 & 6pm

Duplex Cabaret Theatre

Cabaret, comedy and small ensemble theatre mostly with a gay theme or a campy slant. There's a nightly open mic in the downstairs piano bar – if the customers don't ham it up, the bar staff do.
✉ **61 Christopher St, Sheridan Sq, Greenwich Village (3, D4)** ☎ 255-5438 **ⓟ** Christopher St 🚍 M8, M10

Singing Service

Don't scoff at those crooning waiters: Eddie Cantor and Jimmy Durante both started their careers as singing servers in New York City.

Ellen's Stardust Diner

It's not just a diner, it's a linoleum-cabaret joint with waiters who can hold a note just as well as they can hold a 'big bopper burger' or a 'hot diggity dog'. Would you like a tune with those fries?
✉ **1650 Broadway & 51st St, Times Sq (2, K5)** ☎ 956-5151, Telecharge 239-6200 **ⓟ** 50th St (1, 9) 🚍 M6, M7, M10, M27, M50, M104 ◷ 7am-midnight (to 1am Fri-Sat, 11pm Sun) **ⓢ** free

Judy's

Different shows every session at this intimate supper club that attracts cheerful locals and uptown music lovers. The piano bar caters to a diverse crowd, and good food is served till late.
✉ **169 Eighth Ave & 18th St, Chelsea (3, B3)** ☎ 929-5410 **ⓟ** 18th St 🚍 M10 ◷ Mon-Fri 6pm-4am, Sat-Sun 1pm-4am

Oak Room at The Algonquin

From in set to twin set, the oak-panelled, old money venue is the city's classiest cabaret, with top names or quality newcomers. Dinner and show (Tues-Sat); 2 shows a night on weekends.
✉ **59 W 44 St & Sixth Ave, Times Sq (2, L5)** ☎ 840-6800 **ⓟ** Grand Central/42nd St 🚍 M5 to M7 ◷ Tues-Sat, dinner from 7.15pm

The Supper Club

Dinnertime big band bashing and cabaret-style revues give way to highclass swing around the witching hour. Dancing lessons are available 11pm-midnight. Jackets required.
✉ **240 W 47th St, Times Sq, Midtown (2, K5)** ☎ 921-1940 **ⓟ** Rockefeller Center 🚍 M5 to M7, M27, M50 ◷ Fri-Sat 5.30pm-4am **ⓢ** $15 after 11pm

CLUBS

Kit Kat Klub

Large faux-1940s club with a pretty friendly crowd and mixed music from R&B to house. This is one club where you may be able to have yourself added to the guest list just by calling up. No sneakers allowed.
✉ **124 W 43rd St, b/n Sixth Ave & Broadway, Midtown (2, L5)** ☎ 819-0377 **ⓟ** 42nd St (B, D, F, Q) 🚍 M6, M7, M42, M104 ◷ Fri-Sun 9pm-5am

Life

Of-the-moment club (maybe still as you read this) with a prime layout for dancing and dancer-watching. Deep and hard house Wednesday to Friday, cutie pie tea dance Sunday evening. Friday is the hardest night to get past the door police. Dress is smart and trendy.
✉ **158 Bleecker St, Greenwich Village (3, E5)** ☎ 420-1999 **ⓟ** Bleecker St, B'way/ Lafayette St 🚍 M5, M6 ◷ Tues-Sat 10pm-late

Naked Lunch

Not-too-sceney dance bar with afternoon and evening events like barbecues and shows as well as straight up stuff-strutting festas.
✉ **17 Thompson St &**

Grand St, SoHo (3, F5)
☎ 343-0828 ⓟ Canal
St (A, C, E) 🚌 M6
🕐 Tues-Sat 5pm-4am

Nell's
Original European velvet
lounge that attracts a well-
dressed downtown crowd.
Monday is comedy, Tuesday
is torch song karaoke,
Wednesday is Latin night.
Later in the week a posse
of DJs and live bands makes
sure everyone's booty is
bopping. No sneakers,
boots or baggy jeans.
✉ 246 W 14th St, b/n
Seventh & Eighth Aves,
Greenwich Village (3, C3)
☎ 675-1567 ⓟ 8th Ave
🚌 M14 🕐 10pm-4am

Speeed
Different nights run the
gamut from salsa to hip-
hop to tribal and back to
merengue. Parties for Latin
gay porn stars (and their
admirers) are held regularly.
✉ 20 W 39th St, b/n
Fifth & Sixth Aves, Mid-
town (2, M6) ☎ 719-

9867 ⓟ 42nd St, 5th
Ave (7) 🚌 M1 to M7
🕐 Thurs-Sun 10pm-4am

Tunnel
Massive 3-floor club with
different DJs on each level.
Count on a range of house,
hip-hop and groovy clas-
sics. The crowd is mostly
young with a high bridge-
and-tunnel quotient on
weekends.
✉ 220 Twelfth Ave &
27th St, Chelsea (2, O2)
☎ 695-4682 ⓟ 23rd
St (C, E) 🚌 M11, M23
🕐 Fri-Sat 10pm-8am,
Sun 10pm-4am

Twilo
Popular club with 3000
capacity, widely touted as
having the best sound system in the world. Plenty of
room to spin jungle, house,
hip-hop and old-time (70s
and 80s) dance.
✉ 530 W 27th St, b/n
Tenth & Eleventh Aves,
Chelsea (2, O3) ☎ 268-
1600 🌐 www.twiloclub
.com ⓟ 23rd St (C, E)

🚌 M11, M23 🕐 Fri &
Sat 11pm-8am

Vinyl
Party kinda club attracts an
older crowd with an eye on
grooving out rather than
scene-ing in. Funky, tribal
house and old-time radio
hits mix with excellent taste
by a sparkling line-up of DJs.
✉ 6 Hubert St, b/n
Hudson & Greenwich
Sts, Tribeca (3, G4)
☎ 343-1379
ⓟ Franklin St
🚌 M10 🕐 Fri-Sat
11pm-late, Sun 4pm-
late

XVI
Two-level club specialising
in manufactured sleaze.
Thursday night is the fab
Nymphomania go-go club
with sassy caged dancers,
French 60s pop and hilari-
ous Euro soft porn videos.
✉ 16 First Ave, b/n
First & Second Sts,
E Village (3, E7)
☎ 260-1549 ⓟ 2nd Ave
🚌 M14 🕐 8pm-late

BARS & LOUNGES

Barramundi
Australian-owned arty bar
with convivial booths, reasonably priced drinks and a
lovely shady (but early closing) garden. A good place
to start a Lower East Side
bar crawl.
✉ 137 Ludlow St, b/n
Stanton & Rivington
Sts, Lower E Side
(3, E7) ☎ 529-6900
ⓟ Delancey/Essex Sts
🚌 M9, M14, M15, M21
🕐 Sun-Thurs 5pm-4am,
Fri-Sat 6pm-4am

Beauty Bar
Haven't you always wanted
to sip on a cocktail while

sitting under an old
hairdrying cone? Sure ya
did. This bar is in a not-
quite-converted old beauty
salon complete with DJs,
live music and beautician.
✉ 231 E 14th St, b/n
Second & Third Aves, E
Village (3, C6) ☎ 539-
1389 ⓟ 3rd Ave
🚌 M14 🕐 5pm-4am
(from 7pm Sat-Sun)

Belmont Lounge
Hip, snappy and spacious
with lots of nooks for those
with serious gossip or an eye
to romance. There's a garden
for stargazers and food at all
hours if you're not getting

enough vitamins from your
beverages. The 119 Bar next
door is low key: pool, darts
and cheap drinks.
✉ 117 E 15th St &
Irving Pl, Union Sq,
Chelsea (3, B6) ☎ 533-
0009 ⓟ Union Sq
🚌 M1 to M3, M9, M14
🕐 noon-4am

Bowlmor Lanes
Tenpin bowling, drinkies and
a disco soundtrack – everything is fun when you're
wearing 2-tone shoes.
Monday night is glow-in-
the-dark techno bowling.
Cheap games before 5pm.
✉ 110 University Pl, b/n

12th & 13th Sts, Greenwich Village (3, C5) ☎ 255-8188 🚇 Union Sq 🚌 M2, M3, M5, M7, M14 🕐 Mon-Fri 10am-4am (to 1am Tues-Wed, 2am Thurs), Sat 11am-4am, Sun 11am-1am

More please, Bowlmor

Cafe St Barts
Big outdoor terrace next to St Bartholomew's Church open for eats and drinks and occasional live jazz. The holy cow location should keep you on the narrow, if not exactly the straight. The church is open till 6pm for 'quiet contemplation'.
✉ 109 E 50th & Park Ave, Midtown (2, K7) ☎ 888-2664 🚇 51st St, Lexington Ave (E, F) 🚌 M27, M50 🕐 12-11pm (to 4pm Sun)

Chumley's
A former speakeasy serving decent pub grub and US microbrews. It's a sawdust on the floor, jocks at the bar kind of place but it's welcoming and rowdy in the right way. Unmarked brown door in a white wall.
✉ 86 Bedford St, b/n Grove & Barrow Sts, Greenwich Village (3, D3) ☎ 675-4449 🚇 Christopher St 🚌 M8, M10 🕐 4pm-2am

Double Happiness
Double the fun if you go early in the week or early on a weekend night to grab a table in this dank dungeonesque ex-speakeasy with an obscure entrance – look for 'watch your step', a stairway down.
✉ 173 Mott St, b/n Broome & Grand Sts, Chinatown (3, F6) ☎ 941-1282 🚇 Spring St (6), Bowery 🚌 M103 🕐 6pm-4am

Ear Inn
A bar in a largely original federal house dating back to 1817. Tuesday is bikers night with a lot of machinery-ogling; Saturday is poetry night; every night is Guinness night. Food is served.
✉ 326 Spring St, b/n Greenwich & Washington Sts, SoHo (3, F3) ☎ 226-9060 🚇 Canal St (1, 9) 🚌 M10, M21 🕐 11.30am-4am

The Evelyn Lounge
A clubby multiroom cellar with a classy cigar lounge and a martini list with more options than the dinner menu. There's a laid-back crowd during the week, making room for hobnobbing students on the weekend.
✉ 380 Columbus Ave & 78th St, Upper W Side (2, E4) ☎ 724-2363 🚇 81st St 🚌 M7, M11, M79 🕐 6pm-2am (to 4am Fri-Sat)

Kinsale Tavern
Popular bar with 20 beers on tap and live satellite broadcasts of European rugby and soccer. Frequented by a friendly crowd who'll talk baseball or philosophy.
✉ 1672 Third Ave & 93rd St, Upper E Side (2, B7) ☎ 348-4370 🚇 96th St (4, 5, 6) 🚌 M101 to M103 🕐 8am-1.30am (to 3.30am Fri-Sat)

Lakeside Lounge
A slightly grungy, firmly casual hang-out with free bands, cheap drinks and a black and white photo booth – you need 8 quarters to remember this night forever.
✉ 162 Ave B & E 10th St, E Village (3, C8) ☎ 529-8463 🚇 1st Ave 🚌 M9, M14 🕐 4pm-4am

Liquor Store
Friendly corner bar with big street-watching windows. It's a local hang-out early in the week but gets more crowded with interlopers towards the weekend. Plenty of people to talk to and outdoor tables when the weather is kind.
✉ 235 W Broadway & White St, Tribeca (3, G5) ☎ 226-7121 🚇 Franklin St 🚌 M6 🕐 12pm-2am (to 4am Fri-Sat)

Marc Chiaro
One of Manhattan's oldest bars, AKA 'Mulberry Bar', has been in the same family for 90 years. It's a solid drinking place with a handsome wooden bar, a great jukebox (plenty of Sinatra) and a movie-Mafia feel.
✉ 176 Mulberry St & Broome St, Little Italy (3, F6) ☎ 226-9345 🚇 Spring St (6), Bowery 🚌 M103 🕐 noon-2am

No Moore
Big boho space with bar, tables and deluxe round booths. There's a menu but no kitchen: they'll order in takeaway from 8 local resaurants. Just the place when someone wants *tandoor*, someone wants *pad thai* and you want brew and buddies. There's live music – blues, groove and salsa – Wednesdays and weekends.
✉ 234 W Broadway & N

Moore St, Tribeca (3, G5)
☎ 925-2595 🚇 Franklin
St 🚌 M6 🕐 5pm-2am

Pravda
Purposely hard to find,
though queues spilling all
over the pavement have
made the truth a little easier
to behold of late. If you make
it past the door worthies
(dress trendy, look intense),
you're in for boastable martinis (there's a 2 page vodka
list – including Canada's
Inferno Pepper and a home-
grown Rain Organic) and
clouds of cigar smoke.
✉ 281 Lafayette St, b/n
Prince & Houston Sts,
SoHo (3, E6) ☎ 226-
4696 🚇 Broadway/
Lafayette St 🚌 M5,
M6, M21 🕐 5pm-late
(from 6pm Sun)

Red Bench Bar
A shoulder-rubbing chichi

place to be seen nursing an
expensive drink and wearing
the divine little somethings
you snapped up in the boutiques earlier in the day.
✉ 107 Sullivan St, b/n
Prince & Spring Sts,
SoHo (3, F5) ☎ 274-
9120 🚇 Spring St (C,
E) 🚌 M5, M6, M21
🕐 5pm-4am

The Scratcher
Popular with the Irish, it's a
true Dublin-style pub: a
quiet place to read the
newspaper during the day
over coffee but crowded
and raucous at night.
✉ 209 E 5th St, b/n
Second & Third Aves,
E Village (3, D6)
☎ 477-0030 🚇 Astor
Pl 🚌 M15, M103
🕐 11.30am-4am

Wall St Kitchen & Bar
This handsome old bank

building is now a lunch and
after-hours hang-out for
suits who love a beer. There
are 50 beers on draught,
beer flights, a long wine list
and a mid-priced
Mediterranean menu.
✉ 70 Broad St &
Beaver St, Lwr Man-
hattan (3, L6) ☎ 797
7070 🚇 Broad St, Wall
St 🚌 M15 🕐 Mon-Fri
11.30am-11.30pm

WCOU Radio
Low-key hang-out with
cool jukebox and ecstatic
happy hours making it a
good place to sit in the
window and watch avenue
life pass by with a Bud or a
bud. It's commonly known
as the 'Tile Bar' because of
its bathroomy veneer.
✉ First Ave & E 7th St,
E Village (3, D7) ☎ 254-
4317 🚇 2nd Ave
🚌 M15 🕐 5pm-4am

GAY & LESBIAN NEW YORK

B Bar
A big bar/restaurant with a
garden that stays open
through the winter. It's
busy most nights and has a
high beautiful-person fac-
tor. Tuesday is a high-
energy gay/mixed night.
✉ 40 E 4th St & the
Bowery, Lwr E Side
(3, D6) ☎ 475-2220
🚇 Bleecker St 🚌 M103
🕐 11.30am-4am (from
10.30am Sat-Sun)

The Cock
Boozy, cruisy club with a
wild Saturday night through-
the-roof party with DJs,
dancing and drag. The crowd
is old-school East Village:
unpretentious and arty, with
the odd leather-dressed go-
go boy chucked in.
✉ 188 Ave A & 12th St,

E Village (3, C7) ☎ 777-
6254 🚇 1st Ave 🚌 M14
🕐 9.30pm-4am

Crazy Nanny's
Brash bar for gay women
and their friends with a
Monday pool tournament,
Wednesday and Sunday
karaoke (fun atmosphere,
no cover charge), classic
drag on Thursday and exotic dancers on Saturday. It's
crowded and raucous on
weekends.
✉ 21 Seventh Ave S &
Leroy St, Greenwich
Village (3, E4) ☎ 366-
6312 🚇 Houston St
🚌 M10 🕐 4pm-4am
(from 3pm Sat-Sun)

Don Hill's
Varied club where live soul
and pop might give way to

a late-night ostentatious
transvestite party with drag
shows, go-go boys and
anything goes.
✉ 511 Greenwich St &
Spring St, SoHo (3, F4)
☎ 219-2850 🚇 Spring
St (C, E) 🚌 M10, M21
🕐 8pm-late

Hell
Smallish lounge with lus-
cious red drapery and cutesy
photos of celebs with devil-
ish horns. The crowd is
mixed and pretty laid-back,
the feeling is friendly.
Sunday is disco night.
✉ 59 Gansevoort St,
b/n Greenwich & Hudson
Sts, Greenwich Village
(3, C2) ☎ 727-1666 🚇
14th St (A, C, E), 8th Ave
🚌 M11, M14 🕐 7pm-
4am (from 5pm Sat-Sun)

Henrietta Hudson
Dive bar for women with a pool table, DJs and occasional live music. A good meeting place or an easy place to sit and feel comfortably unhassled with a brewski.
✉ 438 Hudson St & Morton St, Greenwich Village (3, E3) ☎ 924-3347 ⊖ Houston St 🚌 M10 ⊘ 4pm-4am

HENRIETTA HUDSON
1991

Greenwich Village for gals

King
The 3 floors are roughly split between cruise bar, dance floor and theme room (you might have to get naked or plait your pubes to enter). Saturday nights are most popular.
✉ 579 Sixth Ave, b/n 16th & 17th St, Chelsea (3, B4) ☎ 366-5464 ⊖ 6th Ave, 14th St (F) 🚌 M5 to M7 ⊘ 5pm-4am

Lure
Popular leather and fetish bar with an exclusively gay crowd and a strictly enforced dress code. Wednesday's entertainment is particularly naughty – it might include body painting, piercing, tattooing or pornographic performances. Dress leather, denim or uniform.
✉ 409 W 13th St &

Ninth Ave, Greenwich Village (3, C2) ☎ 741-3919 ⊖ 14th St (A, C, E), 8th Ave 🚌 M11, M14 ⊘ 8pm-late

Marie's Crisis
A wonderful tavern that caters mostly to older gays. It features piano playing and show tunes that often involve everyone in the place gathering around and joining in for the chorus.
✉ 59 Grove St, near Seventh Ave, Greenwich Village (3, D4) ☎ 243-9323 ⊖ Christopher St 🚌 M8, M10 ⊘ 4pm-4am

The Monster
An up-for-anything club with a piano bar upstairs and a dance floor down below. Drag shows Monday to Wednesday and retro disco on Tuesday. A comfortable place for all ages and races.
✉ 80 Grove St, Greenwich Village (3, D4) ☎ 924-3558 ⊖ Christopher St 🚌 M8, M10 ⊘ 4pm-4am (from 2pm Sat-Sun)

Mother's
Club nights include Friday's Clit Club for gay women – recent themes have included 'Fuzzy Peach Pussy' and 'Fierce Filipinas Kick Ass'. Tuesday is Jackie 60, a long-running night with camp

floor shows and a friendly TV/TS/mixed crowd. Various dress codes are enforced for different nights – call ahead (☎ 929-6060) to check.
✉ 432 W 14th St, Greenwich Village (3, C2) ☎ 366-5680 ✆ www .mothernyc.com ⊖ 14th St (A, C, E), 8th Ave 🚌 M11, M14 ⊘ Tues-Sun 10.30pm-late

Rubyfruit
A civilised gathering place for an older lesbian contingent with a welcoming regular crowd. Dinner is served every night (brunch Saturday only). Weekend entertainment runs from piano bar schmaltz to 50s bop.
✉ 531 Hudson St & W 10 St, Greenwich Village (3, D3) ☎ 929-3343 ⊖ 14th St (A, C, E), 8th Ave 🚌 M8, M10 ⊘ 3pm-2am (from 11.30am Sat)

Splash
Exclusively gay video dance bar with an upmarket crowd and 4 bar areas. There are happy hours and dancers nightly; Monday is reserved for Broadway musical videos.
✉ 50 W 17th St & Sixth Ave, Chelsea (3, B4) ☎ 691-0073 ⊖ 6th Ave, 14th St (F) 🚌 M5, M6, M7 ⊘ 4pm-4am

The Stonewall Rebellion
On 27 June 1969, the Stonewall Inn, a men's bar filled with patrons mourning the death of Judy Garland, was raided by the police. A spirited fightback escalated into 3 nights of riots, galvanising the gay rights movement and conferring sacred site status on Christopher St at Sheridan Square (later renamed Stonewall Place). The Pride March pays homage to the site every year. Today's *Stonewall Inn* (☎ 463-0950), 53 Christopher St (3, D4), though a reasonable gay bar, is not the original.

SPECTATOR SPORT

New Yorkers are a sporty lot, even if they're just watching it on TV in the company of a cold brewski. They fancy themselves the most ardent, knowledgeable and loyal fans anywhere and will happily argue the merits of pitchers, receivers and owners while riding the subway, queuing for brunch or waiting for the opera to start. Baseball and basketball are the most watched sports. Most sporting events can be booked through Ticketmaster (☎ 307-7171).

Baseball

The game that became known as baseball was first called the 'New York game' when its rules were written down in 1846. Baseball traditions that began in New York include the eating of hot dogs at the game (1900) and the playing of 'Take Me Out to the Ball Game' (1908).

The professional baseball teams in the city today are the Mets (National League) and the Yankees (American League). When the Yankees won the World Series in 1996, 3 million people lined Broadway for the parade. Brooklyn is still hurting from the departure of the Dodgers to Los Angeles in 1957. The baseball season runs April to October.

Basketball

Basketball was invented in Massachusetts but New York is its heartland. New York's NBL team is the Knicks – Spike Lee and Woody Allen are big fans. Ticket scarcity, player strikes and the heartbreak of nearly getting there so often have led many basketball fans to turn to the successful New York Liberty women's team. Both teams play at Madison Square Garden.

Football

NY Giants tickets sell out years in advance; season tickets are hotly contested in divorce battles and are left to children in wills. Jets tickets are easier, though not easy, to come by. The season runs from September to January.

Ice Hockey

The New York Rangers play (Oct to Apr) at Madison Square Garden. Their rivals, the New York Islanders, play at Nassau Veterans Memorial Coliseum.

Tennis

The US Open is the year's final Grand Slam event (with the finals played over the Labor Day weekend). The tournament tends to have a show-stopping Broadway aspect – champion players either seem to excel here (Jimmy Connors) or bomb out (Bjorn Borg). At Flushing Meadows, around 600,000 spectators each year watch top players vie for a lion's share of the $14.5 million prize pool. Reserved tickets are only required for Arthur Ashe Stadium, which is sold out months ahead. Call to check for last-minute Arthur Ashe tickets. Scalpers also sell overpriced tickets as you come off the train. Day-session grounds passes are sold on the morning of each day's play – if you are in line before 9am you might snag just one.

Giants Stadium

Part of the Meadowlands Sports Complex, which also includes the Continental Airlines Arena, this 80,000 seat football stadium is home to the Giants and the Jets, and the MetroStars soccer team.
✉ East Rutherford, NJ (4, B1) ☎ 201-935-3900 @ www.meadowlands.com 🚊 Lincoln Tunnel to Route 3, W NJ Turnpike; take ext 16W (Garden St Pkwy) to ext 153A, then Route 3 E 🚌 M'lands bus from Port Authority (2, M4)

Madison Square Garden (2, N5)

This 20,000 seat venue hosts all sorts of events, from concerts to motivational seminars. It's home to basketball teams – the Knicks (Nov-June) and the Liberty (Apr- Sept) – and the New York Rangers ice hockey team (Oct-Apr). Most Knicks tickets are hard to get as they are sold as part of season packages. Liberty and Rangers tickets are easier to come by.
✉ Seventh Ave & W 33rd St, Midtown ☎ 465-MSG, 1 Knicks 465-JUMP, Liberty 564-WNBA @ www.thegarden.com; www.wnba.com/liberty; www.nyknicks.com; www.newyorkrangers.com ⊖ Penn Station 🚌 M4, M10 ⚥ alcohol-free family area

Nassau Veterans Memorial Coliseum

This 16,000-seat ice hockey arena is all enclosed. It's also home to the New York Saints indoor lacrosse team. It's usually possible to pick up tickets for individual games.
✉ 1255 Hempstead Turnpike, Uniondale, Long Is (5, C3) ☎ 516-794-9300 @ www.newyorkislanders.com 🚊 Whitestone Bridge to Cross Is Pkwy S to Grand Central Pkwy E, take ext 31A to Meadowbank Pkwy S to ext M4 ⊖ LIRR to Hempstead, then Bus N70, N71 or N72

National Tennis Center

Planes from La Guardia fly overhead, trains clatter past outside, the crowds aren't necessarily polite, but the atmosphere is often electric. Arthur Ashe Stadium is the centrepiece of a 1997 renovation that turned Flushing Meadows into a truly world-class facility.
✉ Flushing Meadows-Corona Pk, Queens (4, B4) ☎ 760-6200, booking 888-OPEN-TIX/673-6849 or 718-760-6200, court assignment 718-592-5024 @ www.usta.com 🚊 Grand Central Pkwy to Shea Stadium ext, follow signs to Flushing Meadows ⊖ Shea Stadium-Willets Point (7) ⏰ 10am-end play ⑤ 1st week tickets $25; 2nd week: $35 ⚥ yes

Shea Stadium

An ugly duckling but not a bad place to eat peanuts, drink beer and – oh yeah – watch a baseball game.
✉ Flushing Meadows, Queens (4, B4) ☎ Mets 718-507-8499, Ticketmaster 307-7171 @ www.mets.com 🚊 ⊖ see previous listing 🚢 NY Waterways ferry from Sth St Seaport (☎ 800-53-FERRY) ⏰ most games at 1.30 or 7:30pm ⚥ alcohol-free family area

Yankee Stadium (4, A2)

Famous home of the most successful team in baseball's history. Built in 1923 and renovated in 1976, it is still referred to as the 'House that Ruth Built' – it was partly designed to suit his hitting style and seat the fans who came to see him.
✉ 161st St & River Ave, The Bronx ☎ Yankees 718-293-6000 @ www.yankees.com ⊖ 161st St-Yankee Stad 🚢 NY W'ways ferry from Sth St Seaport (☎ 800-53-FERRY) ⏰ most games at 1.30 or 7.30pm ⚥ alcohol-free family area

Yoo-hoo – Yankee heaven

Babe Ruth

George Herman Ruth (1895-1948) is the most famous Yankee. Known as 'The Babe' or the 'Sultan of Swat', the left-handed slugger was baseball's first superstar, an icon whose on and off field charisma helped make baseball the national pastime. Ruth was the first to hit 3 home runs in a game (in the 1926 World Series), was an early inductee into Baseball's Hall of Fame, and starred as himself in the 1942 film *Pride of the Yankees*.

places to stay

Accommodation in New York is tight all year round and there are some exceptional places to stay. Your options include some of the grandest hotels in the world, hip boutique hotels, anonymous but bustling mid-priced places, private guest-houses and cheaper lodges. New York has a desperate shortage of reasonably priced hotels – rooms under $80 a night are usually only found in dives or shared-room hostels.

Price Range

The price ranges in this chapter indicate the cost per night of a standard double room.

Top End $300+
Mid-Range $150-299
Budget   under $150

If you can, book well in advance and confirm your arrival date with the hotel a week before you intend to arrive. When booking, ask about reduced weekend rates and other packages that can include upgraded rooms, complimentary meals and car services. Be sure to allow for taxes, which add a hefty slug to your bill and are rarely included in quoted room rates. As well as 13.25% in city and state taxes, there's a $2 occupancy tax for each normal-sized room.

Booking Agencies

Booking agencies reserve rooms in bulk, supposedly giving them the buying power to pass on large discounts. The mid-range hotel rates they offer don't usually drop much below the rack rate, though they do a better job with higher cost accommodation. The following provide efficient service.

- Express Reservations
  (☎ 303-440-8481, 800-407-3351;
  www.express-res.com)
- Central Reservations Service
  (☎ 407-740-6442, 800-555-7555;
  www.reservation-services.com)
- Hotel Discounts (☎ 800-715-7666;
  www.hoteldiscounts.com)

A well-established New York B&B agency, At Home In New York (☎ 956-3125; athomeny@erols.com), has about 300 guest rooms all over Manhattan. Its rates tend to be a little higher than those charged by the cheapest hotels.

If you are travelling to New York on impulse, or that friend of a friend with a spare bed in his SoHo loft suddenly has the parents arrive from California, get on the phone or the Internet straight away to line something up for your arrival. A last minute bed hunt is more likely to mean a series of dead ends than cheap standby room rates, though you could be lucky. If your first choices are full, consider spending more for a night's accommodation so you can hunt around for something cheaper while you at least have a roof over your head.

The Waldorf-Astoria, more than just a salad.

TOP END & DELUXE

If money grows on your trees, you won't do better than New York's finest hotels. Take as standard impeccable service, excellent climate control, 24hr room service, premium cable TV, data ports, a fax machine and a large tub.

Four Seasons (2, J7)
This IM Pei/Frank Williams-designed limestone monolith is the tallest hotel in New York (52 floors) and has the largest rooms. Children are so welcome they get balloons, milk and cookies on arrival. The public spaces are epic: pop in for a drink even if you're not a guest.
✉ 57 E 57th St, b/w Park & Madison Aves, Midtown ☎ 758-5700; fax 758-5711
@ www.fourseasons.com
🚇 5th Ave (N, R), 59th St (4, 5, 6), Lexington Ave (N, R) 🚌 M1 to M4, M31, M57 ✕ Fifty Seven Fifty Seven Restaurant & Bar, Lobby Lounge

The Michelangelo
An escape from anonymous chains, this hotel is owned by an Italian family with an eye for guest comfort. The rooms are spacious, you could bathe a pony in the tub and there's a limousine service to Wall St.
✉ 152 W 51st & Seventh Ave, Midtown (2, K5)
☎ 765-0505; fax 581-7618 @ www.michelangelohotel.com 🚇 50th St (1,9); 49th St 🚌 M6, M7, M50 ✕ Limoncello

Parker-Meridien
A matter-of-fact eliteness pervades this hotel, from the so-low-key-it's-almost-secret lobby to the 'go away' swingtags. And if the studied elegance of the room isn't enough, suite-dwellers can savour the Central Park view. Tennis players and officials stay here during the US Open partly because of the well-equipped fitness centre and large pool with a view.
✉ 118 W 57th St, Midtown (2, J5) ☎ 245-5000; fax 708-7477
@ nysales@parkermeridien.com; www.parkermeridien.com 🚇 57th St (B, Q, N, R) 🚌 M5 to M7, M31, M57
✕ Norma's, Seppi's

Peninsula
Gorgeous rooms feature one-touch mood lighting, in-room temperature display and a privacy button to deactivate your doorbell. The pool is almost big enough for laps and the Pen-Top bar is tops amongst sunset watching Manhattanites.
✉ E 55th St & Fifth Ave, Midtown (2, J6) ☎ 956-2888; fax 903-3949
@ pny@peninsula.com 🚇 5th Ave (E, F), 51st St 🚌 M1 to M5 ✕ Adrienne, Pen-Top Bar, Gotham Lounge & Bistro

The Pierre
The only trouble with the Pierre is that it's so nice you'll have a hard time leaving your room – no-one's going to be this friendly and attentive once you hit the street. If you go get outside, you'll love the location: b/n Central Park and Madison Ave's top shops.
✉ Fifth Ave & 61st St, Upper E Side (2, H6) ☎ 838-8000; fax 826-0319 🚇 5th Ave (N, R) 🚌 M1 to M4 ✕ The Rotunda, Cafe Pierre

St Regis
Gorgeous beaux-arts building in the heart of the city with large comfy rooms and impeccable, discrete service. The King Cole bar downstairs lays claim to inventing the Bloody Mary.
✉ 2 E 55th & Fifth Ave, Midtown (2, J6) ☎ 753-4500; fax 787-3447
🚇 57th St (B, Q) 🚌 M1 to M5 ✕ Lespinasse

Soho Grand Hotel
The industrial chic entrance – doof and buffed metal – sets the scene. This comfort zone for the young and splashy – and their pooches – prides itself on being pet-friendly. Your mutt or moggy can sleep in your room, and the hotel will supply the petless with a goldfish. There's even a laundermutt on site.
✉ 310 W Broadway, near Canal St (3, G5)
☎ 965-3000; fax 965-3200 @ www.sohogrand.com 🚇 Canal St (A, C, E) 🚌 M6 ✕ Canal House

Waldorf-Astoria
(2, K7) A treasure that is showing some wear and tear, so its cheaper than its counterparts. Its pleasant rooms have sitting areas and kitchenettes – though some can be dim.
✉ 301 Park Ave, Mid town ☎ 355-3000; fax 872-7272 @ www.waldorf-nyc.com 🚇 51st St, Lexington Ave (E, F) 🚌 M1 to M4, M27, M50, M101 to M103
✕ Oscar's, Inagiku, Bull & Bear, Peacock Alley

MID-RANGE

Most of Manhattan's hotels fall into this price range. Expect private bathrooms – usually with a bath – often a fax machine, sizable closets, air-con and voicemail.

Ameritania

Popular with groups and families, this well-staffed hotel has adequate rooms and a Broadway location. Rooms of the same price vary a lot in size – ask for a larger room when booking.
✉ **230 W 54th St & Broadway, Midtown (2, J5)** ☎ **247-5000; fax 247-3313** ⓔ **www.ny citihotels.net** Ⓜ **7th Ave** 🚌 **M6, M7, M10, M104**

Private (non-car) park thrown in at the Gramercy Park.

Michelle Bennett

Clarion Hotel

Aimed at leisure travellers, families and budgeting business folk, this place has all the facilities but none of the flash. The location is great, the kids-free policy enticing and the rooms workable.
✉ **3 E 40th & Fifth Ave, Midtown (2, M6)** ☎ **447-1500; fax 685-5214** ⓔ **ww.clarionhotel.com** Ⓜ **42nd St/Grand Central** 🚌 **M1 to M5, M42**

Comfort Inn

If you want Midtown and you're not planning to lounge around the hotel room, this 'inn' should be fine. The rooms are forgettable but adequate, the service won't

have you screaming nor exclaiming and you can roll home from Broadway.
✉ **129 W46th St, b/w B'way & Sixth Ave, Times Sq (2, L5)** ☎ **221-2600; fax 764-7481** Ⓜ **42nd St (B, D, F, Q), Rockefeller Cr** 🚌 **M5 to M7, M10**

Gramercy Park Hotel

Not as charming as it claims to be but this comfortable old favourite has more character than bland newer hotels. Guests have the bonus of access to locked, lovely Gramercy Park and the Gothic National Arts Club mansion.
✉ **2 Lexington Ave & 21st St, Gramercy Park (3, A6)** ☎ **475-4320;**

fax **505-0535** Ⓜ **Union Sq** 🚌 **M1 to M3, M101 to M103** ✗ **Gramercy Park Hotel Restaurant**

Holiday Inn

Small rooms with no surprises; the location and the price are the drawcards. You're in the middle of Chinatown and easy walking distance to Lower Manhattan, SoHo and Tribeca. Faxes are only provided in suites.
✉ **138 Lafayette St, near Canal St, Chinatown (3, G6)** ☎ **966-8898; fax 966-3933** ⓔ **holinn soho@aol.com** Ⓜ **Canal St (N, R, S, 6)** 🚌 **M1 (p/time), M6** ✗ **Pacifica**

Hotel Gershwin

NYC dream: you enter a red and black super-cred lobby, line up with the groove train for the slooooow elevator (ignoring the Warhol-signed soup can on the wall). You enter a spacious room with modish pop furniture, freshen up in your jaunty bathroom, watch TV from the bed without wrenching your neck. Doze off. Wake up. It was no dream.
✉ **7 E 27th St, Midtown**

Gay & Lesbian Accommodation

You're unlikely to find any hotel in New York blinking an eyelid at same sex couples sharing, though some are more welcoming than others. The *Washington Square Hotel* (p. 105) and the *Gramercy Park Hotel* (this page) are gay-friendly. The *Colonial House Inn* (☎ 243-9669), 318 W 22nd St (2, P4), and the *Chelsea Pines Inn* (☎ 929-1023), 317 W 14th St (3, C3), are popular with gay men. The deluxe *Mercer Hotel* (☎ 966-6060), 99 Prince St (3, E5), welcomes guests in any configuration.

(2, O6) ☎ 545-8000; fax 684-5546 @ gershwin hotel@pobox.com; www.gershwinhotel.com ⊙ 28th St (N, R) 🚍 M2, M3, M5 to M7 ✗ Gershwin Cafe

Hotel Grand Union

Newly refurbished rooms with a comfortable feel, HBO cable TV and large tubs. Not the place to come if you want to be coddled – the staff don't put on any airs but are nevertheless efficient. Family or quad rooms are a good deal.
✉ 34 E 32nd St, b/w Madison & Park Aves, Midtown (2, N7) ☎ 683-5890; fax 689-7397 ⊙ 33rd St 🚍 M1 to M3, M16, M34 ✗ Tony's Burger

The Lucerne

A welcome addition to the neighbourhood, this composed hotel has location, comfort and value all sewn up. Try to snag a street-facing room for more light and better views – the corner suites aren't much pricier than the deluxe rooms.
✉ 201 W 79th St & Amsterdam Ave, Upper W Side (2, E3) ☎ 875-1000; fax 721-1179 ⊙ 79th St 🚍 M7, M11, M79 ✗ Wilson's

On The Ave

Somewhat chaotic on opening, this reinvigorated hotel has the potential to wear in well. The rooms are stylish, well lit, with clever fittings such as stainless steel sinks. The superior rooms don't win for size, they're just a little more ornate.
✉ 2178 Broadway & 77th St, Upper W Side (2, E3) ☎ 362-1100; fax 787-9521 @ www.ontheave-nyc.com ⊙ 79th St 🚍 M5, M7, M104

Roosevelt Hotel

A massive hotel with newly renovated large rooms, many with excellent natural light. There's a small fitness centre, a cigar lounge and Playstation in every room. Adjoining rooms make this a good choice for families.
✉ Madison Ave & 45th St, Midtown (2, L6) ☎ 661-9600; fax 885-6161 ⊙ 42nd St/Grand Central 🚍 M1 to M5 ✗ Madison Club Cigar Lounge, Palm Lounge

The Time

A new hotel frequented by the young and snappy. Its small rooms are stylish, decked out in solid primary colours (check with your aura-therapist before you reserve) with Bose sound systems and impeccable bathrooms (most shower only).
✉ 224 W 49th St, b/w B'way & Eight Ave, Times Sq (3, K5) ☎ 246-5252; fax 245-2305 ⊙ 50th St (1, 9) 🚍 M10, M27, M50, M104 ✗ Palladin

Washington Square Hotel

Cramped rooms in a friendly hotel that rides on its great location and its history (Bob Dylan lived here for a while). If you just need a crash pad after a day of mooching around the Village, this hotel will suit fine.
✉ 103 Waverly Place, b/w Fifth & Sixth Aves, Greenwich Village (3, D4) ☎ 777-9515; fax 979-8373 @ wshotel@ix.netcom.com; www.wshotel.com ⊙ W 4th St 🚍 M5, M6, M21 ✗ C3 Restaurant & Bar

BUDGET

People may begin giggling when you ask about budget accommodation in New York – it is largely a laughable concept. The places listed here offer reasonable, if not luxurious facilities and most are shared-bath affairs.

Amsterdam Inn

Clean budget rooms with TV and phone. Some rooms share a bath, but there are enough communal ones to go around. Beware the 5-floor walk-up if you're way upstairs. No credit cards.
✉ 340 Amsterdam Ave & 76th St, Upper W Side (2, E3) ☎ 579-7500; fax 579-6127 @ www.amsterdaminn.com ⊙ 79th St (1, 9) 🚍 M7, M11, M79

Hotel 17

This slightly grubby labyrinth is popular with slumming minor celebrities and ex-backpackers. Some rooms are real gems – spacious and atmospheric – while others are small and junky. Whatever – it's always packed: take what you can get. No children under 17.
✉ 225 E 17th St, b/w Second & Third Aves, Greenwich Village (3, B6) ☎ 475-2845; fax 677-8178 @ www.citysearch.com/nyc/hotel17

🅔 Union Sq 🚌 M15, M101 to M103

Herald Square Hotel

Purpose-built in the 1890s to house *Life* magazine, the golden cherub that graced the cover of the magazine still sits above the doorway. These days it oversees low prices, good rooms and a constant stream of guests. Singles have a choice of share or private bath; all larger rooms have baths. Great value quad and family rooms.

✉ 19 W 31st St, b/w Fifth Ave & B'way, Midtown (2, N6) ☎ 279-4017; fax 643-9208 🅔 www.heraldsquare hotel.com 🅔 33rd St 🚌 M2, M3, M5 to M7

Hotel Hayden Hall

A large private hotel with great rates on rooms that don't exactly sparkle but aren't grimy either. Single women might feel a little unnerved by the working fella atmosphere but there's not too much to worry about.

✉ 117 W 79th St, Upper W Side (2, E3) ☎ 787-4900; fax 496-3975 🅔 79th St, 81st St 🚌 M7, M11, M79

Hotel Madison

This gruff but well-meaning hotel veers between characterful and depressing. Rooms range from 'cosy' to spacious (if a little dim) and the bathrooms are adequate but bathless. The sign at check-in states 'we accommodate transients', which gives you an idea of your fellow clientele, but the price is right.

✉ 21 E 27th St & Madison Ave, Midtown (2, O6) ☎ 532-7373; fax 686-0092 🅔 madi hotel@aol.com

www.madison-hotel.com 🅔 28th St 🚌 M2, M3

Hotel 31

Reasonably spacious and comfortable hotel popular with backpacking couples splurging for a few days in the big smoke. There's a choice of rooms with shared bathrooms or private – all doubles.

✉ 120 E 31st St, Midtown (2, N7) ☎ 685-3060; 532-1232 🅔 hotel31@worldnet.att .net 🅔 33rd St 🚌 M1, M101 to M103

Hotel Wolcott

The rooms don't live up to the fancy beaux-arts marble-and-mirrors lobby but they're spacious and not bad for the price, especially if you're sharing (some rooms can accommodate four). Ask for the $100 rate on double rooms.

✉ 4 W 31st St, Midtown (2, N6) ☎ 268-2900; fax 563-0096 🅔 www.wolcott .com 🅔 33rd St, 34th St/Herald Sq 🚌 M2, M3, M5, M16

Lil's Guest House

An appealing guesthouse with only 6 rooms but all of them light, spacious and pleasant. All travellers will appreciate the home comforts and the low tariffs but the private bathrooms, fully equipped kitchens and kid-

friendly management make this a great choice for families. Weekly rates available.

✉ 270 E 7th St, b/w Aves C & D, E Village (3, D9) ☎ 777-5270; fax 777-5270 🅔 1st Ave, Delancey/Essex Sts 🚌 M9, M21

Murray Hill Inn

Small but workable good-value rooms with air-con (some sleep 4). It's all stairs up to the 5th floor, so ask for a lower level room if you don't fancy obligatory stair-master sessions. The owners are opening up similar inns in Manhattan – ask about them if this one is full (it often is).

✉ 143 E 30th St & Third Ave, Midtown (2, N7) ☎ 683-6900; fax 545-0103 🅔 murhillin@ aol.com; www.murray-hillinn.com 🅔 28th St (6) 🚌 M101 to M103

Off Soho Suites

This is close to SoHo and excellent value for families or groups – the suites are clean without being fancy and sleep up to 4 in 2 rooms. There's air-con, voice mail and a good-sized kitchen and bathroom.

✉ 11 Rivington St, Lower E Side (3, F7) ☎ 979-9808; fax 979-9801 🅔 www .offsoho.com ✕ Off Soho Suites Cafe 🅔 B'way/ Lafayette St, Spring St (6) 🚌 M9, M15

Travelling with Children

Most hotels welcome children and will set up camp beds in guest rooms at no extra charge. The fancier hotels offer extras like special room service menus, video games and toys. Check the cut-off age for such privileges when reserving your room. A surprising number of New York hotels also welcome kids of the 4 legged variety – see the *Soho Grand* (p. 103).

facts for the visitor

Richard l'Anson

PRE-DEPARTURE
Travel Requirements

Passport
Your passport must be valid for at least 6 months after your intended stay in the USA. Technically, Canadians don't need a passport, but they still need proof of citizenship with photo ID.

Visa
Visas are not required by most visitors, depending on length of stay. Citizens of Australia, New Zealand, Ireland, the United Kingdom and of some other countries may enter for 90 days or less without a visa. Those not covered by the visa waiver exemption and people wishing to stay for extended periods need to obtain a visa from a US consulate or embassy. Ultimately, length of stay is determined by officials at the US point of entry.

Return/Onward Ticket
A return ticket that is non-refundable in the USA is required to enter the country.

Immunisations
No specific immunisations are required to enter the USA.

Travel Insurance
A policy covering theft, loss, medical expenses and compensation for cancellation or delays in your travel arrangements is highly recommended.

Driving Licence
If you intend to drive, you will need a licence from your home country.

Keeping Copies
Keep photocopies of important documents with you, separate from the originals, and leave a copy at home. You can also store details of documents in Lonely Planet's free online Travel Vault, password-protected and accessible worldwide. Visit the Web site at www.ekno.lonelyplanet.com for details.

Tourist Information Abroad

The USA has no national tourist offices abroad. See page 113 for New York-based information services and visit the Web sites listed on page 116.

Climate & When to Go

There are always *lots* of tourists in New York City, although numbers decline slightly in January/ February. The most pleasant and temperate times to visit are May, early June and from mid-September to October. As these times are popular with tourists, hotel prices can be scaled accordingly. Long periods of wet weather are common in November and April. Snow falls are almost exclusively confined to December, January and February. High average temperatures and humidity, together with poor air quality, can make summer in New York an uncomfortable experience. Luckily most hotels, restaurants and shops are air-conditioned.

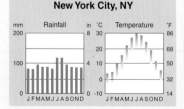

ARRIVAL & DEPARTURE

New York is readily accessible from most places in the world and from within the USA. There are direct flights from London, Dublin, Paris and other European cities, Mexico and Central and South American cities. Flights from Australia and New Zealand travel via San Francisco or Los Angeles. Many flights from Asian destinations travel via Honolulu.

Air

There are 3 international airports servicing New York, and the Air Ride line (☎ 800-247-7433) has information on transport to/from all of them.

JFK International Airport (4, C5)

John F Kennedy International Airport, in south-eastern Queens, is 15.5 miles (45 to 75mins by road) from Midtown, Manhattan. For general inquiries and/or flight information, call ☎ 718-244-4444. There are left-luggage facilities at terminals 1 and 4 for approximately $5 per bag; you can exchange currency at the same terminals from 7am to 10pm.

American Airlines, British Airways, Delta and TWA have their own terminals. All other airlines use the International Arrivals Building. Yellow and white courtesy buses run between terminals every 5 to 15mins.

Airport Access

Car Park The fee in the long-term car park costs $8 per day. Courtesy buses regularly run the 20min trip between the car park and the terminals. In the short-term car park you will pay $2 for 30mins, or $24 per day.

Bus The New York Airport Service (☎ 718-706-9658) runs buses every 15 to 30mins from 5am to 10pm from Park Ave, between 41st and 42nd Sts (2, L7), and every 30mins from 5.40am to 10.10pm from the Port Authority bus terminal (2, M4). You should allow 60 to 75mins for the trip; the fare is $13.

Taxi The fare to Manhattan is a flat $30 plus tolls and tip. The flat fare rate is not available outbound to the airport.

Shared Ride You can expect to pay approximately $16 per person for this service; call SuperShuttle on ☎ 258-3826.

Car Service Expect to pay around $40. Some operators include Big Apple (☎ 718-232-1015), Citywide (☎ 718-405-9393) or Dial (☎ 718-743-2877).

Subway The train ride to Howard Beach-JFK station takes around 1hr from Midtown, Manhattan; from the station catch the Long Term Parking Bus to the terminal.

La Guardia Airport (4, B3)

This airport is in northern Queens, 8 miles (20-45mins drive) from Midtown, Manhattan. For general inquiries and flight information call ☎ 718-533-3400.

Left-luggage facilities are available on the departure level of Central terminal, for around $5 for each bag. Currency exchange facilities are available between concourses B and C and are open from 7am to 9pm.

US Airways and Delta use the Marine Air/Delta Shuttle terminal; all other airlines use Central terminal. Red, white and blue courtesy buses visit the terminals at 10min intervals.

Airport Access

Car Park Long-term parking costs $24 for the first day and $10 per-day thereafter; short-term parking is $2 for 30mins, or $24 per day.

Boat The Delta Water Shuttle (☎ 800-221-1212) runs from the Marine Air/Delta Shuttle terminal to the 90th St, 62nd St, and 34th St piers and to Pier 11 (Wall St). The fare is $15.

Bus Take the M60 public bus service. Alternatively, use the New York Airport Service (☎ 718-706-9658), which has a bus leaving every 20mins between 6am and midnight. It costs $10 and the trip takes 45mins.

Taxi The fare is around $15-25 plus tolls and tips.

Shared Ride SuperShuttle (☎ 258-3826) charges approximately $14 per person.

Car Service Expect to pay around $30 plus tolls and tips. Contact the services listed in the JFK airport section.

Newark International Airport (4, E1)

Situated in New Jersey, 10 miles west of Manhattan, Newark is a 30 to 60min drive from the city. For general inquiries/flight information call ☎ 973-961-6000. Terminal B has currency exchange facilities which open from 7am to 9pm. There is no left-luggage office at Newark.

Terminals A and C are domestic while terminal B is international. All terminals and most car parks are linked by monorail.

Airport Access

Car Park Long-term parking costs $8 per day. You should allow 20mins for the courtesy bus trip to the terminals. Short-term parking costs $2 for 30mins, or $24 a day. A monorail links most car parks to the terminals.

Bus Take Olympia Trails (☎ 964-6233) from the Port Authority bus terminal (2, M4), Penn station (2, N5), Grand Central Station (2, L7) or the World Trade Center (3, J5); the fare is $10.

Taxi It costs approximately $45 from Newark to the city plus $10 for tolls and extra for tips.

Shared Ride Expect to pay around $19 per person.

Car Service This is available from around $48. See the services listed in the earlier JFK airport section.

Bus

Long-distance and commuter buses arrive at and depart from the Port Authority bus terminal (2, M4; ☎ 564-8484), 41st St & Eighth Ave, near Times Square.

Train

Long-distance trains (Amtrak) arrive at Pennsylvania (Penn) station (2, N5; call ☎ 582-6875 for station information or ☎ 800-872-7245 for reservations and schedules). Commuter trains (Metro-North) use Grand Central Station (2, L7; ☎ 532-4900). New Jersey PATH (Port Authority Trans-Hudson) trains (☎ 800-234-7284) stop at several stations throughout Manhattan.

Customs

If you are carrying more than $10,000 in US and/or foreign cash, travellers cheques or money orders when you enter the USA, you must declare it.

You can import 1L of liquor (if you are over the age of 21); 200 cigarettes, 50 cigars (provided they are not Cuban) or 2kg of tobacco; and gifts up to a total value of $100 (or $400 if you are a US citizens).

Departure Tax

Departure taxes are included in the price of your air ticket.

GETTING AROUND

Manhattan's entire grid system is packed with traffic during the day ('gridlock'). The subway is generally the fastest, cheapest way to get around – statistically it's safer than walking the streets in broad daylight. City buses can be useful if you are travelling north-south along the same avenue provided the traffic is moving. Nearly every subway booth has a good bus and subway map. Taxis are the most convenient way to get around after 10pm.

Travel Passes

Metrocard (☎ 718-330-1234) is the most convenient way to pay for travel on New York's public transport system. Regular refillable cards are available for $3 or more. If you spend $15 you get a $1.50 bonus; spending $20 gives you a $2 bonus; and spending $30 scores you $3 – that's 2 free rides!). A 1 day unlimited pass is $4 and a weekly pass costs $17. You can transfer between buses and subways within a 2hr period when using the Metrocard system.

Subway

The subway system (☎ 718-330-1234) runs 24hrs a day over 26 different routes linking 469 stations. It's a rattly, often smelly and uncomfortable network but it does get you around ... usually. Most Manhattan venues are accessible by several subway lines. If you are not using Metrocard, you can buy single-use tokens ($1.50) from station booths.

Bus

City buses (☎ 718-927-7499) operate 24hrs a day, generally north and south along avenues and crosstown along the major thoroughfares. Buses that begin and end in a borough are prefixed accordingly: ie, M5 for Manhattan, Q32 for Queens, B51 for Brooklyn, and Bx13 for The Bronx. Some 'Limited Stop' buses pull over only every 10 blocks or so, but at night you can ask to be let off at any point along the route.

You need exact change of $1.50, a Metrocard or a subway token to board a bus. 'Express' buses ($4-6.50) are primarily for outer-borough commuters, not for people taking short trips.

Train

New Jersey PATH (Port Authority Trans-Hudson) trains (☎ 800-234-7284) are part of a separate fare system that runs down Sixth Ave to Jersey City and Newark, with stops at 34th, 23rd, 14th, 9th and Christopher Sts along the way. A second line runs from the World Trade Center to northern New Jersey. These reliable and inexpensive trains (called 'Hudson Tubes' when they first opened) run every

15mins. The fare is $1, and machines accept coins and dollar bills.

Taxi

Taxis are available for hire when the rooftop licence number is alight (as opposed to the 'off duty' side lights). Fares are metered and posted in each car and kick in at $2; tip from 10 to 15% (minimum 50¢). For trips longer than 50 blocks, instruct the driver to take a road well away from Midtown traffic. Watch for tampered meters that turn over every 20 seconds or so while the cab is stationary.

Limousine

Limousines and car services can be a convenient and cheap way to travel, especially if you are part of a group, you've got a lot to carry or you're on your way to the airport. Affordable Limousine Service (☎ 730-6666) and Carmel (☎ 666-6666) rates are about $45 per hour for 1 to 4 people; a night on the town for 8 costs $120 for 3hrs.

Boat

New York Waterway (☎ 800-533-3779) has several ferry routes, including up the Hudson River Valley and from Midtown to Yankee Stadium (4, A2) in The Bronx. A popular commuter route runs from New Jersey Transit train station, Hoboken (4, C2) to the World Financial Center in Lower Manhattan (3, J4); boats leave up to every 5 to 10mins in peak time; a 10min ride costs $2 each way.

The New York Water Taxi company (☎ 681-8111) runs spring and summer ferries from various points along the Hudson and East rivers and has a combo deal with Gray Line Bus Tours.

Car & Motorcycle

Traffic congestion, the high incidence of theft and the expense of rental, parking and petrol more than offset any convenience afforded by having a car in New York: if you travel in your own vehicle, you are likely to spend 15mins finding a parking spot and 15mins walking to your destination in which case you would have been better off taking public transport.

Major institutions and businesses are generally willing to reserve parking spots for disabled drivers – call ahead to confirm availability. Disabled parking permits for public parking places are only available to New York residents.

Road Rules

Drive on the right hand side of the road. Turn right at a red light only if a sign specifically permits it and don't block intersections – the wrath of other drivers is worse than the stiff penalties you may incur. All front seat occupants must wear seat belts; all back seat occupants under the age of 10 must wear seatbelts or another suitable restraint.

Driving while your ability is impaired by drugs or alcohol is forbidden; specifically, driving with a blood alcohol level of 0.1% or more is against the law. The state maximum speed limit is 55mph (just over 70kmh), however you will need to watch for lower limits in built-up areas and school zones.

Car Rental

Car rental rates in New York are expensive, and cheaper airport deals are rare. Most of the time you will be better off making arrangements for some sort of a package deal before you leave.

The main rental agencies in New York include: Avis (☎ 800-331-1212); Budget (☎ 800-527-0700); Dollar (☎ 800-800-4000); Hertz (☎ 800-654-3131) and Thrifty (☎ 800-367-2277). The agencies may try to sell you personal insurance coverage (about $15 per day) but you don't need to take this out if you have medical coverage.

Motoring Organisations

If you are going to be doing a lot of driving, consider joining the AAA (☎ 757-2000), an America-wide auto club that offers driving directions, motoring advice and emergency road service (☎ 800-AAA-HELP). It also acts as a travel agent. Membership will often entitle you to reduced hotel rates.

PRACTICAL INFORMATION

Tourist Information

You can ring the following numbers for specific information:

Time	☎ 976-1616
Weather	☎ 976-1212
Moviefone	☎ 777-FILM
Clubfone	☎ 777-CLUB
NYC On Stage	☎ 768-1818
Restaurant listings	☎ DINE-123

New York Convention & Visitors Bureau

This bureau is a comprehensive booking and information centre with a Web site (www.nycvisit.com) and a 24hr toll-free line which provides listings of special events and reservation details. Call ☎ 800-692 8474 or ☎ 397-8222 (for callers from outside the US and Canada) then press #5 to bypass the recordings and talk to a representative. The bureau is located at 810 Seventh Ave & 53rd St (2, J5). Staff are helpful and knowledgeable and it's open Monday to Friday from 8.30am to 6pm and Saturday and Sunday from 9am to 5pm.

New York State Travel Information Center

This travel centre (☎ 800-225-5697; www.iloveny.state.ny.us), at 1 Commerce Plaza, Albany NY 12245, can provide lots of ideas for recreation, camping and holidays in New York State.

Tourist Information Centres

There are other information counters and centres at airports, in Times Square (2, L5), at Grand Central (2, L7) and Penn (2, N5) stations and also at the Port Authority bus terminal (2, M4).

Big Apple Greeters Program (☎669-8159; www.bigapplegreeter .org), at 1 Centre St, is a useful service that organises volunteers to introduces visitors to the city.

Other Information

For other sources of information about New York City see Newspapers & Magazines (p. 117) and useful Web sites on page 116.

Embassies

The UN's presence in New York means that nearly every country in the world maintains diplomatic offices here. Most are listed in the white pages of the phone book under 'Consulates General of (country)'. Some embassies include:

Australia
150 E 42nd St, Midtown (2, L7)
☎ 351-6500

Canada
1251 Sixth Ave, Midtown (2, K5)
☎ 596-1783

Ireland
345 Park Ave, Midtown (2, K7)
☎ 319-2555

New Zealand
780 Third Ave, Midtown (2, K7)
☎ 832-4038

South Africa
333 E 38th St, Midtown (2, M8)
☎ 213-4880

UK
845 Third Ave, Midtown (2, K7)
☎ 745-0202

Money

Currency
The monetary unit used is the US dollar, which is divided into 100 cents (¢). Coins come in 1¢ (penny), 5¢ (nickel), 10¢ (dime), 25¢ (quarter) and 50¢ (half dollar; rare) denominations. Notes come in $1, $2, $5, $10, $20, $50 and $100. Some shops are hesitant to accept notes in denominations higher than $20.

Travellers Cheques
American Express (☎ 800-221-7282) and Thomas Cook (☎ 800-287-7362) cheques are widely accepted and have efficient replacement policies. Restaurants, hotels and most stores readily accept US-dollar travellers cheques. Fast food restaurants and smaller businesses will sometimes refuse to accept cheques.

Credit Cards
Visa, MasterCard (both affiliated with European Access Cards) and American Express are widely accepted. Discover and Diners Club less so. For lost cards contact:

American Express ☎ 800-992-3404

Diners Club	☎ 800-234-6377
Discover	☎ 800-347-2683
MasterCard	☎ 800-826-2181
Visa	☎ 800-336-8472

Changing Money
Banks often have better deals than bureaux de change. Always check the rates, commissions and any other charges. Citibank doesn't charge foreign account holders a fee for withdrawing cash from its automatic teller (ATMs) machines.

Tipping

Tips are rarely included as a service charge on a hotel or restaurant bill and *must* be given separately. Many restaurants add a 15 to 20% 'tip' to the bill of groups of 6 or more – make sure you don't double up.

Baggage carriers – (skycaps in airports, hotel bellhops) $1 for the first bag; 50¢ for each additional bag

Bars – at least $1 per drink (more for faster service and stronger drinks for your next order)

Cloakroom attendants – $1 for each item

Doormen, bellboys, parking attendants – $1 for each service performed (including opening a taxi door)

Hairdressers – 15%

Restaurants – 15-20% (not expected in fast food, takeaway or self-service restaurants)

Room cleaners – $5 per day (for business travellers only)

Taxis – 10%

Tour guides – $5 per family/group for a full day tour

Discounts & Discount Cards

Students
Accredited US and international students receive discounts at most attractions. Many restaurants and

stores in university areas also offer student discounts.

Seniors
Seniors can expect reduced transit fares and cut rates on hotel charges, drugstore (pharmacy) prescriptions and museum and cinema prices.

Disabled People
The disabled are entitled to reductions on transport fares.

Families
Many attractions admit children up to 12 years of age free or offer reduced price tickets for families.

Opening Hours

Banks
    Mon-Fri 9am-3.30pm; several Chinatown banks along Canal St are open Saturday and Sunday

Post Offices
    Mon-Fri 8am-6pm, Sat 9am-2pm; the main post office is open 24hrs a day

Offices
    Mon-Fri 9am-5pm

Shops
    Mon-Sat 10am-6pm, Sun 12-6pm; some bakeries and clothing shops close Mon

Pharmacies
    Mon-Sat 9am-6pm; some open 24hrs

Tourist Sites
    Tues-Sun 10am-5pm (varies)

Late-Night Shopping
    Thurs (department stores); many book and speciality stores have regular night hours

Public Holidays

1 Jan	New Year's Day
3rd Mon in Jan	Martin Luther King Jr Day
3rd Mon in Feb	Presidents' Day
Mar/Apr	Easter
last Mon in May	Memorial Day
4 July	Independence Day
1st Mon in Sep	Labor Day
2nd Mon in Oct	Columbus Day
11 Nov	Veterans' Day
4th Thurs in Nov	Thanksgiving Day
25 Dec	Christmas Day

On public holidays banks, schools and government offices (including post offices) close and transportation services, museums and other services operate on a Sunday schedule. Holidays falling on a weekend are usually observed the following Monday.

Time

New York is in the Eastern Standard Time (EST) zone, which is 5hrs behind Greenwich Mean Time (GMT). Daylight-saving starts on the first Sunday in April, when the clocks are advanced 1hr; it finishes on the last Saturday in October.

When it is noon in New York City it is:

9am in San Francisco
5pm in London
6pm in Paris
7pm in Cape Town
3am (the next day) in Sydney

Electricity

The voltage in the USA is 110V and 60Hz; plugs have 2 or 3 pins (2 flat pins, often with a round 'grounding' pin); adaptors for European and South American plugs are widely available; Australians should bring adaptors with them.

Weights & Measures

Americans hate the metric system and continue to resist it. Distances are in feet, yards and miles. Dry weights are measured by the ounce, pound and ton; liquid measures differ from dry measures. Gasoline is dispensed by the US gallon (about 20% less than the imperial gallon). US pints and quarts are also 20% less than imperial ones. See page 121 for a Conversion Table.

Post

The main post office (2, N4; ☎ 967-8585) is at 421 Eighth Ave & 33rd St, Midtown; branches are listed in the back of the Yellow Pages phone directory.

Sending Mail
Stamps are available from post office counters. Domestic/international rates are: 33c/60c for letters, 20c/50c for postcards. Buying them from hotel concierges and vending machines in stores costs 25% more.

Opening Hours
The main post office (2, N4) opens 24hrs; the Rockefeller Center post office (2, K6) is open Monday to Friday from 9.30am to 5.30pm; the Franklin D Roosevelt post office at 909 Third Ave (2, J7) is open Monday to Friday from 9am to 8pm and Saturday from 10am to 2pm. See also the Opening Hours section on page 115.

Telephone

The country code for the US is 1. Public phones are either coin or card-operated; some accept credit cards. Bell Atlantic phones are the most reliable. Use a major carrier such as AT&T (☎ 800-321-0288) for long distance calls. Newsstands and pharmacies sell prepaid phonecards but they can be huge rip-offs, charging per-minute prices way higher than those promised.

Lonely Planet's eKno Communication Card, specifically aimed at travellers, provides competitive international calls (avoid using it for local calls), messaging services and free email. Check out www.ekno.com for joining and access information.

Manhattan land lines now have 2 area codes: ☎ 212 and the new ☎ 646. In this book, all numbers are ☎ 212 unless otherwise noted. If you're dialling another area code, even if both numbers are within Manhattan, you must dial ☎ 1, the area code and the number. For the 4 outer boroughs the area codes are ☎ 718 and the new ☎ 347. Pager and cell numbers (and a small number of land lines) begin with ☎ 917.

Useful Numbers

Directory Assistance	☎ 411
International Dialling Code	☎ 011
Operator	☎ 0
Operator-Assisted Calls	☎ 01
(+ the number; an operator will come on the line once you have dialled)	
Reverse-Charge (Collect) Calls	☎ 0

International Codes

Australia	☎ 61
Canada	☎ 1
Japan	☎ 81
New Zealand	☎ 64
South Africa	☎ 27
UK	☎ 44

Email/www

Internet Cafes
If you can't access the Internet from where you're staying, try a cybercafe – New York is full of them, see the listings on page 83 or check the White Pages.

Useful Sites
The Lonely Planet Web site (www.lonelyplanet.com) has New York City information and links. Other good Web sites include:

New York City Search
    newyork.citysearch.com

New York Times
    www.nytimes.com

New York Convention & Visitors' Bureau
www.nycvisit.com

New York City Council
www.ci.nyc.ny.us

New York City Insider
www.theinsider.com/NYC

Doing Business

All top end hotels have business centres with computers, dataports, faxes and admin staff. Some hotels rent space in these centres to nonguests.

PC Computer Rental (☎ 594-2222) rents PC and Mac desktops and laptops for around $200 per week or $300 per month. A $50 delivery and pick-up fee includes any necessary on-site servicing.

Unique Support Services (☎ 406-0062) offer administration assistants on a daily or half-daily basis. Basic word processing rates start at around $25 per hour. Berlitz Translation Services (☎ 917-339-4771) offers translation and interpretation services for documents, meetings and conferences.

The orange *Wall Street Journal* is the daily business bible. *Forbes Magazine*, *Business Week* and the *Economist* are weekly journals for moguls and movers.

Newspapers & Magazines

The *New York Times* is the nation's premier newspaper; its Friday 'Weekend Section' is an invaluable guide to cultural events. The weekly *New York Observer* specialises in local media and politics. The *Daily News* and *New York Post* are popular tabloids. The *Wall Street Journal* is essential financial reading.

Time Out New York is good for 'what's on', eating out and shop-ping; the *New Yorker* magazine lists art, cinema and music events. Free street papers – *Village Voice* and *New York Press* are best known – have good entertainment listings. *Where New York* (from hotels) is the best free monthly guide to mainstream events and museums.

Radio & TV

New York has over 50 radio stations; WBAI 99.5FM is an interesting independent station; WINS 1010AM and WCBS 880AM have continuous news and weather. The 4 major TV networks (NBC, CBS, ABC and FOX) offer familiar evening prime time fare; alternatives are the local New York 1 and the Public Broadcasting Service (PBS). Cable carries well-known networks like CNN, MTV and HBO. Daily newspapers have TV programs; the Sunday *New York Times* has a weekly TV magazine. *TV Guide* comes out weekly at newsstands and supermarkets.

Photography & Video

Print film is widely available at supermarkets and discount drugstores; 35mm slide film is less easy to find. Camera shops stock b&w film. If you purchase a video, note that the USA uses NTSC colour TV standard, which is not compatible with the other standards (PAL or SECAM) used elsewhere in the world.

Health

New York tap water is drinkable and tastes OK. Even so, many residents drink bottled or filtered water. An encephalitis outbreak in late 1999 prompted citywide spraying and advice that residents should wear long sleeves and mosquito repellent, but generally, New York is as healthy as other big, dirty cities.

Insurance & Medical Treatment

Definitely have medical insurance when you enter the USA, as medical care is extremely expensive. Doctors often expect payment on the spot for services rendered.

Medical Services

New York University Medical Center (2, N9; ☎ 263-7300), 550 First Ave & 31st St (bus: M15), is an urgent-care clinic for less-than-catastrophic injuries and illnesses.

New York Hotel Urgent Medical Services (☎ 737-1212) offers medical services including homeopathic and dental care to visitors; doctors make 24hr house (and hotel) calls. Prices from $200 include most medication.

The following hospitals have 24hr casualty and emergency units:

Bellevue Medical Center (2, O8)
(☎ 562-4141) First Ave and 27th St, Gramercy

Lenox Hill Hospital (2, E7)
(☎ 434-2000) 100 E 77th St, between Park and Lexington Aves, Upper East Side

New York Hospital (2, G9)
(☎ 746-5050) 525 E 68th St, between York Ave and Franklin D Roosevelt Dr, Upper East Side; paediatric referrals available here

Dental Services

The Stuyvesant Dentist Association (☎ 473-4151), 430 E 20th St & First Ave (2, P8), can help with general and paediatric dental issues. See also Medical Services above.

Pharmacies & Drugs

Among the 24hr-a-day Duane Reade pharmacies are those on W 57th St & Broadway (2, J4; ☎ 541-9708) and Sixth Ave & Waverly Pl (3, D4; ☎ 674-5357), near the W 4th St subway entrance. Also open 24hrs, Genovese (☎ 772-0104), 1299 Second Ave & 68th St, does deliveries.

HIV/AIDS

Help, advice and support are available from the Gay Men's Health Crisis Hotline (☎ 807-6655).

Emergency Numbers

Police, Fire, Ambulance	☎ 911
Police Information Operator	☎ 374-5000

Toilets

Public toilets are rare, and commercial establishments provide facilities for customers only. If you're in distress, head to a department store or a fast food restaurant.

A word of advice for foreigners: ask for the 'bathroom' or 'restroom' when you want to know where the loo is. Major attractions and large, new restaurants tend to have decent disabled toilets but many smaller restaurants and bars do not.

Safety Concerns

Don't carry money or valuables in a way that will be an obvious temptation, especially in poor areas.

Subway

Don't leave a wallet in your back pocket on the subway. Before you leave a station, be aware of the neighbourhood you're entering.

Beggars & Scams

Panhandlers and hustlers can target tourists but you shouldn't feel obligated to give money. One of the best ways to help the many New Yorkers in need is to donate some time to the City Meals-on-Wheels program (☎ 687-1234).

Drugs

The street drug scene has been largely cleaned up in Manhattan. You may be offered marijuana in Washington Square Park and along St Marks Place in the East Village, but most dealing and using is done discretely. There's a bit of a scene along Amsterdam Ave (between 100th and 114th Sts) and in parts of Washington Heights; move carefully through these areas at night.

At Night

Many streets in New York stay lively till the wee hours and are not any more dangerous at night than they are by day. Generally, avoid places that are deserted or badly lit – most public parks close at midnight. Central Park, considered a no-go area by tourists at night, is quite safe when there's a concert or a play at Delacorte Theater.

Lost Property

Finding lost property is as much a matter of luck in New York as in any city. It's worth keeping current contact details in belongings. The easier you make it for someone to return your belongings, the more likely it is you'll be reunited with them. If you lose something on public transit call ☎ 712-4500. For taxi lost property call ☎ 692-8294.

Women Travellers

Women need not be particularly concerned about travelling on their own in New York City. Though many shun the subways, this fear is unjustified since the transit system has a lower crime rate than the city streets. At night, you might consider riding in the conductor's car (in the middle of the train). If someone stares or acts in an annoying manner, simply move to another part of the car or near the conductor's booth. Women are far more likely to encounter obnoxious behaviour on the street. Most men will take it no further if you ignore them and walk on.

Tampons and pads are widely available, though there's a smaller selection of tampons in the US than in Europe or Australia. The contraceptive pill and 'morning after' pill are available by prescription only.

Information & Organisations

The following provide medical services and advice specifically for women:

Brooklyn Women's Services (☎ 718-748 1234), 9201 Fourth Ave, Brooklyn (4, E3)

Columbia Presbyterian Center for Women's Health (☎ 326-8540), 16 E 60th St (2, H6)

NYC Department of Health Women's Health Line (☎ 230-1111), 280 Broadway (3, J5)

Gay & Lesbian Travellers

New York is one of the most gay-friendly cities on earth and several neighbourhoods – particularly Greenwich Village and Chelsea in Manhattan and Jackson Heights in Queens – are populated by many gays and lesbians. The age of consent for homosexual sex is 17 (the same as for heterosexual sex).

Information & Organisations

The free listings magazines *HX*, *Next* and *LGNY* are available at most restaurants and bars. *Time Out New York* (Wednesday) has a good events section. The literary magazine *Christopher Street* and the lifestyle magazine *Metrosource* are also free at many bars.

Useful counselling, referral and

information centres include:

Gay & Lesbian Hotline
☎ 989-0999; glnh@glnh.org

Lesbian & Gay Community
Services Center
☎ 620-7310

Senior Travellers

New Yorkers tend to be respectful towards older people – you'll usually be offered a seat on public transport and be treated with consideration while you're out and about.

Information & Organisations

The American Association of Retired Persons (AARP; ☎ 800-424-3410), 3200 E Carson St, Lakewood, CA 90712, offers hotel and car hire discounts (10-50%) to over 50s. Membership costs $8 per year for US residents and $10 per year for foreigners.

The mayor's Senior Action Line office (☎ 788-7504; Mon-Fri 11am-1pm) is run by volunteer advisers.

Disabled Travellers

Federal laws require that all government premises have good elevator and ramp access for wheelchairs and hearing loops for the hearing impaired. Almost all major venues have good facilities for visitors using wheelchairs and all city buses are able to carry wheelchair passengers. Only some subway stations are accessible (see MTA maps, Web site or call ☎ 718-596-8585).

Information & Organisations

Useful publications include the city's Access Guide for People with Disabilities and Access for All, available in bookstores. Other helpful organisations include:

Big Apple Greeter
☎ 669-8159

New York Society for the Deaf
☎ 777-3900

People with Disabilities Office
☎ 788-2830, TTY ☎ 788-2838

Public Transport Accessible Line
☎ 718-596-8585, TTY ☎ 718-596-8273

Society for the Advancement of Travel for the Handicapped (SATH) ☎ 447-7284, www.sath.org

State Commission for the Blind
☎ 961-4450

Language

American English has borrowed words from the languages of successive waves of immigrants who made New York City their point of arrival. From Germans have came words like 'hoodlum', from Yiddish-speaking Jews words like 'schmuck' (a 'fool'), and from the Irish words like 'galore'. The large Hispanic population has made Spanish a semi-official second language, though a popular Spanish-English hybrid has not yet evolved, but everyone knows that bodega is slang for a convenience store. Some words and phrases that originated in NY are:

Big time – an all-out effort or massively good thing; eg 'I'm going to get a big-time raise'.

Enough already – a less than polite request to stop; eg 'Enough already with your questions'.

Kick-ass – excellent.

Schlep – a long walk or the act of wandering around aimlessly; eg 'We schlepped around all day looking for that hat'.

Step lively – a subway conductor's command as he closes the doors on a train.

Straphanger – a standing subway rider.

The whole 9 yards – an all-out effort, no costs spared; construction worker lingo derived from the maximum capacity of a cement truck, which is 9 cubic yards.

Conversion Table

Clothing Sizes
Measurements approximate only; try before you buy.

Women's Clothing

Aust/NZ	8	10	12	14	16	18
Europe	36	38	40	42	44	46
Japan	5	7	9	11	13	15
UK	8	10	12	14	16	18
USA	6	8	10	12	14	16

Women's Shoes

Aust/NZ	5	6	7	8	9	10
Europe	35	36	37	38	39	40
France only	35	36	38	39	40	42
Japan	22	23	24	25	26	27
UK	3½	4½	5½	6½	7½	8½
USA	5	6	7	8	9	10

Men's Clothing

Aust/NZ	92	96	100	104	108	112
Europe	46	48	50	52	54	56
Japan	S		M	M		L
UK	35	36	37	38	39	40
USA	35	36	37	38	39	40

Men's Shirts (Collar Sizes)

Aust/NZ	38	39	40	41	42	43
Europe	38	39	40	41	42	43
Japan	38	39	40	41	42	43
UK	15	15½	16	16½	17	17½
USA	15	15½	16	16½	17	17½

Men's Shoes

Aust/NZ	7	8	9	10	11	12
Europe	41	42	43	44½	46	47
Japan	26	27	27.5	28	29	30
UK	7	8	9	10	11	12
USA	7½	8½	9½	10½	11½	12½

Weights & Measures

Length & Distance
1 inch = 2.54cm
1cm = 0.39 inches
1m = 3.3ft
1ft = 0.3m
1km = 0.62 miles
1 mile = 1.6km

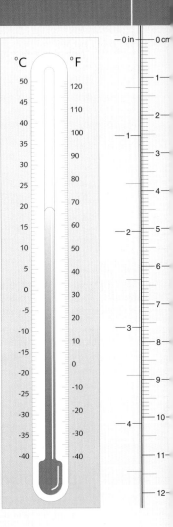

Weight
1kg = 2.2lb
1lb = 0.45kg
1g = 0.04oz
1oz = 28g

Volume
1 litre = 0.26 US gallons
1 US gallon = 3.8 litres
1 litre = 0.22 imperial gallons
1 imperial gallon = 4.55 litres

THE AUTHOR

Dani Valent

It might have kicked her butt from Battery Park to Harlem and back again but Dani Valent can't kick New York. Her blood runs thick with cawfee, her bagel count is in six figures and the Yankees and Mets slug it out in her dreams. An Australian resident who well knows how long the flight from Melbourne to JFK takes, she has been writing Lonely Planet guides since 1995.

ABOUT LONELY PLANET GUIDEBOOKS

The story begins with a classic travel adventure: Tony and Maureen Wheeler's 1972 journey across Europe and Asia to Australia. Useful information about the overland trail did not exist at that time, so Tony and Maureen published the first Lonely Planet guidebook to meet a growing need.

From a kitchen table, then from a tiny office in Melbourne, Australia, Lonely Planet has become the largest independent travel publisher in the world, an international company with offices in Melbourne, Oakland (USA), London (UK) and Paris (France).

Today there are over 400 titles, including travel guides, city maps, cycling guides, first time travel guides, healthy travel guides, travel atlases, diving guides, pictorial books, phrasebooks, restaurant guides, travel literature, walking guides and world food guides.

At Lonely Planet we believe that travellers can make a positive contribution to the countries they visit – if they respect their host communities and spend their money wisely. Since 1986 a percentage of the income from books has been donated to aid projects and human rights campaigns.

ABOUT THE CONDENSED GUIDES

Other Lonely Planet Condensed guides include: *Amsterdam* (due July 2000), *California, Crete, London, Paris* and *Sydney*.

ABOUT THIS BOOK

Series developed by Diana Saad • Edited by Lyn McGaurr and Gabrielle Green • Design & layout by Andrew Weatherill, with assistance from Csanád Csutoros • Maps by Charles Rawlings-Way • Cover design by Indra Kilfoyle and Simon Bracken • Software engineering by Dan Levin • Publishing Manager Mary Neighbour • Thanks to Angus Oborn, Brett Pascoe, Emma Miller, Fiona Croyden, Mary Hagemann, Richard I'Anson, Shelley Preston, Simon Bracken, Tim Uden and Valerie Tellini

LONELY PLANET ONLINE

www.lonelyplanet.com or AOL keyword: lp
Lonely Planet's award-winning Web site has insider info on hundreds of destinations from Amsterdam to Zimbabwe, complete with interactive maps and colour photographs. You'll also find the latest travel news, recent reports from travellers on the road, guidebook upgrades and a lively bulletin board where you can meet fellow travellers, swap recommendations and seek advice.

PLANET TALK

Our FREE quarterly printed newsletter is full of tips from travellers and anecdotes from Lonely Planet authors. Every issue is packed with up-to-date travel news and advice, and includes a postcard from Lonely Planet co-founder Tony Wheeler, mail from travellers, a look at life on the road through the eyes of a Lonely Planet author, topical health advice, prizes for the best travel yarn, news about forthcoming Lonely Planet events and a complete list of Lonely Planet books and products.

To join our mailing list, email us at: go@lonelyplanet.co.uk (UK, Europe and Africa residents); info@lonelyplanet.com (North and South America residents); talk2us@lonelyplanet.com.au (the rest of the world); or contact any Lonely Planet office.

COMET

Our FREE monthly email newsletter brings you all the latest travel news, features, interviews, competitions, destination ideas, travellers' tips & tales, Q&As, raging debates and related links. Find out what's new on the Lonely Planet Web site and which books are about to hit the shelves.

Subscribe from your desktop: www.lonelyplanet.com/comet

LONELY PLANET OFFICES

Australia
PO Box 617, Hawthorn, Victoria 3122
☎ 03 9819 1877 fax 03 9819 6459
email: talk2us@lonelyplanet.com.au

USA
150 Linden St, Oakland, CA 94607
☎ 510 893 8555 TOLL FREE: 800 275 8555
fax 510 893 8572
email: info@lonelyplanet.com

UK
10a Spring Place, London NW5 3BH
☎ 020 7428 4800 fax 020 7428 4828
email: go@lonelyplanet.co.uk

France
1 rue du Dahomey, 75011 Paris
☎ 01 55 25 33 00 fax 01 55 25 33 01
email: bip@lonelyplanet.fr
minitel: 3615 lonelyplanet

World Wide Web: www.lonelyplanet.com or AOL keyword: lp
Lonely Planet Images: lpi@lonelyplanet.com.au

index

*See separate indexes for Places to Eat (p. 126), Places to Stay (p. 127),
Shopping (p. 127) and Sights (p. 128, includes map references).*

PLACES TO EAT

sights index